POLAND'S
SELF-LIMITING
REVOLUTION

POLAND'S SELF-LIMITING REVOLUTION

Jadwiga Staniszkis

Edited by Jan T. Gross

Princeton University Press
Princeton, New Jersey

Copyright © 1984 by Princeton University Press
Published by Princeton University Press,
41 William Street, Princeton, New Jersey 08540
In the United Kingdom: Princeton University Press,
Guildford, Surrey

All Rights Reserved
Library of Congress Cataloging in Publication Data
will be found on the last printed page of this book
ISBN 0-691-09403-9

Publication of this book has been aided by
the Whitney Darrow Fund of Princeton University Press

This book has been composed in APS-5 Trump
Clothbound editions of Princeton University Press books
are printed on acid-free paper, and binding materials
are chosen for strength and durability.
Paperbacks, although satisfactory for personal collections,
are not usually suitable for library rebinding

Printed in the United States of America by
Princeton University Press, Princeton, New Jersey

Contents

R S H 403318 Suk 85.6.10

CONTENTS

Editor's Preface

In June 1980, Princeton University Press received for consideration a manuscript written by a Polish sociologist, Jadwiga Staniszkis, entitled "The Dialectics of the Socialist Society: Poland's Case." Subsequently the manuscript was sent to me for review and advice concerning its publishability. The book was, undoubtedly, extraordinarily difficult reading for an American not entirely preoccupied with the mysteries of Soviet and East-Central European politics. I admired the audacity of the Social Science Editor at the Press who had become sufficiently interested in the manuscript to initiate the review process, and I later learned that editors at the Press had been in touch with Staniszkis in 1978, when she was visiting the United States as an ACLS fellow, and again in 1980, when she was in this country as an Eisenhower Fellow, and had examined two earlier versions of the work.

Despite stylistic problems and the uneven quality of the translation, the manuscript I reviewed was fascinating. In my reader's report, I wrote: "Staniszkis's book is the best, most original, thought-provoking analysis of an East-Central European society and its politics that I have read in a long time. It goes beyond analyses derived from the totalitarian model approach and it is also more sophisticated than analyses using the interest group approach to study 'socialist' societies. The book is an attempt to describe and understand the authoritarian regime in Poland as a sort of corporatist society. As a sociologist of organizations the author succeeds in analyzing an intricate system of mechanisms that have been generated by a social system in order to compensate for irrationalities due to ideological restrictions placed upon it. She has been sensitive to the manifestations of symbolic manipulation in the process of social control and able to analyze such phenomena as *simulation* of interest group representation or *ritualization* of periodic crises of the regime. In these analyses she has demonstrated how the system succeeded in incorporating and, as it were, domesticating what would be seen by a less astute observer (or a traditionally thinking social scientist) as developments disrupting and threatening the system's stability. Undoubtedly, Staniszkis has written a major contribution that substantially broadens our understanding of the so-called 'people's democracies.'" At that time the manuscript was returned to the author with suggestions for major revisions.

The revised manuscript, now entitled *Poland's Self-Limiting Revolution*, was returned to the Press in November 1981. In the meantime, the only genuine workers' revolution ever had taken place in Poland. As one of the six advisers called to the Gdańsk Shipyards during the August 1980 strike to advise the workers in their negotiations with the government, Jadwiga Staniszkis became one of the revolution's important participants *and* most astute interpreters. Her manuscript grew, as it were, with the unfolding of events in Poland. The new manuscript was an original contribution rather than merely a revision of the earlier manuscript. The analysis continued to be original and thought-provoking, but the treatment—largely devoted to Polish society in 1980 and 1981—covers one of the most significant political phenomena in the history of postwar Europe.

The manuscript at this stage was also reviewed by Walter D. Connor and approved for publication by the Editorial Board of Princeton University Press in March 1982, in the knowledge that it might be difficult to work with the author during the considerable editorial revision required. The imposition of the state of war in Poland made it impossible to communicate with Staniszkis for the foreseeable future. At this stage I agreed to work with the Press to prepare her manuscript for publication.

Throughout the editorial process, I and Gail Filion, the Social Science Editor, who copyedited the manuscript, have striven to remain faithful to the author's original version. The problems of accurate interpretations were heightened by the roughness of the translation in some sections. As a result, we may occasionally have sacrificed readability in order to preserve phrasing that, while not idiomatic, seemed to express the author's intention adequately. Infrequent textual emendations are indicated by square brackets. The majority of our explanations are rendered in editorial footnotes, lettered rather than numbered to distinguish them from the author's own footnotes. In one or two instances we have removed parenthetical material from the text to the author's footnotes.

Sections of the manuscript had been composed at different times. Chapters VI, VII, and VIII constituted parts of the original version of the manuscript that were revised and incorporated into this new version. The other chapters were written as events occurred. A late-arriving epilogue is dated by the author "January 1982" one month after martial law was imposed on Poland. In order both to preserve the sense of immediacy the author felt as she wrote these chapters and to signal to the reader the development of the book, we have noted at the beginning of chapters the date on which we believe they were composed.

We have not communicated directly with Staniszkis since early in December 1981. Her last letter to Gail Filion urged us to proceed with the publication of her manuscript, making whatever editorial changes were necessary. Needless to say the text would be more intelligible if the author herself had had the opportunity to work on its final draft with the editors. The imperfections are, in a way, a small casualty in the state of war imposed by Communist rulers on Polish society.

JTG
New Haven
March 1983

POLAND'S
SELF-LIMITING
REVOLUTION

Introduction

THE CREATION OF SOLIDARITY[a]

On July 1, 1980, the Polish government introduced changes in prices and in the system of meat sales that effectively doubled the cost of some types of meat. Strikes began immediately, and continued spontaneously all over Poland. Local authorities, sometimes even factory managers, were soon empowered to settle strikers' demands for pay hikes—amounting to 5 or 10 percent of their salaries. This decision of the Polish authorities—to delegate power to grant concessions to its local representatives—was intended to stem the wave of strikes by settling them promptly, on a case-by-case basis. Instead, it encouraged additional strikes for—as there was no general, legally binding procedure to negotiate labor disputes, in this case for higher wages—only those workers who *actually* went on strike got pay increases. By mid-July, large areas of the country (e.g., the town of Lublin and vicinity) were affected by strikes, as clusters of factories stopped working. Railway traffic, including railway lines to the Soviet Union, were blocked. In addition to pay raises, striking railway workers demanded family allowances equal to those enjoyed by police and the military, as well as new elections to trade union chapters. Meanwhile, the Workers' Defense Committee (KOR) was issuing statements warning that

[a] This section was written by Jan T. Gross.

hidden inflation would soon absorb salary increases and that workers ought to defend their constitutionally guaranteed rights, including the freedom to form associations, such as trade unions. By the end of July, press reports about "work stoppages" or "disturbances of work rhythm" — as the official propaganda called them — multiplied. Strike prevention committees were set up in factories threatened with strikes; supplies of cheap meat were rushed in and local chapters of the official trade union would step in and negotiate raises for the workers. At the same time, on July 27, the First Secretary of the Polish United Workers' Party (PUWP), Edward Gierek, left for a three-week holiday in the Crimea. Thus far there were no repressions against striking workers. In some factories promises of up to 20-percent pay raises were won by the strikers. But the government's tactic did not bring anticipated results.

At the beginning of August, strikes spread to Gdańsk shipyards and port facilities. On August 14, the strike began in Gdańsk shipyards. The initial demands were for the reinstatement of crane operator Anna Walentynowicz (fired on August 9) and electrician Lech Wałęsa (who lost his job earlier). Demands were also made for a cost of living allowance, a raise of 2,000 zlotys per month, family subsidies equal to those of the police, and the erection of a memorial monument for the victims of the 1970 strikes. Since the 1970 strikes (a wave of workers' protests that brought about the replacement of Władysław Gomułka by Edward Gierek at the helm of the Communist party in Poland and resulted in mass killings of strikers on the Baltic coast), both Wałęsa and Walentynowicz were known and respected by their fellow workers as outspoken champions of workers' rights and interests. Lech Wałęsa immediately emerged as the main spokesman for the strikers, heading the strike committee. On the next day, authorities imposed a communications blackout on the city of Gdańsk. The KOR expressed solidarity with the strikers and protested the cut-off in communications. On August 16, after management agreed to the demand for raises, but stated that it was not empowered to speak to other demands, Lech Wałęsa declared the strike over. Soon he realized that a significant portion of the shop crew wanted to continue the strike. He then called for a resumption of the strike, but in the confusion, the majority of the workers left the shipyard. That night several delegations from striking factories arrived at the shipyard. The MKS (Interfactory Strike Committee) was formed, and a provisional list of demands was formulated. Workers who left earlier in the evening began to return.

By Monday, August 18, one hundred and fifty-six factories had joined the MKS. Strikes spread to the coastal city of Szczecin. Gierek broadcast a speech over radio and television. A government commission, chaired by Deputy Prime Minister Tadeusz Pyka was sent to Gdańsk. It refused to meet with representatives of the MKS; instead it offered to deal with each factory's representatives separately. Seventeen factories belonging to the MKS began a series of separate discussions with Pyka, only to break them off on the next day, under pressure from their striking constituencies. On August 20, authorities arrested 14 members of the KOR. On August 21, Deputy Prime Minister Mieczysław Jagielski replaced Tadeusz Pyka as head of the party-government commission in Gdańsk. Longshoremen issued a statement revealing that, as early as the second day of the strike, Polish officials had notified shippers that this was an authorized strike, thus permitting them to claim damages from their insurance companies. Otherwise, the Polish government would have to pay penalty for delays in loading and unloading ships. A letter of support, signed by 64 intellectuals, was delivered to the MKS by professor Bronisław Geremek and Tadeusz Mazowiecki, editor of the Catholic monthly *Więź*. Together with Bohdan Cywiński, Tadeusz Kowalik, Waldemar Kuczyński, Jadwiga Staniszkis, and Andrzej Wielowiejski, who joined them later in the shipyards, they formed a commission of experts to assist the Gdańsk MKS in the negotiations with the government. On August 22, Jagielski agreed to begin talks with the Gdańsk MKS. Simultaneously in Szczecin shipyards, a government commission headed by Deputy Prime Minister Kazimierz Barcikowski began talks with the local MKS. They were presented with a list of 36 demands including freedom for arrested members of KOR. Factories approached by government ministers with proposals for separate talks declared their intention to negotiate only through MKS.

On August 23, the first issue of the *Strike Information Bulletin "Solidarity"* appeared, printed in the shipyards by the Free Printing Plant of Gdańsk. Among other things, it carried the text of the International Labor Organization's conventions concerning the right to organize and the right to strike. Three hundred and eighty-eight factories had already joined the MKS. At 8 p.m. the government commission headed by Deputy Prime Minister Jagielski arrived at the shipyard. Talks with the Presidium (Executive Committee) of the MKS began. Lech Wałęsa chaired the meeting. The talks in their entirety were broadcast over the public address system.

On August 24, a delegation from MKS arrived in Szczecin shipyards. Both MKS's agreed that the demand for free trade unions was non-negotiable. The Fourth Plenum of the PUWP's Central Committee met in Warsaw. Several people were demoted from the Politbureau, the Prime Minister was replaced; Gierek kept his post, but the main report at the Plenum was given by Stanisław Kania, who succeeded Gierek as First Secretary of the PUWP on September 5. On Monday, August 25, telephone lines to Szczecin and Warsaw were restored, and the MKS decided to continue talks with the government commission, which were suspended until the government stopped the communications blockade of Gdańsk.

Strikes spread throughout the entire country. An MKS was

formed in the city of Wrocław. It expressed solidarity with the list of demands of the Gdańsk MKS. On August 28, four MKS's existed in Poland: in Gdańsk (over 600 enterprises), in Szczecin (over 200 enterprises), and smaller ones in Wrocław and in Elbląg. At the Ursus plant in Warsaw, a Workers' Solidarity Committee was formed. Representatives from large factories from all over the country continued to arrive at the shipyards. Solidarity strikes were threatened in Kraków and Katowice steelworks and in several coal mines. On August 30, an agreement was signed in Szczecin, and the strike was declared over. On August 31, a formal agreement concerning the 21 demands put forward by the strikers was signed in Gdańsk. Jagielski signed a statement declaring that all persons detained by the police during the preceeding two weeks, whose names were on the list delivered by the MKS to the government commission, would be released by noon, September 1, 1980. The signing ceremony was shown on national television.

ONE YEAR LATER: THE ANATOMY OF REVOLUTION
[Written in October 1981]

Most discussions of Polish events are bound to involve consideration, explicit or not, of their revolutionary nature. The word "revolution" suggests an analogy with the great modern prototypes, the French and Russian revolutions. Such an analogy imposes a model of what revolution should be. In this book I will describe the peculiarities of the mechanisms and the dynamics of revolution in a post-totalitarian regime, with its characteristic ideological vagueness, its multidimensionality, and the different rhythms of its political, social, and cultural processes.

The ambiguity of the present situation in Poland and the difficulty of forecasting its outcome stem from the fact that this situation results from the interplay of five phenomena, each with its own dynamic. First, there is the "self-limiting revolution," which can be analyzed in terms of its own dynamic or in the context of the more general process of an evolution of forms of a class war in a system based on state ownership of means of production; and, secondly as the dialectic of social protest, when each successive strategy resolves at least some of the tensions generated by the previous one and produces tensions of its own.[1]

A second phenomenon that must be considered is the complex, confused, and generating authoritarian temptations response of the ruling group to the most recent events in this self-limiting revolution. The dynamics of the ruling group's reaction can be seen in three characteristic moments. These were the effort in October 1980 to reformulate arguments supporting their own legitimacy from an eroded concept of a vanguard party to a "social contract" justification of power. A second moment occurred in the January-February 1981 attempt by the communist party to change its polymorphic structure and to withdraw from at least some areas of state administration and economic activity in order to divide responsibility and avoid an accumulation of tensions. The third moment began more recently and seems to have been accepted by some groups in the Soviet power elite. This is an effort to redefine the institutional arrangement of the regime in order to stabilize the system. It involves a shift from the communist party to the state as the core of the institutional system. An unsolvable crisis of the Polish communist party's identity, in which nearly all of its old functions are impossible in the new political circumstances and no new functions have been elaborated, is reinforced by the party's self-effacing posture due to its inability to uphold the myth of unity of interests in the context of deep internal conflicts. This crisis of identity was followed by a severe legitimacy crisis

[1] See Jaime Reynolds "Communists, Socialists and Workers: Poland 1944–48," *Soviet Studies* (1978), no. 4, pp. 516–539.

8

and the system's unsteerability and led to the efforts[2] of General Wojciech Jaruzelski's regime to build from below a new organization that would be more an army-state than the party-state it was before. In a sense this activity recalls the process in which the power vacuum was filled in post-revolutionary Russia. The military control commissions sent by Jaruzelski to villages and small towns all over Poland fill the same role played by Communist party commissions in post-revolutionary Russia, trying to control a disorganized, atomized collection of local authorities. The political crisis in Poland serves as a type of a laboratory where the following questions have to be answered: How can this unavoidable institutional shift, following the regime's evolution from a totalitarian toward an authoritarian-bureaucratic regime, be smoothly conducted without provoking a counter-mobilization of the party apparatus? How can this apparatus be demobilized? What type of legitimacy can be created for the army-state?

A third phenomenon affecting recent events in Poland has been accelerated cultural modernization containing elements of a cultural revolution in which, for instance, the overcoming of semantic differences in protest situations was perceived by workers as an end to a hierarchy built on semantic codes.[3]. The workers' identification with Solidarity as well as their emotional

[2] For instance, the military "operational groups" sent in mid-October 1981 to control the lower levels of state administration.

[3] The classical definition of cultural modernization is a rapid change of ontology caused by a shift in an identification. A new framework of identification created by membership in Solidarity changed an ontology characteristic of traditional, status-oriented society. The latter was based on mythological discontinuities in perceiving social hierarchy, on the generalization of local problems onto the whole system (not on abstract concepts of roles and functions), on thinking in terms of groups not institutions and in terms of condensed, personalized symbols, not abstract concepts.

Cf., for instance, the work of Perry Anderson: *Lineages of the Absolutist State*, London, N. L. B., 1974; *Passages from Antiquity to Feudalism*, London, N. L. B., 1974; and (ed.). *Towards Socialism*, Ithaca, N. Y., Cornell University Press, 1965.

involvement in problems of other social groups (demonstrated by their participation in solidarity strikes) helped to overcome their narrow status orientation and fragmented social perspective. The charisma of Solidarity as an institution led workers a step away from the traditional, personalized, and hero-oriented culture, "we" versus "them." A dramatic dimension of the Polish situation is rooted in the blocking of political as well as economical emancipation and modernization: it is typical of Poland that all revolutions and counterrevolutions were experienced through changes in culture and morality rather than in the form of thorough institutional reforms or new philosophical visions. The inner dynamic of this cultural modernization process, including its rapid end and reversal when deep economic crisis again fragmented society, should be analyzed as well. The rapid increase of frustrations rooted in workers' low tolerance of uncertainty and the accelerating process of social disorganization so characteristic of late Autumn 1981 can also stop this process. The search for scapegoats (not without anti-Semitic overtones) creates surrogate conflicts channeling tensions that cannot find expression; the continual resort to violence that survives all "renewals," remains frozen in the memory of the party apparatus and creates a social climate that is a far cry from the ideal of a rational modern society.

The fourth phenomenon is linked to a contradiction that is built into the political system in Poland. This system operates according to two conflicting functional imperatives. The first imperative is to prevent the articulation of interests different from official definitions, a necessity in an organization such as the Polish Communist Party built on the ideological myth of a unity of interests and operating with no formal organizational mechanisms that allow negotiation of internal conflicts. The only way to keep such organizational structures stable is to prevent free articulation. The main instruments here are the demobilization of members of such an organization and organizational blockage of the articulation process. Such totalitarian tendencies have their own rhythm; they seem to be more vigorous at times when the ruling group's policy is more pragmatic and thus less ideological. In periods of high mobilization or politicization of the society, the pressure on a party to appear unified (and efforts to demobilize its members) is more intense. One example is the passivity, even ritualization, of the lower echelons of the Polish United Workers' Party (PUWP) that was ordered from above after the August 1980 strikes in order to prevent the party from being penetrated by the rapidly politicized social atmosphere. This ritualization was supposed to work as a barrier between the PUWP and the rest of the society. The actual attempt to redefine the political system has been followed by increased organizational pressure of party unity. But the political system possesses another functional imperative that creates an opposite pressure. In order to stabilize the system over the long term, some reforms and changes are necessary. The totalitarian tendency that prevents free articulation and is based on a myth of infallibility makes every change extremely difficult. To maintain the system's potential for change, some independent spheres must be tolerated or they have to be reconstructed from above. This process of artificial negativity allows a regime to introduce necessary reforms. A "public" temporarily invoked on the political stage helps also to disarm opponents in factional rivalry inside the ruling elite. As events in the late 1970s proved, however, processes such as the reconstruction of public opinion from above tend to get out of control. They also generate tension within the executive strata of the power apparatus. The unofficial character of these processes is perceived by party and state bureaucrats as a threat to their security. In a way, the strikes of August 1980 were also a sign of the counter-mobilization of this executive strata against the detotalization-from-above [stepping back from attempts at total control] policy of Edward Gierek, first secretary of the PUWP, 1970–1980. The interplay of these two contradictory processes is one of the most important sources of the actual tensions in Poland and for the frustration of both sides: society as well as the power apparatus.

The fifth phenomenon that must be analyzed in order to understand the dynamics of Polish revolution is the downward spiral of the economic crisis. We observe in Poland a surreal turning back of the clock. Both the state economy — the reversion to a barter system and the rapid decrease of agriculture marketability — and society's reaction to this situation ("active strike" tactics and consumer cooperatives) as well as the ruling group's longing for the restoration of obligatory food levies from the countryside recall the situation in Russia after the revolution.

Now, a year after the strikes of August 1980, it seems nearly impossible to stabilize a quasi-liberal, authoritarian-bureaucratic regime in Poland based on a "social contract" legitimacy on the one hand and on a conciliatory pattern of problem solving on the other hand. The totalitarian temptation of reverting to organized coercion is openly formulated.[4] Some of these voices represent the *ultima ratio* of party-state power. Some are a rigid response caused by an ideological interpretation of Solidarity's claims.[5] Others are linked to institutional-sectoral interests.[6] Such temptations are reinforced by the desire of party members for a more active policy and for an end to the serious status problems linked with a tactic of permanent "retreat."[7] These attitudes are often justified by some of today's PUWP leaders by invoking formulas derived from their communist youth as

[4] See voices on the Fourth Plenum of the PUWP Central Committee in *Trybuna Luda* (October 16–18, 1981).

[5] Rakowski's response is of this type; he overinterpreted Solidarity's demand for control of food distribution as fighting for economic power (August 6th meeting). This led to deep conflict.

[6] An example is the speech of Politbureau member Milewski, former internal affairs minister, Fourth Plenum.

[7] See the speech at the Fourth Plenum by Albin Siwak.

"true-believers," when the use of coercive means was legitimated by the popularity of the ruling group's policy.[8] For some
PUWP leaders a "hard line" policy seems to be the only feasible
way out of chaos and economic crisis. Kadar's example in 1956
is sometimes invoked in this connection.

Paradoxically, this shift in attitude and, following it, a rapidly
deepening polarization[9] is occurring independently of the inner
dynamic and functioning of Solidarity. On the contrary, Solidarity seems now to be more open to cooptation,[10] more demobilized and disintegrated than before, in spite of the highly politicized rhetoric at its first Congress, the momentary eruptions
of frustrated masses,[11] the status politics of its functionaries, and
a fundamentalist mentality of its rank and file members that
makes communication so difficult.[12]

The current tendency of the regime to exercise a "hard line"
policy is above all the result of tensions within the power apparatus. This tendency is reinforced by the international situation.[13] The situation is similar to that in Czechoslavakia thirteen

[8] Barcikowski's speech at the meeting with party apparatus (February 20,
1981).

[9] During the Fourth Plenum, 13 members of the Central Committee at the
PUWP gave up their Solidarity cards.

[10] Wałęsa's careful avoidance of controversial (from the government's point
of view) figures in the National Commission Presidium; Kuroń's longing for a
"National Salvation Government" (see his article in *Niezależność* [September
18, 1981], as well as his interview in *Sztandar Młodych* [October 15, 1981].

[11] Hunger marches in Łódź and Warsaw in August 1981, racial fights with
Gypsies in Konin, strikes during food crises in Katowice and Żyrardów in September 1981.

[12] Characteristic was a strike in the Szczygłowice mine in September 1981,
which was connected with the miners' rejection of higher pay for working on
free Saturdays (in order to avoid being treated by the rest of society as overprivileged strata). This incident, which included a threat of violence against the
branch union activists who openly supported the idea of additional money in
television interviews, can be perceived as a crusade against evil temptations.

[13] See Zamiatin's interview in *Stern* (September 1981), after the Haig-Gro-
myko meeting, and a rapid change of the tone after the Sadat killing, with
Suslov's article in *Novyi Mir* (October 14).

years ago. The only difference today is that the "other side" is inside, and, if we can talk about "intervention," it is an economic, invisible one.[14] When the Soviets intervened in Czechoslovakia in August 1968, the Dubček regime had already seriously limited plans for its radical reforms, excluded some of the most controversial figures,[15] and seemed to be disintegrating and divided.[16] However, the aggression of the "other side" was caused by the interweaving of many small streams of frustrations and group interests that were often so petty they could not be affected by the moderation of Dubček's policy. [17] The analogy with the present Polish situation is very close: the policy of moderate leader of Solidarity, Lech Wałęsa, cannot influence or reduce the status problems of the party apparatus that are caused by the fact of Solidarity's existence. In 1968 in Czechoslovakia, all these frustrations sometimes related to local issues, slowly built up and exploded when they reached a critical mass. An intensification of a propaganda paper war played a role there: after a while all verbal arguments wore down to the expression that "something should be done."

The crisis of the power apparatus in Poland has several

[14] Note the following versions of the so-called stabilization plan: between March and June we observed increasing rigidity in the treatment of individual farmers in order to protect the collective farms, the halt of plans for radical cuts in investment — due to defense obligations, a threat of introducing a "balanced exchange" with the Soviet Union if the political situation does not change (actually the deficit on the Polish side is 1.5 billion rubels), the September visit of Nicolai Bajbakov in Warsaw, the picking up by COMECON partners of some unfinished Polish investment projects for their own use using Polish energy supplies (by accident these are very energy-intensive steel mills, necessitating the reallocation of 3 million tons of coal from Western to Eastern markets, which harms our credit problem).

[15] For instance General Prchlik.

[16] Over the "2,000-words letter."

[17] See Jiri Valenta, *Anatomy of Intervention*, Baltimore, Md., Johns Hopkins University Press, 1978.

dimensions. First of all, on the government level, it is revealed in a deepening disintegration of the state administration,[18] combined with a paralysis of machinery that cannot control actual events. As we will see later, it is the severity of the economic crisis that has such detotalizing impact on the system. This has been followed by a spreading chaos, politicized by factional infights.[19] What is more, a tactic of decentralizing responsibility to deal with local problems on a district level (undertaken in order to avoid an accumulation of tensions) practically destroyed the steering capacities of the Jaruzelski regime. On the party level a profound crisis of identity is occurring in which all traditional functions of the monoparty are seriously reduced and new roles have not been elaborated. Internal conflicts in the PUWP are more and more open.[20] First Secretary Stanisław Kania's political base was swept away.[21] The propaganda as well as

---

[18] See the conflicting statements of two government agencies on the "Social Council in Economy" requested by Solidarity. The chairman of the Economic Committee of the Ministry Council, Krzak, promised to negotiate the idea, but Urban (Jaruzelski's press attaché, linked with Rakowski) vigorously rejected the same idea on the same day (October 16, 1981).

[19] At least some strikes after the Ninth Congress were provoked; for instance, the distribution of food in Katowice and Łódź was disrupted by distributing food coupons one week after they were due.

[20] Kociołek (First Secretary of the Warsaw's party Committee) collected nearly 800 signatures from delegates demanding the Tenth Party Congress. Siwak's (a Politbureau member) proposal to invite Kociołek, who was not elected to Central Committee, to the Politbureau resulted in the angry exit of a few Politbureau members who opposed it (Kubiak, Grzyb, Łabęcki).

[21] The October 18 resignation of Kania from the post of first secretary was a result of these conflicts. Also, more liberal district secretaries (for instance Fiszbach) are criticized by "old communists" groups in their regions. Secretaries from the biggest factories, who supported Kania during his conflict with Olszowski in March 1981, recently criticized him openly for cutting off all possibilities of a change of the party formula. See for instance the meeting in Cegielski factory on August 20, 1981, transmitted by television.

coercion apperatuses are increasingly unreliable.[22] Even the so-called "branch" union[b] (the remains of the old "transmission belt" structure) split recently over a problem of internal democracy.[23]

The main element of the crisis, however, is a power vacuum. The problem is not how to rule but to rule at all: the economy as well as the executive strata seem to be fully out of control. What is more — and this is probably an immediate cause of the present shift toward the "hard line" policy — proposals for filling in the power vacuum are more and more openly formulated.[24] In addition, a peculiar characteristic of the Polish revolution that could be labeled "institutional revolution" gained strength when the power vacuum deepened. The tactic of institutional revolution might be termed "open conspiracy." In it, goals such

[22] Independent Unions (Solidarity) were organized within the police. Deep conflict between the Association of Journalists (SDP) and the government led to the expulsion from the PUWP of the SDP's chairman, Stefan Bratkowski. Jaruzelski decided to extend the army service of recruits for two months because the new induction to the armed forces would bring people who had already been influenced by Solidarity. The latter corresponded with discussions at the Fourth Plenum concerning the possibility of introducing a state of emergency (October 17, 1981).

[23] The Secretary General of the branch union criticized openly the overcentralization of his organization and was expelled October 17, 1981.

[24] The Catholic Church, some members of PAX such as Reiff, the Peasant party, plus Kuroń independently proposed in September 1981 organizing the "National Salvation Government." Rumors circulated about direct contacts between Solidarity (and the Church) with Moscow.

[b] A craft union. Solidarity was an oddity among labor unions in that it was organized territorially. When the old labor unions collapsed in Poland, in the Summer and Autumn of 1980, two union structures were set up — Solidarity and the so-called craft or branch unions. In part, this was an attempt by the authorities not to be completely left out of the game, and in many instances old, compromised unions re-named themselves into some allegedly new craft union. In addition so-called autonomous unions were established which had a nationwide "craft" constituency (medical personnel or teachers and university professors, for example) but which were pro-Solidarity and thus wanted to differentiate themselves from branch unions.

as a peaceful evolution toward a pluralistic system are formulated openly, but the ruling group's opportunity to counteract is greatly reduced as a result of the methods used by this peculiar revolution (labeled recently by the government as a "paper putsch").[25]

Transformation of Solidarity

The open conspiracy stage in the evolution of Solidarity was preceded by the period of institutionalizing the movement (September 1980 to March 1981), which I have called a "self-limiting revolution," and by the period between April 1981 and July 1981, during which an identity crisis of the movement became aggravated.

Self-limiting revolution. The most striking characteristic of the initial period of the movement's history was the painful process of cramming that radical wave of protest and class war into a "trade union" formula.[c] Nearly all other features of the move-

---

[25] See Urban's comment about Solidarity's proposal to organize the Social Council on Economy, October 16, 1981.

The most efficient of these methods are: 1) exploitation of loopholes in the Polish legal system that are characteristic of an authoritarian-bureaucratic regime, to which they provide a necessary flexibility without formal changes in the institutional structures; 2) invocations of legality based on popular feelings of justice and, following it, breaches of law twisted with formulations of new laws, combined in carefully selected cases with appeals to the authorities to abide by the law; 3) taking the legal façade of the existing political system — the Constitution, the international conventions to which Poland adhered, etc. — at its face value in order to enforce its observance; 4) setting up institutional bodies that themselves may serve as future vehicles of change (e.g., self-governing groups at the factory level); and 5) filling with its own activity all the spheres of the power vacuum.

[c] A reference to the fact that Solidarity was established and gained legal recognition in Poland as a *trade union.* Yet, obviously, it was something very different from a trade union — even in Western democracies. Given the circumstances of Polish politics (where an Independent Self-governing Trade

17

ment stemmed from this self-limitation of the Polish revolution. For instance, its symbolic politics (which took the form of attacks on local PUWP bosses and did not try to undermine the political institutions as such) provided a peculiar alibi for regional Solidarity leaders who had to pay with their own authority for the policy of moderating the movement, persuaded by its top authorities and experts from the intelligentsia. Other features included the predominance of status-oriented policy over interest-oriented policy[26] and the full mobilization of rank-and-file members. The latter activity contained elements of cultural revolution, Solidarity was not only perceived as a vehicle of upward mobility[27] for the whole working class but it seemed to satisfy anti-hierarchical desires. Workers rapidly decided to talk, some of them imitating the vocabulary of their leaders, who demonstrated for the first time an ability to converse on the same level of generalization as the ruling group and intelligentsia. Many workers, however, made a conscious effort to change their habits of speech and to overcome limita-

[26] The conflict over work on free Saturdays was perceived above all as a sign that Solidarity was being treated seriously by the government (January 1981).

[27] Research by Marody (Warsaw University) conducted in a Warsaw Steel mill in December 1980 indicated that Solidarity was perceived as, above all, a vehicle of upward mobility.

Union was already an oddity) it had to preserve the appearance of being just a trade union. It was, for instance, hard-pressed to demonstrate (at different times both to its supporters, who wanted to give the government no pretexts to attack the union, and to its enemies, who were looking for such arguments) that it was not a political organization, that it did not meddle in politics — an obvious impossibility in a quasi-totalitarian state where the political sphere is ill-defined and tends to encompass everything and certainly whatever a genuine trade union might do to protect the interests of its constituencies. Still, until full political freedoms were restored in Poland and people could also associate freely in political parties, Solidarity had to pretend to be a labor union *and* remain responsive to a huge volume of accumulated grievances and demands of its members that went far beyond the scope of issues that a trade union could handle *qua* trade union.

18

tions rooted in a restricted semantic code.[28] The hierarchy that was built on differences in semantic skills, so powerful in Poland, seemed to be gone. Orwellian "newspeak" was also gone, and many words had their former meaning restored.

Another characteristic feature of this initial period was a lack of ideology due to the tactical silence on the part of the self-limiting revolution. This silence was covered up, however, by the specific mentality of the members, a mentality that itself played the role of ideology. This peculiar non-ideological climate of Polish revolution has several sources. One is a ritualization of ideology and deep suspiciousness of all ideologies typical of the post-totalitarian regime. A second source is the peculiar, non-ideological style of the political opposition within Polish society in 1970, a loose coalition of the system's opponents from different milieus. The relative absence of ideology (when ideology is defined in traditional terms) is also evident in Solidarity; more than 55 percent of workers cannot label their political attitudes, and most of the 36 percent who support opposition groups (KOR, KPN) cannot give any ideological reason other than the argument that the "Opposition tells the truth."[29]

This initial stage of Solidarity's development ended with the so-called Warsaw Agreement on March 31, 1981, following the Bydogoszcz crisis.[d] That agreement was formulated in a peculiar

[28] Compare Basil Bernstein, "Language and Social Classes," *British Journal of Sociology*, (1960).

[29] Odrobińska's research in Gdańsk Shipyard, June 1981.

[d] Representatives from farmer's trade unions (not legalized at the time) and from Solidarity were invited to a meeting of the Bydgoszcz People's Council to discuss a number of grievances. Their case was the last item on the meeting's agenda — "other business." With three items still left on the agenda, however, Edward Berger, chairman of the council, suddenly adjourned the session. Solidarity representatives demanded to be heard and proceeded to draft a resolution with a number of councilors who remained in the hall. A militia detachment, accompanied by a group of plainclothesmen, was brought in and repeatedly asked Solidarity representatives to leave the building. Finally, they intervened, beating up the invited guests, leaving some of them unconscious.

style in which nothing was unequivocally promised and at the same time nothing was unequivocally rejected. The language of this agreement, which was negotiated mostly by the experts of both sides, was in a typical intelligentsia style — full of allusions, mutual meaningful winks, and unbinding signals. The bargain was obviously not ended after the agreement was signed; its semantic style left room for both sides to maneuver. For the working-class members of Solidarity, the agreement was a shock. It was a compromise over an issue so strongly felt about that it generated readiness all over the country, to general strike. The obscure language of the agreement, which made it impossible to deduce from the text what was won and what was lost was therefore especially frustrating. A hierarchy built on semantic skills reappeared and proved as stable as before. When nearly all expressive functions in the movement were executed by its middle class members, workers felt their own creation had been expropriated.[30] They no longer perceived Solidarity as the vehicle of upward mobility. Faith in the cultural revolution disappeared. The initial stage of Solidarity's development ended with a visible demobilization of its rank and file members.

[30] Jankowski's research, Szczecin, June 1981.

Jan Rulewski, Mariusz Łabentowicz, and Michał Bartoszcze were among the victims. Bartoszcze, an elderly peasant, required several days of hospitalization. The incident developed into a major crisis, with the government unwilling to prosecute or even identify those who had made the decision to assault Solidarity representatives, and rank-and-file Solidarity members pressing for an all-out general strike to confront the government over a number of unkept agreements and unresolved issues that the union was negotiating with an increasingly procrastinating government side. The agreement which was finally negotiated with the government on March 31 (the Warsaw Agreement) produced, in turn, a very important internal crisis within Solidarity itself. At issue was the secretive nature of the negotiations by the Solidarity delegation including Wałęsa himself and its lack of consultation even with the National Coordinating Commission. A small group of Solidarity negotiators presented the union with a *fait accompli.*

Identity Crisis   The next stage, in the evolution of Solidarity, April to July 1981, was marked by an identity crisis that cropped out in many forms at the same time. That crisis was primarily due to the fact that, although Solidarity had a considerable political (mainly blocking) power, it did not participate in economic decisions and thus lacked economic power. The limited political revolution that took place in Poland was not followed by a social revolution that changed a structure of a domination based on state ownership of the means of production. Moreover, paradoxically, the very existence of Solidarity strengthened one of the principal causes of the present economic and political crisis: the central control of the means of production. The institutionalization of this conflict and the specific role of shock-absorber played by Solidarity made it possible for the government to survive without making far-reaching changes in its own structure and function. What was more, the union looked indifferently at the deteriorating economic situation in which no decisions were made by the paralyzed government, and Solidarity's great but negative power was useless.

The second dimension of the identity crisis consisted in the deadlock of the self-limiting revolution. The ruling group had already been unmasked and hence was much less sensitive to status issues connected with the popular protest. Furthermore, it was the people and not the ruling elite who had to pay the economic costs of the strikes; the ruling group owned the means of production but without an owner's responsibilities; it participated only in the gains. Also almost all the victories won by Solidarity during this stage of the conflict were superficial; the ruling group made promises that it did not intend to keep, and hence Solidarity victories were pointless. The deadlock of the self-limiting revolution was also due to the narrow trade-union formula used to label the movement's activity. This tactical silence dangerously increased the gap between Solidarity's everyday activities (its short-term goals often simply reactions to the other side's tactics) and the myth that the movement was destroying the ruling group's monopoly of power through universal refusal of obedience (as was the case of the strikes in August 1980), without any intermediate goals between the two.

The third source of the identity crisis can be seen in the way the movement functioned, especially two elements of that formula: inner solidarity and the passive tactic of watching the actions undertaken by the authorities and protesting them whenever necessary, but without taking responsibility for the system's functioning. The commitment to solidarity not only prevented differences within the movement from being openly discussed and resolved by negotiations but was also responsible for a kind of sham radicalism in the elections of the union's regional functionaries. When differences of interests and opinions could not be discussed, the only way to select union officials was to overemphasize those few differences that could not be concealed, such as PUWP membership. As a result, nearly all PUWP members were barred from functions in the union in spite of the fact that, in elections to Solidarity commissions on factory level, more PUWP members were elected than had originally joined the founding groups of Solidarity during the strikes in August 1980. The second element of the formula also proved to be a trap; doctrinal passivity combined with the avoidance of responsibility infected Solidarity with the same paralysis then gripping the government. What was more, this was a direct opening to cooptation. As one of the leading Solidarity functionaries said in an interview, "When we do not have our own conception of how to solve economic and social problems we protest against bad government programs, but after a while we must collaborate in their realization."[31]

[31] Grzegorz Pałka, from the Łódź region of Solidarity, member of Solidarity Presidium, *La Republice* (September 1981), in an interview with J. Strzelecki.

"Open Conspiracy" Stage: Mass Movement or Political Party of activists? The tension created by this multidimensional identity crisis within Solidarity led the movement to the third stage of its evolution, with a resulting change in the strategy of its leaders. This change could be observed not only at the meetings of the National Commission of Solidarity but also during its First Congress in September-October 1981.

First of all the trade union formula was expanded by implicit recognition that Solidarity is a social movement, which made it possible for the movement to speak out publicly on political topics.[32] This in turn led to an eruption of radical rhetoric and to the open manifestation of two different mentalities that served as substitutes of ideologies. One was the pragmatic orientation, rooted in the tactics of institutional revolution, efficient but at the cost of avoiding matters of principle. The other was the fundamentalist orientation, which can be described as a moralistic approach. All declarations are taken at their face value and practically no dissonance is tolerated between declarations and actual conduct. For instance, Solidarity statutes contain a formula accepting "the leading role of the Polish United Workers' Party." During the first part of Solidarity's First National Congress, the demand was formulated for free elections to the Diet (Sejm). Pragmatists treated the two statements as marking the range within which bargaining was possible. For the fundamentalists, especially at the factory level, the contradiction creates serious status problems for Solidarity, as a tension-generating contradiction that must be thoroughly explained and solved. The fundamentalists do not think in terms of political tactics and are generally unconcerned with politics; if a phenomenon is evaluated negatively, this very fact suffices, in their eyes, to eliminate it. The assumption that only one side can be right,

---

[32] An amendment added a formula stating that Solidarity would defend its members in "citizenship as well as workplace situations."

together with their own sense of moral rightness, makes them believe that if evil is identified it must be destroyed, or even that it will destroy itself. This is why the fundamentalists underestimate a need for political strategy and are in practice less radical than the pragmatists, in spite of being severe critics of the system.[33] In addition, their maximalistic attitudes make them defenseless in the face of a reality in which society is overgrown by the state, in which every third man is a manager of something. It is also nearly impossible to operationalize such a maximalistic program.

There is a world of difference between the pragmatic and the fundamentalist mentalities with regard to political imagination. For the pragmatists the state means political institutions and political games. The fundamentalists perceive the state in terms of personal values, sovereignty, dignity,[34] and are indifferent to political games and to reasoning in terms of institutional revolution. Of the program adopted at the First Congress of Solidarity in the Fall of 1981, the item that has caught on at the union's basic level has been the notion of "settling accounts" for government policy in the 1970s — and not the institutional reforms that are the most important part of this program. The fundamentalist attitude is accordingly more common among people of worker origin, the rank-and-file members of Solidarity. The fundamentalists treat verbal declarations, promises, definitions, etc., as more real than the pragmatists do, and that is why, although more amenable in theory, they irritate the ruling elite with their rhetoric more than do the pragmatists. At the same time, however, the fundamentalist orientation may offer the ruling elite a channel to express its frustration at the open conspiracy of the pragmatists.

[33] See the Mazowsze daily *Wiadomości Dnia* (September 24, 1981), which printed the program of the fundamentalists.

[34] Social Research Center of Mazowsze; research done by Andrzej Radźko (June 1981).

Another new element in the present stage of the evolution of Solidarity that increases the possibility of a confrontation with the power apparatus is the union's more active approach to such issues as self-government, union control of food rationing, and the right to determine the distribution of the products of voluntary work on Saturdays, which are legal holidays. In addition, a considerable modification of status politics within the movement combined with symbolic gestures and a shift toward reform of the existing institutions is taking place, including for instance, a demand for a Labor Chamber in the Sejm. However, this development involves mostly the reorientation of Solidarity activists (with its army of nearly 40,000 paid functionaries) with a noticeable demobilization of the rank-and-file members. The latter are not involved in conflicts and games inside the movement and are poorly informed about Solidarity contacts with the government. Even if they were better informed, they would not understand because of their fundamentalist mentality. Many rank-and-file members feel alienated[35] and that they have been used as a kind of levy en masse to be raised and then dismissed. Tired of the hardships of everyday life, they are less and less inclined to get involved in the activities of the union. The fight for authentic self-government seems more important for the union's activists than for its masses. It is worth emphasizing that the shifts in Solidarity's tactics not only increased tensions in the union's relations with the ruling group but generated conflicts and tensions within the movement itself.

A good example is the history of the idea of self-government. The factory-level functionaries of Solidarity were pioneers in recognizing the traps of the union's passive tactics, and the first to taste the impasse of self-limiting revolution. Some of them from more than 50 big enterprises organized a horizontal

---

[35] According to Odrobińska's data, more than 70% of the workers felt that they had no influence on social life (June–July 1981).

arrangement called Network (Sieć),[36] in order to elaborate a concept of a "social enterprise" that would combine the idea of radical workers' councils with a far-reaching program of economic reform. The radical tactics of Network included the organization of factory-level workers' councils with very broad powers and the influencing of future legal regulations. Network's initiative did not meet a friendly reaction either from the state administration or the Solidarity functionaries. From the point of view of the regional leaders, such horizontal structures undercut the hierarchial order. The National Commission was more neutral, but it showed no support until late July 1981. Its interest in the idea of self-government increased rapidly following an abortive meeting with Deputy Prime Minister Mieczysław Rakowski on August 6, 1981, and the subsequent mass media campaign criticizing Solidarity as not interested in lifting the country out of crisis.[e]

[36] Network was created in March 1981 at the initiative of Gdańsk Shipyard and Mielec WSK factory.

[e] On August 3, 1981, the Committee of the Council of Ministers for Union Affairs headed by Deputy Prime Minister Rakowski met for talks with the Presidium of the National Commission of Solidarity. After a day of speechmaking rather than negotiations, the talks were adjourned until August 6. When they resumed, constructive discussions considerably narrowed the differences over a number of very important issues that had soured government-Solidarity relationships for several months. Suddenly, however, Minister for Labor Union Affairs Stanisław Ciosek presented a list of 13 postulates that were commented upon by Deputy Prime Minister Rakowski. They amounted, as Lech Wałęsa immediately observed, to a request that Solidarity cease functioning as an independent union. Then both delegations proceeded to draft a joint communiqué. However, when the final draft was read, the version previously agreed upon had been unilaterally amended in several places by the government delegation. Then the Solidarity delegation proposed a brief communiqué stating simply that talks had been held between the two sides and that government representatives had been invited to the next meeting of the entire National Commission, where their results would be discussed. According to the transcript of the proceedings, Deputy Prime Minister Rakowski replied:

The approach to self-government by the National Commission and some of its advisers was, however, different from that of the Network. Network saw the workers' councils as a means of activating rank-and-file members of Solidarity, as an instrument to socialize means of production and to fill the gap between the union's political and economic power. Above all, the councils were the only possible way to accelerate economic reform. The National Commission supported the idea of self-government mostly to demonstrate its general interest in pulling the economy out of crisis, and by doing so to build a more positive image of the union. National Commission leaders and some advisers who were active in opposition before August 1980 were also interested in a political aspect of the self-government idea, namely as a serious limitation of nomenklatura, in which election of managers would replace their nomination from above.[f] The over-politicization of the self-government idea

---

"This is not a joint communiqué. I am not going to sign it because I did not write it. This is not a joint communiqué, but you may of course publish it. The joint communiqué that was accepted I have later amended together with General Jaruzelski, motivated by state interest the way we understand it. Good night." He left the room when one of the Solidarity delegates, the head of the Mazowsze region, Zbigniew Bujak, protested against police searches that had been conducted in the apartments of several Solidarity activists while the two delegations were negotiating. Rakowski refused to accept the protest but said he was informed of the matter and invited the Solidarity delegation to an adjoining room, where books and journals confiscated by the police were piled up on the tables. "I wonder where the paper [which was a rationed article] comes for these uncensored publications. Goodnight, gentlemen," said Rakowski, and left. On the next day the government media informed the public that Solidarity had broken off talks with the government.

[f] Nomenklatura is a procedure, not regulated by any legislative act or document, requiring that all appointments to key positions in all sectors of society — administrative, economic, military, political, cultural, etc. — obtain prior approval of the executive bodies of the PUWP's committees. The higher the position, the higher the party committee in whose nomenklatura a given position is.

diverted the National Commission's attention from the legal arrangements of factory status vis-à-vis the central administration. The lack of interest was visible during both the negotiations in the Sejm and in the decision of the Presidium of the National Commission that caused so many conflicts during the second part of the Solidarity Congress.[37] It must be added that the self-government problem was treated by some leaders and advisers of Solidarity as an arena where their conciliatory attitudes, linked to rumors about a possibility of a creation of the National Salvation Government,[g] could be demonstrated. This reinforced conflicts within the union because rank-and-file members as well as the factory-level activists (most of them with the fundamentalist orientation) were unable to understand and accept such games with the ruling group. Such internal division also reinforces the possibility of a confrontation with the power apparatus, especially when the National Commission — in order to avoid an accumulation of tensions, — pushed down to the factory level the most conflict-generating negotiations about self-government. We must remember that the ruling group used the same tactic and created district crisis management groups with broad competences.[h]

The present atmosphere of confrontation seems to be caused not only by these trends in the evolution of Solidarity but also, or even primarily, by the processes taking place within the Polish United Workers' Party.

---

[37] The decision gave up all reform-oriented claims of Network.

[g] This was an initiative to create some form of coalition government that would include representatives of Solidarity, the Church, and the PUWP. Meeting between Lech Wałęsa, Primate Józef Glemp, and General Jaruzelski spurred rumors that some such solution was imminent.

[h] A danger of local conflicts is reinforced by the fact that, after the Ninth Congress of the PUWP when Kania's main competitors were not chosen to the Central Committee, nearly all factional infighting was conducted on the level of district party committees.

Dynamics of the Political Regime in Poland

The evolution of the Polish political system after the wave of strikes in the summer of 1980 proceeded in a series of spontaneous processes rather than as a series of purposeful, reform-oriented actions. The most characteristic feature of this evolution was the transformation of the polymorphic status of the PUWP, with the party's effort, observable between late January 1981 and the Bydgoszcz crisis in March 1981,[38] to divest itself of sole responsibility for the functioning of the economy and of public administration. These were ad hoc efforts to divide the responsibility for the running of the country between party and government and thus to avoid a confrontation with Solidarity. They were not the implementation of a reform-oriented policy. According to this tactic, the PUWP was supposed to adopt "hard line" measures (to satisfy the Soviet Union's expectations) while Jaruzelski's government maintained the social contract approach. After a careful examination of this evolution, one must agree with Juan Linz's thesis that "authoritarian regimes in reality are [. . .] likely to be complex systems characterized by heterogeneity of models influencing their institutionalization, often contradictory models in uneasy coexistence."[39] The inner transformation of the totalitarian and, later, the authoritarian-bureaucratic regime in Poland can be analyzed in dialectical terms underlining the system's contradictions and their dynamics.

The main contradiction of the system is linked with the state-ownership of the means of production. The inner dynamics of

[38] I have analyzed that crisis, which was provoked by one faction of the power elite to stop the described evolution, in my article in *Bulletin of Scottish Politics* (Spring 1981)

[39] Juan J. Linz, "Totalitarian and Authoritarian Regimes" in Fred I. Greenstein and Nelson Polsby, eds., *Handbook of Political Sciences*, Addison-Wesley, 1975, pp. 175–411, 283.

social relations built on such type of ownership took two forms: In Poland the evolution of the forms of social protest began with a stage of artificial negativity,[40] in which opposition was constructed from above in order to permit the political system to introduce the necessary changes. During this stage, a public was invoked from above during the political crises of 1956 and 1968 to participate in the political ritual drama. After its job had been accomplished, the public was more or less smoothly demobilized (see Chapter VIII).

The artificial negativity phase was followed by a populist phase, December 1970, and, in the late 1970s, by a corporatist form of interest articulation that was transformed in August 1980 into a class form of protest in which the exploited and powerless opposed those in power who were at the same time the controllers of the means of production.

Each form of protest gradually produced tensions that transformed it into the succeeding, more mature form of protest. The tactic of artificial negativity, based on the pattern of regulation through crisis,[41] not only exploited nearly all the instruments of symbolic manipulation at the end of the 1960s but obviously went out of control. The populist form of protest absorption that followed it not only demanded a costly and unselective economic policy but produced serious status problems for the executive strata of the power apparatus. The corporatist form was very convenient from the point of view of the ruling group: its structure prevented the formulation of more general, political claims. Its relative efficiency from the social point of view, since nearly all strategic groups were bought off, was, however, paid for in terms of moral ambiguity, a rapid increase of social differences, and the segmentation of society as well as the economy. The tension within the executive strata, now linked with increasing uncertainty in everyday functioning, grew even

[40] See Paul Piccone, "One Dimensionality," *Telos* (Spring 1978).

[41] See my article "On Some Contradictions of Socialist Society," *Soviet Studies* (April 1978).

faster than during previous forms of class war. The next and most recent form of social protest took the shape of the social movement Solidarity, with its nearly 10 million members.

The second dimension of the same contradiction took the form of economic-political cycles, with the peculiar pattern of regulation through crisis. During such periods of regulation, downward revisions of investment and production plans were undertaken that temporarily decreased tensions and helped to prolong state ownership of the means of production. In the late 1970s, the stabilizing impact of the corporatist techniques of protest absorption, on the one hand, and easy access to hard currency credits, on the other hand, led to the abandonment of necessary regulation. As a result we have now in Poland a global economic crisis that is fully out of control.[42]

[42] Another contradiction of the "real socialism" is built into the structure and functioning of the political subsystem. The dialectical development of this contradiction can be described by the following events:

1) The creation of an artificial reality, based on a totalitarian utopia that included a myth of the unity of the interests of society and the state and the ideas of supercentralization in order to mobilize all resources;

2) the attrition of the system's reserves and the gradual emergence of all the traps of such an artificial construction;

3) an elaboration by the ruling group (through trial and error) of instruments to deal with at least some of the traps generated by the system. The most important among them: artificial negativity, the politics and detotalization from above (ritualization of ideology), a reconstruction of some social interests in the form of lame, irresponsible pluralism, and a corporatist structure of interest articulation. Another method of dealing with the traps of totalitarian utopia was a pattern of crisis management and even regulation with the help of crisis. Such a pattern appeared in 1956, 1968, and 1970. This pattern was based on two characteristic features of the Polish society: First, there has existed a culture of symbolic gesture in which different social strata possessed different symbolic imaginations. This trait helped in the past to segment society and to provoke conflicts involving only specific groups. Second, a strong Catholic Church can serve not only as a shock-absorber but may be treated as an accountable partner in negotiations by the ruling group. The latter feature of the Church still exists; the former no longer exists due to the rapid change of ontology linked with the shift of identification from status-groups to Solidarity as organized society. The politics of detotalization from above produced many tensions; in a sense the August 1980 eruption of discontent was a by-product of evolution.

Evolution of the Political System after August 1980

In the late 1970s Poland was a typical case of an authoritarian-bureaucratic regime that could well be described in Juan Linz's terms: "Political system with limited, not responsible political pluralism, without elaborate and guiding ideology but with distinctive mentalities . . . and in which a leader or occasionally a small group exercises power within formally ill-defined limits but actually quite predictable ones."[43] An additional feature was the polymorphic pattern of the communist party that had developed in the early 1950s. This pattern was characterized by a low specificity of the PUWP as an institution, which was merged with the state administration and with the various organizations intended to transmit political ideology and instructions to the masses. Typical of the political system during this phase was the peculiar feudalism, in which the performance of political functions depended upon constellations of personal influences, those functions being, moreover, vaguely separated from one another. This neo-feudal character of the system was reinforced by segmentation typical of the corporatist forms of articulation of interests.

The rash of workers' strikes in August 1980 changed nearly all these characteristic features of the political system in Poland. Not only did lame pluralism turn into almost-responsible pluralism (the 40,000 paid union officials in Solidarity wielding considerable political blocking power), but the ruling group nearly surmounted the principal defect of authoritarian regimes, namely the lack of a distinctive formula for its legitimacy. The "social contract" concept took the place of the myth of the vanguard. But this process does not seem to be a lasting one; the inner dynamics of the liberalization process generated counteractivities in the power apparatus that make the stabilization of the social contract more and more difficult. After

[43] Linz, p. 264.

August 1980, a new stage occurred in the feudalization of the system. The profound economic crisis led to a rapid weakening of central authority. Enterprises became much less sensitive to both financial and direct commands. Moreover, there has been a rapid growth of commodities and services beyond the control of the ruling group.[44] The aggravating economic crisis has had thus the peculiar effect of greatly weakening the totalitarian character of the system.

But the most interesting new phenomenon observable since August 1980 is the inner transformation of the Polish United Workers Party, which has tried unsuccessfully to divest itself of its polymorphic status. In July 1981, at the party's ninth Congress, populism was mistaken for democracy and a superficial victory over the party apparatus ended, in fact, in a visible consolidation of the latter. More important still, all chances to elaborate a new model for the functioning of the PUWP were lost. Pressure for the stronger ideological orientation of the party stemming from the Katowice Forum of "true communists" seminars was rejected by pragmatists in the Politbureau as moving toward an open polarization and confrontation with Solidarity and Church. A formula dictated by secretaries from big enterprises, which envisioned the party as a movement against the state bureaucracy, was also rejected. On the contrary, the ninth Congress of PUWP took as its own the government's stabilization plan that formulated no tasks for the party organizations especially on the basic, factory level. This explains the strong tension now observable within the PUWP, which can neither abandon its polymorphic status nor continue to function as it has in the past. This dilemma was pointedly formulated by a

---

[44] It must be borne in mind that the ruling group has nothing to exchange or offer: special privileges have been canceled by Solidarity, funds for investments are no longer available, and the security of managerial jobs depends more on one's good relations with Solidarity than on obedience to orders coming from above.

member of the local PUWP committee in Łódź in an interview granted to *Głos Robotniczy*, a party daily: "In order to rebuild its authority, the Polish United Workers Party should now play the role of an opposition party." This would be an extremely difficult formula for a governing party with so strong a status orientation as the PUWP.

The crisis within the PUWP is aggravated by the fact that the five roles characteristic of the communist party in a totalitarian regime (politicization of the masses, use of trade unions as fully controlled transmission belts, recruitment and training of a new political elite, guidance and leadership through the permanent presence of party members in the authorities of many institutions, and direct control over the economy) have now become seriously limited. At the same time, as we saw, no new roles have been worked out. This crisis of the party identity is, from my point of view, the main reason for the authoritarian, or even totalitarian temptations of some of its activists who try to substitute the old functions with an ethos of a fight. These problems, insoluable in terms of the formula on which the functioning of the PUWP is based, are deepened by the emergence of Solidarity. Even without the latter, however, the inner dynamics of the party would have lead to the present point.

THE LEGACY OF POLISH SOCIETY

Polish political life is very difficult to understand. Most of the labels are misleading: For instance the activities of the fundamentalists (who are radical critics of the system) are less radical than those of the pragmatists. The "hard-liners" within the PUWP indirectly support, for ideological reasons, Solidarity's fight against nomenklatura. They act like this because they want to appear fully competitive on the political arena without the bureaucratic protective "glass jar" of nomenklatura. On the other hand, Catholic Church advisers of Solidarity seem uninterested in the idea of self-government; they prefer a more hierarchical order and do not want social revolution.

This brief analysis of the Polish drama is not intended to provide answers to questions about the future of the Polish revolution. But the knowledge of the latter's multidimensionality, as well as an understanding of the situation not contaminated by moralistic and emotional elements, should help one to grasp what has recently occurred in Poland. It is worth emphasizing that a lack of a developed market, both in the economy and in politics, the prototraditional legitimacy of power,[45] and a strong status order built on distance and exclusiveness seemed, until quite recently, to be the main features of a social system in Poland, locating it closer to traditional than to modern societies. The etatization of the economy in the 1940s, without genuine revolution, not only did not change these features but even reinforced them. Solidarity, as the first institutionalized effort to mobilize and organize the whole society, can be perceived as an important step in overcoming perspective rooted in the previous status-oriented framework of social identification.

A few of the main characteristics of this framework should be mentioned. First is the stress on the discrete and discontinuous qualities of social stratification with a tendency to mythologize the stature of some status groups, for instance the intelligentsia. This tendency resulted from the lack of social contacts between groups of different statuses, on the one hand, and because of basic cultural differences, for instance in terms of semantic skill, on the other hand. A second feature of this peculiar outlook was a tendency to perceive society in terms of the generalized problems of one's own status group, not in abstract terms based on institutionalized roles and functions of the sys-

[45] Staniszkis, *Soviet Studies* (April 1978), p. 264.

tem as a whole.[46] One effect of this one-dimensionality was a faith in the existence of a simple criterion of correctness that had to be discovered and could not be obtained by negotiations in a process of mutual compromise. A third characteristic was a segmented perspective connected with underestimating the links between subsystems; this fragmented perception led to a tendency to use detachment as a way of coping with social reality. This trait was based on a cultural matrix rooted in over one

[46] See Kenneth Jowitt, The *Leninist Response to National Dependency*, Research Series No. 37, Institute of International Studies, University of California, Berkeley, Calif., 1978, p.47.

[47] Very useful is an analytical perspective proposed by Jowitt in ibid. Jowitt suggests that the Communist party in Russia undertook the task of modernization understood as a change in the framework of identification. A vehicle of such modernization was, according to Jowitt, a peculiar organizational formula of this party characterized by the "possession of qualities that at least in a formal or structural sense are consistent with the defining features of the very society it [the party] wishes to transform. It is the possession of these features that gives the charismatic entry into the society he wishes to change."

Jowitt lists the organizational features of the Leninist party that had to invoke the emotions characteristic of the status-oriented perspective in order to overcome the very same perspective. These characteristics are: charismatic impersonality (a first step from the personal-hero-orientation of a status-oriented society toward the institutional impersonality of a modern society); a stress on a charismatic leader that makes it possible to mix the two conflicting funtional imperatives — the secular, empirical and the sacred, utopian — and to overcome the trap of "one correct line"; a material revolutionary legality based on a popular feeling of justice, to legitimize the party's activity, that is so appealing to a traditional society.

The very same characteristics appeared in the structure and method of functioning of solidarity. A similar effort to transform a traditional into a modern society (in Solidarity's case a half-conscious one) is responsible, in my view, for the similarity of mentalities and methods between Solidarity and the Soviet Communist party in the revolutionary phase of its development. In a sense Solidarity can be perceived as an alternative to the Leninist response to general development problems, with, however, some striking similarities due to a similar technique of an exploiting the political culture of status-oriented society. In both cases we observe the creation — in order to overcome a narrow status orientation — of suprahstatus (Solidarity or party membership) vis-à-vis the rest of society, with a strong polarizing effect. Maintaining the movement's impetus through status — rather than interest — politics is another example of

hundred years of partition, when the society existed without its own state and nearly all social programs were built on a myth of the possibility of organizing a substitutional society.[47]

---

exploiting — in order to modernize — the culture typical of a traditional society.

Jowitt shows how such a status-oriented policy, intended as an "entry ticket" that would make possible contact with groups of a traditional orientation, became the essence of the Communist party. The very same dilemma can be observed today in Solidarity. The inner dynamics of the movement as well as the deepening of the economic crisis seem to have had the reverse effect on the process of the modernizing the framework of social identification. A sense of emergency reinforces a narrow, status-group orientation. Solidarity's shift from its revolutionary negation phrase (characterized by the rejection of the system perceived in very synthetic, abstract terms) toward the "institutional revolution," reformist stage, again invokes the fragmented perspective on the social system, with an impact on these spheres that can be reformed and with silence on others that cannot be touched due to "geo-political" factors and "self-limiting" policy. What is more, a hierarchy built inside Solidarity has given different opportunities to particular status groups; for instance the intelligentsia has monopolized nearly all the expressive functions in the movement. This was one reason for the end of the cultural revolution phase of the movement, which in its previous phases served as an important emotional vehicle to overcome status-oriented perspective.

CHAPTER I

Origins of Solidarity[1]

[Written in September 1980]

EVOLUTION OF FORMS OF WORKING-CLASS PROTEST

The 1970s in Poland was a period of deep transition in the political system. The evolution of forms of working-class protest is a
good illustration of both the direction and the mechanisms of
this change. Generally speaking, it was an evolution from a populist form, based on one enterprise (December 1970), through a
corporatist network of interest representation (1976–80), toward
a class form of articulation of interests (the inter-enterprise
strike committee, MKS, at Gdańsk and Szczecin, August 1980)
and a class agreement between the MKS and the Government
Commission on August 31 and the decision of the Council of
State (Rada Państwa) on registration of independent unions (September 13).

In my article in *Soviet Studies* (April 1979) I analyzed some
characteristic features of a populist form of working-class protest: structural silence and shame of language on the workers'
side, status reversal and momentary status-leveling as techniques of protest absorption used by the government side and,
as a result of the latter, deep tensions at the intermediate level
of both party apparatus and administration. In the mid-1970s, a
new form of interest representation evolved. It met all the cri-

[1] This chapter is reprinted with permission from *Soviet Studies*, April 1981,
vol. 33, no. 2, pp. 204–231.

teria of a corporatist type of politicization of society and structuring of interest articulation. The corporatist structure was organized on a functional rather than a horizontal class basis. "Organic" groups such as the Catholic Church, some professional associations and political clubs (for instance the Experience and Future Club, 1978, or the Catholic Intelligentsia Club) acted separately. There were direct contacts ("consultations") between Gierek's team and workers from more than one hundred of the largest Polish enterprises who had shown their blocking power in the strikes of 1970 and 1976. The claims of all these groups are highly specialized and were mediated by the ruling group. This led to a segmentation of problems and a feudal differentiation of privileges and special treatment.

This corporatist structure of interest representation was authoritatively recognized but not legalized as a part of the political process. Corporatist groups, owing to their semi-legal participation in politics, did not have any specialized political apparatus, and their impact on politics was more a result of the style of the particular ruling team than of lasting institutional arrangements. What is more, because of their highly specialized social base, such groups were unable to discuss general political and economic problems with the ruling group. They served as advisers or consultants but did not actually participate in decision making. The initiative for contacts was usually taken by the ruling group, which also chose the topics of consultation. This form of interest representation had many advantages for the ruling group: it helped to segment society and to stabilize the situation by retarding the growth of social tension with the help of a sequence of decisions based on different (and often conflicting) standards and criteria. It was also easier to manipulate a segmented society by playing off one part against another or by the selective use of symbolic gestures on the one hand and of sanctions on the other. Furthermore, such a form of interest articulation reinforced the legitimacy of *both* sides involved in the negotiations, the party as well as societal bodies (because the voluntary contact of the party by corporatist groups meant that it was recognized by society as a power center). And last, but not least, the tensions at the middle level of the party apparatus and administration were relatively less than when a populist form of protest absorption was used.

But in the summer of 1980 a rapid change occurred. Workers at Gdańsk and Szczecin for the first time in the history of the Polish People's Republic formed a representation of interests on a class basis and against the institutionalized representation — the communist party. Through negotiation, a new, more independent (but still recognizing "the leading role of the party") and class, rather than corporatist, form of interest representation was created on August 31 and — which is important — legalized on September 13. Also, individual clubs and quasi-political groups informally united in an Inter-organizational Joint Committee (September 1980), closely connected with Catholic groups.

This chapter is a sociological comment on some aspects of this transition, written from the standpoint of a direct observer. (I spent 9 days in Gdańsk shipyard, 23–31 August, as an expert on the MKS side during the negotiations with the government commission.)

Both the internal dynamics and the dilemmas of the evolution described above were particularly obvious during the wave of workers' protests in Poland in July and August 1980. Two different patterns of workers' protest could be observed. The first moves during the initial wave of strikes in July 1980 took the classical corporatist form described above. Separate strike committees were organized in individual factories. Individual demands (mainly local ones for wage increases) and individual solutions were formulated. This occurred because the authority to take decisions concerning a return to the old prices of meat (the direct cause of most of the strikes) was delegated to the level of the chairmen of particular districts (*Województwa*). Strikers' solidarity was built on a functional rather than a class basis. In addition, two elements appeared that are typical of situations in which strikes are held for the first time: minimal organization, or — in other words — the principle of acting as a crowd, and the characteristic "shame of language" consisting of a disinclination to use the terms and symbols over-exploited by the façade language of propaganda. All this resulted in excessive modesty of claims, as in the case of the 1970 strikes in Gdańsk.[a]

All these characteristics were visible in strikers' movements in Warsaw (city transport and some factories), Lublin (railways, city transport and a few enterprises), Łódź, Mielec, Kraków, and some coal mines (Silesia). This pattern of protest determined the character of the bargaining, which involved a relatively low level of the power structure, compared with the populist pattern

[a] On the 13th of December 1970, the Council of Ministers announced a decree on price changes — increases for a large assortment of foodstuffs and decreases for some other items, such as washing machines and television sets. The next day the Gdańsk shipyard struck. On December 15, the army was sent against striking workers. On December 16 and 17 other towns on the Baltic coast were engulfed in workers' demonstrations that were pacified by the armed forces. According to the official announcement, 45 people were killed and 1,165 people were wounded. Unofficial estimates put the number of dead at several hundred. On December 19, Władysław Gomułka was replaced as first secretary of the PUWP by Edward Gierek. Several of Gomułka's closest associates were also replaced in the party leadership. On January 19, a propaganda broadcast was made concerning an alleged production target pledge made by workers of the Szczecin shipyards. On January 22, the shipyards were on strike. The next day, the entire city went on strike. The strike committee decided to speak with only the highest authorities. On January 24, Edward Gierek together with a new prime minister, Piotr Jaroszewicz, and a retinue of highest officials (including then-Defense Minister Wojciech Jaruzelski) came to the shipyards. After a nine-hour encounter, the strike was declared over. (A tape recording of this meeting has been smuggled to the West and published, hence we have a verbatim account of the whole event.) Scattered strikes continued all over the country. High officials visited factories to quell the discontent. On February 15, 1971, an official announcement was issued, returning food prices to their pre-December 13 level.

41

of 1970–71. This decentralized form of protest absorption greatly reduced the tensions felt by local community and enterprise managers and party apparatus. Such tensions are increased in the populist pattern of protest absorption, when the bargaining takes place above the heads of that level and at the expense of its prestige and authority. On the other hand, the more decentralized, corporatist form eliminated not only tensions but also elements of status reversal (or status leveling), in which the powers of the structurally inferior are manifested in momentary dominance through the leveling, and the situation in which the high are humbled and the humble exalted by the privilege of plain speaking. This status reversal was one of the most important features of protest absorption in December 1970 and January 1971. The possibile use of symbolic gestures and symbolic manipulation by the representatives of the power structure was also dramatically reduced in the corporatist pattern: the relative distance between the bargaining parties was too small and the position of the power holders too low for the use of such general terms as "the national interest" or "reasons of state." The result was that claims were mostly material (economic) in character — a 15–25 percent increase in wages, promises of improvement in the conditions, hours, and organization of work.

A different form of protest appeared in the second wave of strikes, which began in the middle of August in the Gdańsk and Gdynia area and, in a period of ten days, swept over the whole country. Gdańsk, Gdynia, and Szczecin, which was the first to follow, were areas where the populist pattern had developed in the early 1970s. Recent strikes there reveal the tensions in the evolution from a populist form based on factory representation toward the corporatist structure of interest representation preferred by the ruling group. Those workers who had participated in the populist pattern in the past again favored the populist form of bargaining but this time for different reasons, based on class representation. Those who have tasted the magic of status

reversal do not want to talk with relatively low-level representatives of the administration. What is more, their cumulative
experience during the ten years after December 1970 showed
them clearly that mere economic demands (and progress) were
not enough — and the relatively decentralized corporatist pattern was not adequate to meet their political demands. Probably
also they could not forget the painful "structural silence" during the meeting with Gierek in 1970 (see my 1979 article in
Soviet Studies). One of the leaders of the Inter-enterprise Strike
Committee (MKS), Lech Wałęsa, himself an activist in the 1970
and 1976 strikes in Gdańsk shipyard, apparently wanted to
show the government side the incredible improvement in the
organization of strikers and their ability to speak out at a meeting with the same level as in December 1970.

Two stages can be observed in the development of the tactics
of the MKS. The first tactic chosen was a compromise between
populist and corporatist forms of protest, according to which
every local strike committee could negotiate individually with
the managers of its factory, but only on local problems. Negotiations on 21 common points[2] were to be pursued at a central

[2] List of demands of the Gdańsk MKS submitted to the president of the
Gdańsk district and to the Prime Minister E. Babiuch on 18 August 1980:
  1) To accept free unions, independent from the party and from employers,
     according to the 87th Convention of the International Organization of
     Labour ratified by the Polish People's Republic (PRL).
  2) To guarantee the right to strike and safety for all strikers as well as for
     persons helping them.
  3) To respect the freedom of speech and publication guaranteed by the Con-
     stitution of the Polish People's Republic, i.e., to end retaliation against
     independent publications and to give access to the mass media to the rep-
     resentatives of all religions.
  4) a. To restore to their previous positions:
        — all employees dismissed after the 1970 and 1976 strikes:
        — all students expelled for their political opinions.
     b. To liberate all political prisoners (including E. Zadrożyński, J.
        Kozłowski, M. Kozłowski).
     c. To end reprisals because of opinions.

level, i.e., by MKS itself. If local negotiations were concluded before the central ones, workers at the specific factories would have to remain on strike for reasons of solidarity.

However, after a few days, MKS decided that this decentralized and more or less corporatist form would not succeed — owing to the lack of experience of workers from small factories who had never before been on strike, and because of attempts by some managers to organize competitive, coopted strike committees in their factories. MKS decided that tactics should be changed and local negotiations suspended till the end of the central ones. Furthermore, Gdańsk workers had learned in 1970 and 1971 that an agreement concluded on the basis of one enterprise lacks any guarantee. This opinion was reinforced during the first days of the bargaining with a branch subcommission of the government commission directed by Deputy Prime Minister Tadeusz Pyka (August 15–20). At that time MKS already existed, but its main function was to coordinate the activity of

---

5) To give information about the existence of MKS in the mass media and to publish its demands.
6) To undertake actions aimed at leading the country out of the crisis situation, beginning by:
   a. making publicly known all information concerning the socio-economic situation of the country;
   b. opening up the possibilities of participation in discussion of a program of reforms to all social groups;
7) To pay for the time on strike as for holidays and from the central union's fund.
8) To increase everybody's basic wage by 2,000 zlotys monthly as a compensation for previous inflation.
9) To guarantee an automatic increase in wages proportional to future inflation.
10) To guarantee full supply of food and to export only surpluses.
11) To liquidate the so-called "commercial" meat prices and to stop selling goods for hard currency in the "internal export" market.
12) To have appointments to managerial posts on qualifications, not on party membership, and to abrogate all the privileges of the party apparatus, police and internal security police by:
    — equalising family allowances
    — liquidating all closed systems of distribution.

the associated strike committees, not to speak out in their name. Separate negotiations were still permitted. Nearly all the agreements concluded at the enterprise level were immediately broken by the government side. For instance that part of agreements which guaranteed the existence and independent functioning of the strike committees (transformed into workers' commissions) until basic changes in the legislation regulating union activity were introduced was arbitrarily and unilaterally replaced by the government side (during typing) with a statement that such committees should be coopted into the existing (and discredited) enterprise councils (*rada zakładowa*). In such a situation, all the strike committees associated in MKS (of which there were already more than 200) decided that MKS, with its eighteen-member presidium led by Lech Wałęsa, would be the exclusive representative of the interests of all workers and that separate talks with the government side should be suspended.

---

13) To establish special coupons for meat and all meat-derived products (till the market situation returns to normal).

14) To introduce old age pension after 35 years of work for men and 30 for women irrespective of age, in other words to establish the pensionable age for women at 50 years and for men at 55.

15) To increase pension paid according to old rules to the level of those paid according to the new rules.

16) To improve the conditions of work of the medical service in order to ensure better medical care for the working population.

17) To ensure an adequate number of places for the children of working mothers in nurseries and kindergartens.

18) To establish paid maternity leave for a period of three years.

19) To reduce the waiting time for flats.

20) To increase travelling allowances from 40 to 100 zlotys per day and to increase the premium for absence from home.

21) To establish all Saturdays free of work.

Postscript: after a discussion among MKS members and under pressure from Mr. Borusewicz, a member of the Committee of Workers Defence (KOR) from Gdańsk, the MKS (on the night of 17 August) decided to drop the demands for free elections to Parliament and for abolition of censorship as unrealistic in the present conditions.

This was the first turning-point in the events described: Lenin's "immovable object," the communist party, labeling itself the avant-garde of the working class, found itself confronted by the *organized* representatives of the very same class. This created not only a political problem of a new quality but also an ideological precedent. The choice of the form of negotiations and of interest representation has been the main axis of conflict, both between the striking workers and the ruling group and among the members of the Politbureau of the PUWP. Those who preferred the corporatist form and the mere economic solution (including Gierek himself) opposed those who understood that without an agreement on a class-based form of negotiation and without the acceptance of the political claims, the crisis could not be solved but only strangled by force. On the other hand the corporatist solution — as I have tried to show — seemed to be the only solution that could be endorsed without a fundamental and radical change in the nature of the political system itself and thus probably the only solution that would not lead dangerously close to the situation in Czechoslovakia in 1968.

Before I undertake a more detailed description of the Gdańsk case, it is worth noting here that one of the most important problems in Poland today is the problem of *dignity*. The development of forms of working-class protest must also be interpreted in that dimension. The deep gulf between egalitarian slogans and a social reality that is full of hierarchies, together with the growing cohesion of the social structure and characteristic predominance of an "ego-defensive" personality type, born out of an authoritarian context and particularly sensitive to all the various dimensions of power relations, makes the problem of dignity and its preservation a crucial, if sometimes subconscious, drive of social activity. The country has witnessed a variety of forms of penetration of hierarchies by those in low positions and the alternation of victory and defeat in this respect.

The status decomposition of the early 1950s (when working-class origin was a substitute for formal education), with mass upward mobility, was not enough to overcome all the threats to the dignity of workers built into the totalitarian system. Other classes did not even have recompense in the form of upward mobility.

The violent status reversal that took the form of acts against all symbols of power during the events of October 1956[b] represented not only efforts by the masses to rebuild their dignity, but also an attempt by the mass media to canalize and discharge the popular auto-aggression, characteristic of every change from above in the totalitarian system.

During the early 1970s the elements of status leveling and status reversal were present in the populist techniques of protest absorption. In 1976 there was a conscious attempt by the ruling elite to break the dignity of the striking workers by making a public spectacle of begging on television and by severe sanctions against any signs of social solidarity. In 1980 nearly all the techniques directed against the class form of interest representation in the Gdańsk area were also threats against the workers' conception of dignity, in which the term "solidarity" was a crucial one.

It took a few days before MKS was officially recognized and the negotiations undertaken. In the meantime the local administrations and party apparatus tried to crush the solidarity of the striking workers, represented by MKS. Promises and bribery were mixed with menace and pressures. Only 17 of nearly 300 strike committees at that time decided to bargain separately, but even those talks were broken off when the government formu-

[b] October 1956 is also referred to as "Polish October." This was the month of the historic Eighth Plenum of the Central Committee of the PUWP that marked the return to power of Władysław Gomułka. It stands as a symbol for the end of the Stalinist era in Poland and, at the same time, of hopes embodied in the so-called "revisionist" or democratic conception of socialism.

lated as a main condition of eventual concessions on its side that all links with MKS must be severed. This was a victory for solidarity.

The government decision to form a new commission with Deputy Prime Minister Jagielski as its chairman and to begin talks with MKS (August 23) was a second turning point. At that moment MKS represented 370 strike committees and more than 400,000 workers. This decision was accelerated by the spread of a wave of strikes over the whole country. In a petition sent to the Central Committee of the PUWP, 260 intellectuals declared their support for MKS (August 20). The Political Science Association and the Polish Sociological Association circulated letters exhorting the government to negotiate with MKS. What is more, the presidium of MKS controlled practically the entire Gdański-Gdynia area: it decided which part of the public transport system would work (with placards saying "we are on strike too, but we are working to make your life easier"), and its commands directed the supply of provisions not only to the striking workers but also to the whole network of food stores in the Gdańsk and Gdynia area. Internal organization among the striking workers occupying shipyards and factories was improving rapidly: both a daily supply of food and an internal security and information service (printing more than 30,000 newsletters daily) were organized. All these showed that the workers could wait.

It took one week from the beginning of the official negotiations between the government commission and MKS (August 23) to the moment the agreement was concluded (August 31).

For me personally it was a week pregnant not only with public significance but also with private turmoil: on August 24 I arrived at the shipyard in Gdańsk, invited by MKS to serve as an expert on the workers' side during the meetings with Jagielski's commission. Other members of the experts' group were: T. Mazowiecki (editor-in-chief of the Catholic monthly *Więź*),

A. Wielowiejski (Secretary of Warsaw Catholic Intelligentsia Club), B. Geremek (professor of history, connected with the unofficial Flying University—TKN), W. Kuczyński and T. Kowalik (economists, also connected with TKN). I stayed in the shipyard for 9 days, until the end of the strike. This gave me a chance to observe not only the inner dynamics of the bargaining but also the inner transformations of the workers' movement itself. The latter were partly connected with the arrival of the experts and of the opposition (KOR from Warsaw, the local Bratniak, and the Young Poland Movement) and semi-opposition activists (DIP—"Experience and Future Club" from Warsaw) and—as a result—with an artificial over-articulation of the movement and a shift from radical, anti-bureaucratic and anti-hierarchical semantics (close to Saint Simon's concept of control by labor over the class of parasites) toward liberal semantics, underlining human rights problems, but relatively less radical in relation to the political framework existing in Poland. Also an initial peasant-type religiosity among workers, humble and not ostentatious, changed into the promotion of rights for the institutionalized Catholic movement in Poland (discounted later by the Catholic deputy Zabłocki at a session of Sejm on September 5) and more demonstrative identification with the Church as an institution (for instance the placing of a rosary on Wałęsa's neck before the moment of signing the agreement). This shift probably diminished the chances of long-term survival of the workers' movement. In my opinion (and I abstract here from my personal value judgments and interests) the best guarantee for that movement was to create strong links with the anti-bureaucratic movement in the Communist party (which at the same time was anti-clerical, ideologically oriented, and opposed to Gierek's "window-dressing" liberalization), represented by the faction headed by Olszowski and Grabski. The latter were coopted into the Central Committee at the Plenum of August 25.

Furthermore, the transformation of the workers' movement at an expressive level, as described above, was — paradoxically — followed by growing authoritarianism and a decline in the democratic character of the movement itself, especially in the relations between its leader Lech Wałęsa, its 18-member presidium, and the 600 delegate-members of MKS (one third of whom were party members), representing 400,000 workers. Less information was sent from the presidium to MKS (for the sake of the negotiations, as one of the experts suggested), and the previous routine of twice-daily meetings between the presidium and all 600 members of MKS was disrupted. The consequence was that fewer votes were taken in the presidium and none in MKS (except one, at the beginning of the talks, on the question of continuing them in the situation where the basic condition of negotiations, the end of the blockade of Gdańsk telephones, had not been fulfilled by the government side). When participating in the meetings of the presidium, I also observed discussion on the need for censorship of the shipyard daily newsletter *Solidarność*, not fully controlled by MKS (again for the sake of bargaining). At the end of the strike an internal split appeared in the presidium, connected with the political compromise formula, and some efforts were made not only to restrain broad discussion in MKS but even to eliminate the potential opponents who disagreed with the text of the compromise on point one (independent unions) and questioned the way in which it had been concluded without public discussion at a plenary meeting of all members of MKS. To avoid open confrontation, an additional, selective control over entry to the building where MKS had its headquarters was introduced on the day the compromise was concluded.

In the light of the facts described, it is very difficult to say unequivocally whether the workers' movement was more democratic or authoritarian in character. On the one hand we could observe in Gdańsk the paradox that the workers' movement was becoming increasingly oligarchic and undemocratic while its claims were couched in increasingly liberal-type semantics. My thesis of artificial over-liberalization of the workers' semantics in Gdańsk is supported by a comparison with the Szczecin situation, where nearly all contacts between the striking workers and the outside world were cut off. As Professor A. Tymowski (who spent one day in Szczecin as an MKS expert working on the topic of minimum wages) underlined in his speech at the meeting of the Warsaw branch of the Polish Sociological Association in September, the workers there did not understand and did not support his proposal to introduce in their claims a demand for "openness and candor" in all future decisions connected with minimum wages. For them, to have their own independent organization which they could *trust* (even an oligarchic one) was a sufficient guarantee of honest representation of their interests. Because of this, Szczecin workers, when acting spontaneously and without external interference, did not indicate the necessity of one of the most basic democratic guarantees, namely the *public* nature of decision making in the social policy sphere. This lack of democratic culture (or rather, lack of democratic imagination) and the strong emphasis the workers placed on such elements as leadership, trust, and mobilization could easily lead to authoritarianism. Also, the strong impact on the unity of the movement (with Wałęsa's characteristic comment on the meeting of the presidium: "It was supposed to be democracy, and somebody has a different position. . .") increased this danger. On the other hand, any such tendency was blunted by two factors. First of all, the Polish workers' movement operated in an authoritarian context. Workers, when drawing up a list of their demands, defined their position *against* (or rather, — in the face of) the social and political atmosphere existing in Poland. The undemocratic and authoritarian nature of the Polish political system, by means of contrast, reduced their own authoritarianism, deeply rooted in the workers' culture and way of socialization. This led to the spontaneous articulation of some democratic demands (for instance, the abolition of censorship). The second factor was connected with the deeply egalitarian and anti-hierarchical character of the workers' movement: it was this, rather than liberal political culture, that dictated the demands for rotation in all high positions.

It is not worth describing the day-by-day bargaining in Gdańsk. I prefer to leave such description to the notes.[3] Here I

[3] The calendar of bargaining in Gdańsk was as follows: 23 August. First meeting of the MKS presidium with the government commission, Deputy Prime Minister Jagielski, with a stony face, repeated the arguments used earlier by Gierek in his TV speech, describing the workers' claims as economic in character and rejecting any possibility of creating independent unions. His answers to other demands were moderate: 'the government will propose programs . . .' The whole meeting was transmitted by shipyard radio to all striking workers. Before Jagielski went into the meeting he was forced by the workers to walk from the bus in which he arrived with the rest of the delegation along a few hundred metres long line of workers loudly shouting the name of their leader, Wałęsa.

After the first meeting we all had an overwhelming feeling of deep disappointment and pessimism. The group of experts began to prepare an alternative, minimum variant for bargaining (if the idea of independent unions were rejected, we wanted to move to a proposal for thorough reform of the existing unions).

We knew nothing at that time about a letter sent the same day from the Gdańsk Party Committee to the Central Committee of the PUWP. The arguments in that letter, repeated the next day in the speech by T. Fiszbach (first secretary of Gdańsk party committee) at the IV Plenum of the PUWP Central Committee, for the first time described the situation in Gdańsk in political terms as a deep crisis of authority. Basic changes in the Politbureau were postulated as 'demanded by the working class', which nota bene was not true. Fiszbach's speech was a signal for personal changes in the Politbureau. At the plenary meeting of the PUWP Central Committee (24 August) Tadeusz Grabski (expelled from the Central Committee in May 1978 for his critical position on Gierek's policy — among other things — on 'window dressing' liberalization and 'clericalism') and Stefan Olszowski (removed from the Politbureau at the last party congress in February 1980 as Gierek's main competitor for the post of first secretary of the Central Committee) came back. J. Szydlak, who only a few days before, as chairman of the Central Council of Unions had rejected the workers' claims for independent unions at the meeting of the Gdańsk Dis-

would like to analyze just one aspect of the negotiations, namely — the introduction of a political preamble, underlining acceptance of the leading role of the communist party, into the formula for independent unions. My analysis has two aims: to show the characteristic features and to project some light on the

---

trict Union Council (19 August) with the argument 'We fought too hard for power to divide it now with somebody else . . .', was dismissed from his position of secretary of the Central Committee. Tadeusz Pyka was dismissed as deputy prime minister. All these events increased the workers' hope slightly but they underlined that nothing had changed *for them*.

The next day was disappointing again: for many hours the workers waited for a call from the local authorities fixing the time of the next meeting with Jagielski's commission. When a message arrived at last it was a new shock, after already heightened expectations: the *wojewoda* said in Jagielski's name, that the phone blockade would be lifted "depending on progress in bargaining", and he added: "If you do not talk on our conditions, the whole world will be informed that the Gdańsk workers do not want to negotiate." This was interpreted by the workers as a new trial of strength, because an end to the blockade was one of their conditions to be fulfilled by the government side before the beginning of the talks. In spite of the tone of the ultimatum in the government statement and a relatively fresh memory of blood on the streets (December 1970) MKS responded unanimously "no talks". Two hours later the time of a second meeting between Jagielski's commission and MKS was fixed.

The tone of the 25 August bargaining was different. The workers, mostly silent at the previous meeting (when Jagielski presented his answer to their 21 demands) started talking, first about the cyclically recurring political crises and independent unions, as the only guarantee of *continuous* representation of working-class interests without the need for such violent eruptions as the present strike and, second, about the deep disequilibrium of the Polish economy, where only 26% of the goods produced were consumer goods and the rest mere 'production for production's sake'. Once again, independent unions as a representation of working people's interests were described by the workers as the only guarantee of avoiding such a situation in the future. And — last but not least — the workers talked about the need for economic reforms (even painful reforms) and independent unions, having authority among workers, were presented as the only guarantee of successful implementation of such reforms.

Jagielski also changed his tone: for the first time a slight hope of creation of new unions emerged when he used the phrase 'we need renewal of a *type* of union activity'. After the first meeting a working group was created.

problem of the self-consciouness of the participants in the movement; and to analyze the role of experts in the Gdańsk negotiations.

After the second meeting with Jagielski's commission (August 25), a small working group was created to elaborate the conception of independent unions. I participated in two meetings of that working group as one of three experts on the MKS side (with T. Mazowiecki and T. Kowalik) and three members of the MKS presidium: B. Lis (a worker from "Elmor," an activist in the old union), A. Gwiazda (an engineer, since 1978 an activist in the illegal Independent Unions) and S. Kobyliński (a warehouseman). On the government side there were the *wojewoda* of Gdańsk, Kołodziejski; the minister of the engineering industry, Jedynak; and the vice-minister of that industry, Kuczyński; with Professor Pajestka (ex-chairman of the Planning Commission, dismissed a few months earlier for his criticism of Gierek's economic policy); Professor Rajkiewicz (Gierek's adviser on social policy); and Professor Jackowiak (representing the point of view of the old unions).

The first meeting was a very technical one. We discussed in a hypothetical manner "if independent unions are created, such and such legislation should be changed." Also discussed were the difference between the existence of unions (on the basis of Convention No. 87 of the ILO) and their functioning (when changes in the existing law would have to be introduced to regulate access of the new unions to the material basis for activity, labor courts, control of safety at work at enterprise level, and access to central institutions — to exercise supervision over central decision making). The workers declared that if such additional legal regulations were not introduced, they would merely "exist and strike."

The first conflict between the two sides were connected with the registration of the new unions. One of the government experts tried to convince us that the only legal possibility was

registration in the existing monopoly central union organization — CRZZ. Our side rejected this possibility. At the end of the
meeting a compromise was reached — the Government itself
would find a possibility of registration independent from CRZZ.

Another controversy concerned the MKS demand for a guarantee, in the text of the agreement, of the right of all Polish
working people to organize independent unions. The government side vigorously rejected such a formula, arguing that it
would look like Czechoslovakia in 1968, when the Dubček
team was later criticized for "encouraging from above. . . ." The
government side suggested between the lines that they preferred
to be forced from below. Members of the MKS presidium were
surprised: "It will cost a lot of money. . . ." They were right:
because of the absence of such a general formula, 200,000 miners from the Rybnik district stayed on strike for two days after
the Gdańsk agreement to obtain their own unions. In September
1980 there was an attempt in Warsaw to organize unions without strikes — but at the time of writing it has not yet been
successful.

During the first meeting of the working group, a peculiar
half-relaxed atmosphere and gentle, ironic tones predominated.
One of the reasons was that the experts on both sides (except
one who tried very hard to involve us in legal traps and formulae, making acceptance of our point by the Politbureau
impossible) were more or less members of the same Warsaw
society: the government experts as somewhat critical but still
loyal professionals, we as perhaps more openly critical, but still
accepted in Gierek's "window dressing" liberalization pattern.
We could very easily have changed places (if only our political
attitudes were taken into account). This atmosphere made the
negotiations easier: elements of truth existed already, leaks from
both sides helped us work more smoothly. There was, in addition, a surreal atmosphere of familiarity that facilitated bargaining; it created a peculiar detachment from the context of our

talks and such facts as the crude blackmail of the telephone blockade, in which our collocutors were involved or at least informed. On the other hand, this atmosphere dangerously increased internal loyalty within the bargaining group: it was one of the main reasons why, for the sake of the talks, the workers were not informed about crucial details and changes made in the working group. We ended the first meeting in an optimistic mood.

Meanwhile, as we waited for the next round of bargaining (Deputy Prime Minister Jagielski went to Warsaw to discuss the text elaborated at the working group's meeting) new events occurred. Leaflets from unknown sources were distributed with the slogan "You will have independent but surely poor unions," rumors were spread about police blockades and food shortages in some provincial factories occupied by strikers. What is more, pay day occurred, and managers refused to pay the wages due for the first two weeks of August when the shipyard and other factories were still working. Lack of information from the working group (only an enigmatic "talks will be continued") and disruption of the daily routine of presidium meetings with MKS (transmitted to all workers) increased the atmosphere of uncertainty and boredom. One of my memories from these few days when talks were being conducted mostly in the working group is a characteristic picture of silent faces waiting for hours glued to the large windows of a hall where delegates of MKS had their seats and entry was only by special pass. I cannot forget those faces, bleached in a darkening air, and the motionless, patient crowd melting into the darkness around the building where talks were conducted. If I feel any solidarity and obligation, it is an obligation to do everything for those silent faces.

Information from the outside world also reached us via foreign journalists (we felt as if we were on an island). Ryszard Wojna, a political commentator and Central Committee member, declared on television that "the party cannot rule unless its links with the working class are rebuilt." Some of us interpreted this as a dangerous accusation that the party was out of control, reminiscent of Czechoslovakia in 1968. But it could also have been pressure for a quick agreement. In addition rumors appeared about the possibility of proclamation of a state of emergency if the strike did not end before September 1. Critical statements in *Rude Pravo* and TASS (about "anti-socialist forces") also created fear of a violent pacification of the Gdańsk situation.

RADICALISM AS A PROBLEM OF IMAGINATION
(THE ROLE OF EXPERTS)

Fed with such information, we were not surprised when at the beginning of the next meeting of the working group (August 27) the government declared: "Your demand for independent unions has become an ideological precedent." Characteristically, most of the members of the delegation looked sad; as one of them said earlier: "The idea of authentically independent workers' unions was a kind of challenge for the younger and more enlightened generation in the party apparatus, annoyed with bureaucratic routine. Some of them probably thought of such unions as a potential ally in their fight with rigidity and command-type style, both above and below them." But now, without further comment and with stony faces, the government side asked the MKS to define the political formula for independent unions, namely — their attitude toward "the leading role of the communist party" and "the unity of the working-class movement."

This was probably for all of us (except the workers, who at that moment did not understand that it was a third turning-point in the situation) the moment when we were conscious of a stone wall that designated the limits of possible reforms.

We (experts) understood that the government side wanted us

to introduce a formula that would subordinate one, spontaneous, representation of the working class (MKS) to another, institutionalized, representation (the communist party). For the ruling group, and probably for Moscow, this was a solution to the political problem created by the existence of working-class representation on both sides of a negotiating table and to the ideological precedent created by that fact.

Paradoxically, the government side could not address such claims directly to the workers. The reaction of the members of the MKS presidium present at that time showed that even they did not think in terms of an ideological precedent. For them MKS was mostly a pragmatic creation for the efficient coordination of the movement and to ensure the safety of strike committees in small enterprises. Factually representing class interests, they did not think in class terms. It is worth underlining here that previously — in December 1970 — the workers (when protesting on a single-enterprise basis) used the term "class" legitimacy in their protest. They *imitated* the Marxist semantics to make their protest more efficient and safer. Now that they felt their strength and had created real class representations, they rejected such semantics as a prosthesis no longer needed. Paradoxically, they acted as a class but did not label themselves in class terms.

One of the workers, Kobyliński, surprised by the government side's pressure and the rapid change from the relaxed air of the previous day to that day's deadly serious atmosphere, asked: "Why? We thought that such problems would be elaborated in practice, step by step. We do not want to play the role of a political party."

But we experts were not surprised. And our understanding was a kind of corruption. We knew that the government side could not explain to the workers the political significance of MKS as a precedent, because such understanding would increase the worker's strength. On the other hand, unless they explained to the workers how crucial such a formula was, the government side would never get it from them. The experts, understanding the situation in the same categories as the ruling group, and — at the same time — trusted by the workers, were expected by the government side to play the role of the bridge. My personal position was that we should explain the situation to all the workers in the presidium and leave the choice to them. If they rejected the political formula needed to get new unions, they should bargain for a different one (for instance "social ownership of the means of production and power to the people," plus a declaration that they would not play the role of a political party). If this was not accepted they should change to the variant of reform of the existing union structure. The idea of independent unions should be kept as a pure, utopian dream for the future. Of course, in such open confrontation the possibility of bloody pacification increased. And we all understood that the workers should end the strike with a feeling of victory; this was necessary for their dignity and for the future.

Partly because of such considerations (and probably because of their own past — full of compromises — and possibly because of a subconscious aversion to the utopian and anarchic thinking of the workers) the majority of the experts tried to convince members of the presidium that such a political formula "did not mean anything," so "let us use their double-talk." Laziness, fatigue, articulation problems and — last, but not least — some workers' trust in the experts and others' fear of the consequences of their own principal attitudes were decisive. An "editorial" group was formed. I decided to stay apart.

Later on, events moved very fast: the political preamble was sent to the government side and was accepted (in the meantime more than 200,000 miners went on strike to show their solidarity with the Gdańsk MKS). There was no vote on the preamble in the presidium nor in the MKS. In the latter it was only read (without comment that it was a final version) but not discussed.

On August 30 both sides (Deputy Prime Minister Jagielski and Lech Wałęsa) signed the final agreement on the principal demand and two others (the right to strike and a guarantee of safety for all workers and "helping persons" involved in the strikes). Jagielski emphasized in his final speech (after signing the text of the agreement) that "the ideological orientation of the new union is clear — they stand by the positions of our Constitution, the steering role of the PUWP and they accept our alliances."

Paradoxically, that commentary, rather than the text of the agreement itself, was a kind of alarm for the workers. After the meeting Jagielski told the presidium that he must go to Warsaw to "get the approval of the Central Committee." When he left, a violent discussion burst out among members of the presidium and some MKS delegates, full of statements like "it is betrayal of the interests of the working class." Wałęsa's answer was characteristic (he probably understood the full sense of compromise for the first time): "We still have the chance that the Central Committee will reject it. . . ." Later on the presidium (for the first time without experts) decided, first to check all the proposals for the agreement which had not yet been discussed with Jagielski, but were already formulated in the working group and, secondly, to send immediately to the Central Committee (via *wojewoda* Kołodziejski) an additional clause: "Full independence of the unions will be guaranteed." But it was too late, and this formula was not added to the final text of the agreement.

Wałęsa decided to face the MKS, a faction of which was not satisfied with the formula of the agreement. His incredible talent for crowd manipulation passed a difficult test at that moment. He had to create the feeling of victory. And so he said: "We will have a building of our own, with a large signboard: Independent Unions. Later (when commenting on the lack of guarantee for the whole country) he said "we will help them, but now we must strengthen ourselves." When talking about the political formula, he added: "It would be better without it, but it was necessary and we must all understand that." He also proposed (was this a compensatory reaction to cancel out blame for compromise?) demanding the release of the members of KOR and other groups who had been arrested, in the terms of an ultimatum. The entire hall shouted "Yes, yes." In a flash Wałęsa (who felt that the crowd was his again) reformulated his statement: "We must give him (Jagielski) some time, it should not stop our talks." The next day (August 31) all the other points in the agreement were signed. The workers got a government promise that the right to court appeal would be introduced into new censorship regulations, and the government also agreed to prepare a proposal for a thorough and egalitarian reform of old-age pensions, family allowances, and minimum wages by the end of the year. New regulations on paid holidays for young mothers and additional resources for health care were promised. On the crucial point of an increase in wages, there was still disagreement. The workers wanted an "allowance for the higher cost of living" of 1,000 zlotys for people with incomes up to 3,500 zlotys monthly , and 500 zlotys for the rest, from the state budget. The government side preferred separate bargaining in particular branches of industry and — as a rule — wage increases by means of promoting all workers one category. Such a formula is not only less egalitarian (higher categories receive larger increases) but also creates a burden on enterprise funds and can lead to future reductions in the work force. What is more, bargaining in a branch structure is not possible for the MKS and Independent Unions with their territorial and class base. By contrast, such a form is convenient for the old unions. During the meeting with Jagielski, Lech Wałęsa personally decided to accept the government proposal, in spite of the opinion of other members of the presidium. At that moment a worker sitting next to me said: "We made a mistake in giving Leszek power." It was a practical lesson in the need for democracy. Some delegates were crying "what can I say to my workmates waiting in the factory?" We must remember that it was only the Gdańsk shipyard, where the MKS was located, which was like a gigantic festival with TV cameras, journalists and a parade of prominent figures from the Warsaw cultural establishment. In other places the strike involved mostly silent and patient waiting. In many enterprises nobody was allowed to go out of the factory; there was often a lack of food and always lack of information (are the Russians moving?), boredom and uncertainty. At the same time there was great determination, lack of verbal exaltation and, momentarily only, feelings of participation in something very important — when people from the other world outside arrived with food, money, and flowers and were crying when leaving.

FIRST WEEK OF SOLIDARITY

The two weeks following the Gdańsk strikes were pregnant with new events.

First of all the workers of Bydgoszcz and Lower and Upper Silesia also got their own unions. The movement to create such unions spread over the country: some of them were being created from divided branch unions, some were interbranch, as for instance the new union of teachers and scientists, which introduced in its charter the obligation to promote professional ethics and the autonomy of science.

The Gdańsk MKS, transformed into unions, was in a phase of enjoying existence. But the promised new legal regulations did not yet come (except registration on September 13). The independent unions had no access to the property accumulated by their members in the old structures, no access to everyday institutions like labor courts, safety authorities, etc. People who wanted to move to the new unions were pushed to repay loans from the old unions immediately. All wage bargaining was conducted by the old unions in a branch structure. The political formula of acceptance of the "steering role of the party" made it difficult to find an autonomous area of activity; even relatively low positions in the formal structure (like foreman) are in the nomenklatura of the enterprise party organization. In most places the new unions had the rights only to exist and to strike.

One of the main events of those two weeks was the serious "illness" of Edward Gierek and the nomination of Stanisław Kania to the post of First Secretary of the Central Committee of the PUWP (September 5). Many rumors circulated about the situation in the Politbureau. Was Olszowski blocked by pressure from Cardinal Wyszyński? Would Olszowski become a Polish Kadar? Could we avoid a Polish Budapest 1956?

[Written in December 1980]

The first part of the chapter was written in September 1980. Now, more than three months after the Gdańsk agreement, I would like to comment on the present dilemmas of institutionalization of the workers' movement. We must remember that the structure of the new Independent Trade Unions, Solidarity, is influenced not only by the pressures of conflicting internal and external forces but also by the continuing failure of the Polish economy. Deep economic disequilibrium has led to a situation where radical reform seems not to be immediately possible. This could stabilize the present attitudes of workers, which are characterized by an unwillingness to participate in decision-making routines at the enterprise level. The workers' years of experience under the mobilization regime gave them good reasons to resist participation in an illusory and window-dressing self-government. Their past experience also taught them that only decisions made in a crisis situation could halt the uncontrolled drift of the economy for a time. The same is true of social needs: in a system of production for production's sake, social needs are taken into account by decision makers only under extraordinary pressure (for instance, a strike). Such attitudes, together with the absence — up to now — of legal clarification of the status of the new unions (except the right to strike), could lead to expansion of strikes as a normal manner of functioning of the new unions (demanding and protesting).

Other key problems connected with the process of institutionalization of Solidarity include a clash between the territorial (class) formula based on solidarity and the reviving branch structure which arose spontaneously during the implementation of point 8 of the Gdańsk agreement. The point introduced wage negotiations at the industrial branch level. Such a branch structure for the new unions is also supported by the government side (as being closer to the corporatist pattern of interest articulation preferred by the ruling group and less politically dangerous than class-based articulation). So far, this branch structure, inflating the original, strike-generated territorial structure, has not been fully controlled by the National Commission of Solidarity (created on September 17, 1980).

Another crucial problem is the formalization of the hierarchy of the new unions. This has two aspects: first, it concerns the relationship between regional MKS and the National Commission, originally created for the purpose of coordination, protection of the weaker MKS, and representation during the registration procedure, but now negotiating and making decisions in the name of all members of Solidarity, who number nearly ten million. The powers of the National Commission are not clear. Recently some members of the National Commission, including Wałęsa, attempted to change the territorial boundaries of certain MKS from regional units which appeared spontaneously during the summer strikes, to boundaries overlapping with the administrative, district-based structure of the state administration. Such a move would weaken the strongest MKS (like Jastrzębie, with its 3–5 million members) and merge the weakest, dramatically changing power relations in the new unions — of course to the advantage of the National Commission. This initiative failed due to strong resistance by the regional leaders. Another dilemma of the process of building a hierarchy is rooted in tensions characteristic of the institutionalization of any charismatic movement. In all regions, tensions may currently be observed between the MKS presidium, on the other hand, and its plenum (delegates from enterprises) and local union activists, on the other, with the latter pushing for more open operation and for institutionalized guarantees of control from below and the former unwilling to give up the charismatic features of its position. It is worth underlining here that the pressures from the mass of union members runs counter to that from local functionaries and activists. Rank-and-file members want to keep the charismatic character of the movement as long as possible, while local functionaries and activists demand further and complete institutionalization and openness, without the secrets and myths about top leaders unavoidable and necessary in a charismatic movement.

The third dilemma of the process of institutionalization is connected with the character of the government, which is the unions' partner in negotiations. An absolute power in a corset of unclear and decentralized authority and unable to control both economy and party is an extremely frustrating bargaining partner, not decisive and not consistent. What is more, the centralized state is reflected in the new unions' structure. Local units of Solidarity have no chance to taste power when all negotiations are at the National Commission level. Only a strike gives a sense of "making a difference by one's own activity" (this was one slogan on the gates of Huta Warszawa during the November strike). This motive led to a wave of wildcat strikes (which ceased recently only because of fear of Soviet intervention).

The last but not the least problem connected with the institutionalization of the new union is the quality of "self-limiting revolution," that has characterized the workers' movement since August. The union formula that was forced on that movement evidently thwarts some of the more politicized (younger) workers. Recurring political postulates and actions (for example, the recent organization of a special commission to analyze the problem of political prisoners in Poland or another to find the officials responsible for the December 1970 massacre in Gdańsk) are evidence of this. Such radical attitudes on the part of many workers (often cooled down by both intelligentsia experts and the leaders of the new union) could in the future play the role of a bridge between the grass-roots workers' movement and the anti-bureaucratic and very radical movement which have appeared in many local PUWP units in the last two months.

Before I say a few words about this new tendency in the PUWP I would like very briefly to show the links between the present situation in the party and the evolution of forms of working-class protest that I described earlier. The changes in the pattern of working-class protest are a good example of the process by which social forms wear out, when a new form solves at least some of the problems produced by a previous one but at the same time itself generates new tensions and problems. The populist pattern of protest articulation and absorption not only created the status problems of the middle-level apparatus but also had imprinted in itself a kind of self-negating drive. That pattern, justifying itself through welfare policies, was completely dependent on economic prosperity. But, on the other hand, it was by definition unable to set a consistent and rational income and investment policy (which should be more selective) and quickly eroded its own economic base. The corporatist form of interest articulation and protest absorption is more selective in its allocation policy and furthermore, produces fewer status problems for the executive strata in the party and administration. But it also generates tensions of its own which lead toward the gradual wearing out of that pattern as well. The corporatist mode of interest representation helps to segment not only problems but also solutions (or quasi-solutions) and to slow down the growth of social tensions by a sequence of decisions based on different (and often conflicting) standards. This led to the semi-feudalization of society observed in the mid-1970s in Poland, with segments of society operating on the basis of different rules, status arrangements, and special privileges. The main costs of this were accelerated erosion of the legal system and a rapid increase in social stratification (with growing differences between particular regions, branches of industry, and social groups, according to their relative bargaining power). In such a situation, when the most strategic groups were bought off under a screen of special treatment, relative social peace existed in spite of an incipient economic crisis.

The first signals of this crisis appeared as early as 1973, with a rapid increase in compulsory savings and foreign debts, a deficit in foreign trade, and declining growth productivity. But decisions to revise investment plans downward come too late to balance the economy effectively. Both the corporatist form of protest absorption (which created an illusion of social stabilization) and the availability of foreign credits are responsible here. But this is not the end of the list of costs of the corporatist pattern: it is worth emphasizing that the tensions at the middle level were as high as before. The unofficial and semi-legal character of the corporatist links between state and society increased with risk and uncertainty at the executive level of both party and state hierarchy. For these reasons, we saw in Poland a few unsuccessful attempts at countermobilization by apparatchiks, frustrated by the system's shift toward a corporatist-type regime. My opinion is that the July–August events, directed against Gierek's policies and aiming at more formal rules of the game (both in the sphere of interest representation and of internal relations in the PUWP), also signaled such countermobilization.

I think that the workers' protest, authentic as it was, also played an instrumental role in that countermobilization of the executive strata of the apparatus. It is characteristic that the new first secretary Kania, in his speech at the Sixth Plenum (October 4–5) promised to formalize the rights and obligations of the particular levels of the apparatus so as to make the functioning of the party more transparent. The apparatus also seemed to be interested in institutionalizing and giving a more open character to government relations with the Catholic Church, which became politicized in the mid-1970s. As a result of that pressure a joint Government-Episcopal Commission was created (October 1980) and more information released not only to the apparatus but also to the press about mutual contacts.

At that time a new movement developed within the PUWP. It called itself a renewal movement directed against the bureaucratization and depoliticization of the PUWP, which was a characteristic of the 1970s and was also rooted in the corporatist pattern. In its most extreme forms, this renewal movement had the character of a rebellion against the apparatus. It began in mid-October in Toruń and Bydgoszcz (partly as a counterreaction inspired by one of the factions in the Politbureau to the possible threat of Euro-communist tendencies of so-called revisionists, already expelled from the party). After a few weeks the movement spread widely and became fully autonomous and out of control. At first the chief demand of that movement was new democratic elections of party secretaries in basic units. Later, with the help of spontaneously created horizontal agreements between party units, it was also able to push effectively for personnel changes at the PUWP city committee level. Another aim of the first stage of the movement's development was an extraordinary party congress and the introduction of new rules for the election of delegates (by direct election) in all party units with at least 750 members, and election at conferences at which only those who got their mandates in secret elections conducted in basic party units have the right to vote. This rule would eliminate the chances of a repeat of the present situations where nearly 50 percent of Central Committee members (who are supposed to control the apparatus) are members of that apparatus, and a further 25 percent are managers, fully dependent on the party apparatus. This first demand was to take from the apparatus the right to make political decisions. Second came a demand for an increase in the role of elected bodies in the party and for working through loosely structured elected commissions in every field where it was possible. According to this postulate even the Politbureau should play the role of a coordinating rather than a decision-making body. The third demand was for obligatory rotation in every position of power in the party. What is more, it emphasized that any cumulation of managerial positions should be forbidden. The final postulate of the movement was repoliticization of the party, followed by a verification of its members (with the help of ideological criteria).

Most of the activists in this movement used institutional justification of their demands (guarantees of party debureaucratization, etc.). But some of them (for instance the Sigma Club at Warsaw University) also used ideological arguments. The Sigma Club activists labeled the Gdańsk events a "conservative and Stalinist movement, because the workers accepted a bureaucratic, Stalinist definition of socialism, based on the division of labor. Workers wanted only to limit and control managers, not to liquidate the managerial role as such" (meeting of Sigma, September 5, 1980). The attitudes of Sigma people have not changed: quite recently they formulated the opinion that Solidarity, if left alone, would only cause "a social democratic limitation of state capitalism" (meeting on November 27). This served as an argument for the necessity of closer links between the unions "with their trade-unionist mentality" and the anti-apparatus movement in the PUWP, represented by Sigma, the Toruń group, and many others (for instance "Kuźnica" in Kraków or the party groups in the Marchlewski and Fonica factories in Łódź). It is worth stressing that at present (December 1980) nearly 1 million members of Solidarity, out of ten million, are party members.

The hope for a possible alliance with workers, which is cherished by the ideologists of the anti-apparatus rebellion, is built on a few facts. First of all, they are themselves much more radical than the experts of Solidarity (linked with the Catholic Church, playing the role of a loyal opposition under the Kania regime). Second, the strongly anti-hierarchical and anti-institutional attitudes of the movement within the party correspond to similar attitudes of rank-and-file members of Solidarity who want to retain as long as possible the movement character of their organization, to work by fluent commissions, etc. Third, there are similar strongly egalitarian accents in both movements. What is more, Sigma people hope that their own anti-bureaucratic position would help in overcoming the barrier of workers' hostility toward the bureaucratized and monopolistic party.

Recently we could see a countermobilization by the party apparatus, trying to find its own contacts with Solidarity with the help of its less discredited members and a somewhat more radical program than that formulated at the Sixth Plenum (for instance, proposing not only new elections but also changes in voting regulations). It should be emphasized that the contacts between party apparatus and Solidarity are mostly at the level of activists in the new unions, whereas the members of the anti-apparatus movement are trying to forge links with rank-and-file members of Solidarity. The reasons for this are obvious; while the former have a similar need for transparency in their organizations, the latter are interested in retaining their movement quality and mobilization as long as possible. This does not exhaust the peculiar parallelism of the PUWP and Solidarity. Both are acting in an ambiguous situation full of a kind of bashful silence, with self-limiting revolution (i.e., Solidarity at its present movement of development) facing an absolute power trying to limit itself. What is more, neither institution is eager to name the differences and conflicts in its own ranks and both have a tendency to repress rather than negotiate such conflicts. Last but not least, both organizations at the present stage of their development avoid labeling their own activity. The party cannot talk openly about its successes in pacification and cooptation of some units of the new unions, because this would mobilize workers again. On the other hand, Solidarity, which took on (under party pressure) the corset of a political organization, cannot name openly its purely political actions. The effect of this is to deepen discontent among the rank-and-file members of the new unions who, due to the highly centralized character of negotiations in a centralized state, have no chance to taste the power they know they have.

Finally I would like to emphasize once more that the frustrations of workers, of the party apparatus, and of rank-and-file members observed before August 1980, were rooted in the same reasons. The corporatist techniques of protest absorption deepened stratification and led to the incipient economic crisis that frustrated workers. But, at the same time, the same corporatism eroded the legal system and strengthened the semi-feudal character of society and state, leading to deep frustration among the apparatus. It also reinforced the depoliticization of the party on the one hand and its corruption and bureaucratization on the other. Both reasons led to the mobilization of rank-and-file party members now observed.

It is impossible at the time of writing to foresee future developments in Poland. Some of us here think that we are in the situation of Italy in the early 1920s (before Mussolini) with the same double-tying of government and very similar erosion of the legal system typical of every situation of change in an authoritarian regime, where the whole legal system was designed to support an absolute ruling group. There are very similar dreams about a "movement" which would overcome all institutional differences, and very similar tensions when facing a weak but at the same time absolute power. Others are thinking about a different analogy: Russia under Kerensky. The main reason for such an analogy is the presence of a highly disciplined and ideologically oriented movement in the party, reminiscent in many aspects of the early Bolsheviks, including their peculiar mixture of activism and passivity (when even worse social facts were perceived as "necessary" because — with the help of dialectical development — they would lead to their opposite). The strong impact of direct democracy on members of that group and their utopian (totalitarian utopian) character are also reminiscent of the early communists.

POST SCRIPTUM

This first chapter was completed in mid-December 1980. The further development of the political situation in Poland went toward rapidly increasing polarization: Solidarity versus party and state. The anatomy of this process will be analyzed in the following chapter.

Self-Limiting Revolution

Winter 1980–Spring 1981

[Written in Autumn 1981]

To understand the inner dynamic of the situation in Poland during winter 1980 and spring 1981, one must analyze its two most
characteristic processes. The first is the painful, zigzag development of a self-limiting revolution, in which the "trade union"
formula has proved too restrictive for a radical workers' movement. This has resulted in frustrations, in surrogate conflicts in
which every issue is turned into a political issue, and in Solidarity's regional leaders playing a symbolic type of politics in order
to preserve their own authority, an authority that is constantly
threatened by pressure from above for "de-radicalization."'

The second process, which began only recently, is the fragmentation and deconcentration of power (which entails deconcentration of responsibility), a process steered by the authorities
in order to avoid open confrontation within society. Initially,
this appeared to be a sign of the party's withdrawal from the
state and the economy. This process signals the end of the practice and the theory of the polymorphic party, which in the past
used its many tentacles to take over all institutions. The party
paid for its polymorphism through depoliticization, bureaucratization, and disintegration. During the winter of 1980, the
party tried to politicize itself again, and to learn once again how
to fight. Kazimierz Barcikowski, a Central Committee secretary,
urged a meeting of PUWP activists on February 20, 1981: "Don't

be afraid to use polarizing methods!" This was an astonishing echo of the "revolutionary" legitimacy accepted in the party apparatus in the late 1940s, when to say that a leader was "popular" implied that he was not revolutionary enough.

At present, the party seems to have abandoned the social contract legitimation (as expressed in the Gdańsk Agreement of August 1980) to the prime minister, General Jaruzelski, and his government. Probably under pressure from the Soviet Union, the party will instead play the unpopular role. This strategy of deconcentrating power was the only way for the party to avoid a total confrontation with Polish society. The change, however, has produced many tensions within the ruling apparatus. These tensions are being used as levers in factional conflict within the leadership. A faction led by Stefan Olszowski, for instance, argues that the party should not withdraw from the state and the economy, leaving them to the government, but should take the opposite approach of restoring and reinforcing its polymorphic structure.

The decision to adopt a power-segmenting strategy was made only after other possibilites had been discarded. The first was to change the nature of party legitimation from the utterly eroded and ritualized "revolutionary" form to a quasi-legal one. This did not succeed. The second was to demobilize and segment society through neo-corporatist techniques (for instance, by bargaining separately with specific professional groups or branches of industry). This did not work either. The third was to employ the Polish Catholic Church as both a negotiator and shock-absorber. However, the Church declined to continue playing this role in 1981 following a conflict with the ruling group over the registration of Farmers' Solidarity as a peasants' trade union.[a]

---

[a] The Catholic Church spoke up for peasants' rights to associate freely in their own unions if they wished to do so. The government stalled on recognizing peasants' right to establish Rural Solidarity, arguing, among other things, that because they were self-employed, peasants did not need to organize

To understand the present situation in Poland, a whole set of political forces must be analyzed. In trying to chart the social forces that existed in Poland in Spring 1981, I will include such obviously active elements as Solidarity, the communist party apparatus, the rank-and-file members of PUWP who were mobilizing against the apparatus, the peasants' movement, and the politicized Catholic Church. Another factor, though more passive and less articulate, was very important because of its latent interests and indirect activity: the managerial stratum. I will also give a brief account of the internal tensions and modes of operation of these forces in the months following the crisis of August 1980.

Second, I will analyze some of the processes typical of the 1970s in Poland that account for the frustration and mobilization of these forces. These are:

1) the changes in the nature and dynamics of the economic cycle that have led to a new, "creeping" crisis;

2) the transformation in the forms of social protest, and the corresponding evolution of the techniques of protest absorption used by the ruling elite. These have ranged from populism through corporatism to class confrontation;

3) the internal processes of the Polish United Workers' Party;

4) the changes in the official policy toward private farming that began in the mid-1970s;

5) the slowdown in upward social mobility as it has affected both individuals and groups.

The framework will be a sketch of the present Polish economic situation and a brief summary of the dilemmas that confront the ruling elite. These dilemmas are rooted in the efforts,

---

against non-existent employers. Before it finally yielded to the peasants' demands, the government was willing to recognize their right to form an association rather than a union. The law, however, has nothing to say about an association going on strike.

unsuccessful thus far, by the ruling elite to change the basis of its legitimacy. This was to have been a change to a quasi-legal, social contract legitimation. These efforts, however, were sabotaged both by the executive level of the party, through the conservatism of the middle-level apparatus and its defense of its entrenched local interests, and by pressures from the Soviet Union and other East European countries. Factional in-fighting and the Polish ruling group's recollection of the circumstances that had led to the Soviet intervention in Czechoslovakia in 1968, also rendered its attempts inconsequent and erratic. The regime's manipulation of the mass media in order to produce an acceptable image for consumption abroad and its campaign to keep Solidarity off television (both of which policies generated severe internal tensions) probably derived from a fresh assessment by Polish leaders of what had taken place in Czechoslovakia.

STRAINS WITHIN SOLIDARITY, WINTER 1980–1981

The political stage in Poland during this period was crowded with social forces in a state of high mobilization. The workers' movement, Solidarity, had developed out of a wave of strikes that affected more than 4,000 enterprises in August 1980. The restrictive character of the trade union formula defining the movement was increasingly evident.[1] The strikes over the free

[1] The results of survey research carried out by the social research center of Mazowsze during the November confrontation on a purely political matter (the arrest of one of Mazowsze's printers, which coincided with the demand for punishment of those responsible for the massacres of December 1979) shows that this kind of activity is part of the "independent union" formula, even though it may go beyond the purely trade union formula. More than 70% of the rank-and-file members gave this opinion. The author of the research was Ludwik Dorn.

Saturdays dispute in February 1981, the fourth confrontation[2] with the ruling elite since the Gdańsk Agreement, were in many ways surrogate conflict, a projection of the internal tensions created by a self-limiting revolution. The main price for the restraining, demobilizing instructions which were handed down from the Solidarity's National Coordinating Commission was paid by the union's regional activists, who found their authority diminished. The leaders of the National Commission, including Wałęsa, remained protected by the charismatic legitimacy they had acquired during the summer 1980 strikes.[3]

Another source of tensions and problems for the regional Solidarity leaders arose from the fact that the structure and behavior of Solidarity reflected — as if in a distorting mirror — many features of its political environment. Negotiations were highly centralized because the decision centers of the party and the state administration were located at the summit of the hierarchy. Moreover, the negotiations were often secret — thus beyond the control not only of the regional activists but of National Commission members as well. This secrecy arose from the yawning gap between the formal constitutional distribution of power within the ruling elite and the location of actual power. During the negotiations, there was a kind of gentlemen's agreement between both sides not to expose this reality to the public. This came out clearly during the November 1980 negotiations to find a political formula that would allow Solidarity's statutes to be legally registered. If that particular bout of bargaining had been open to public scrutiny, it would have destroyed the myth of the independence of the Supreme

---

[2] Earlier strikes occurred in September 1980 over the unclear legal status of the Gdańsk Agreement; in October over the registration issue; and in November, as mentioned above.

[3] E.g., the decision to stop all strikes in December 1980, or to cancel solidarity actions with Rural Solidarity. The National Commission's view was that the strikes at Bielsko Biała and Jelenia Góra were a breach of union statutes, even though they were supported by the local factory-level party organizations.

Court.[4b] These difficulties were compounded by the inefficiency of the information flow throughout the union and by undefined, informal procedures of the National Commission, a confusion that extended to the tasks allocated to its ad hoc working parties.[5] These combined with some degree of manipulation by non-elective elements in the National Commission,[6] who tended to be less radical than the rank-and-file Solidarity members.[7c]

[4] A formula introducing a statement that the union accepted the "leading role of the party" was inserted as an addendum, not as an integral part of the statutes. The negotiations were conducted with the help of high Church and party officials including Bishop Dąbrowski and Werblan, chairman of the Marxist-Leninist Institute.

[5] Nearly 65% of Solidarity members feel they are insufficiently informed about the activities of the National Commission. It is interesting that the union activists feel even more deprived of information, although their access is much easier than that of the average Solidarity member. The reason is the higher aspirations and the higher politicization of the activists.

[6] For instance, "points of order" were manipulated eliminating some items from the agenda; others were reserved for points in the meeting at which no vote can be taken.

[7] Fifty-four percent of the rank-and-file Solidarity members, according to the Mazowsze poll conducted in January 1981, thought that the National Commission was too soft in its negotiations with the government.

[b] Solidarity and the government negotiators agreed that the Supreme Court would reverse a lower-court decision that arbitrarily inserted a clause recognizing the leading role of the PUWP into the Solidarity statute before legalizing it.

[c] The National Coordinating Commission was elected at the Solidarity Congress; its Presidium was selected through the following procedure: Wałęsa nominated a number of individuals, his "cabinet," whom he wanted in the Presidium. The candidates had to be approved by a 50% + 1 vote of the National Commission. Eleven of Wałęsa's twelve candidates were approved in the secret ballot. In addition, the chairmen of the six largest regional Solidarity organizations were to join the Presidium, also pending approval by the National Commission. All secured sufficient votes to be included. In addition to the 18-member Presidium, two non-elective officers had influence on the workings of the National Commission — its secretary, Andrzej Celiński, a close collaborator of Wałęsa, and the press spokesman, Marek Brunne. Thus, the secretary of the National Commission and two-thirds of its Presidium were nominated by Wałęsa.

All these factors eroded the authority of the activists in the regional Solidarity committees (MKZs). It became hard for regional delegates at the National Commission meetings to voice the opinions of the rank and file.[8] The regional leaders were in an especially uncomfortable position as they waited for the first union elections at regional level, due to take place in April 1981.[d] As a result, at Łódź and Radom, there was a fresh wave of confrontations with the local party and state authorities, which could be interpreted as signs of mounting frustrations.

These internal tensions were reinforced by the extremely high expectations of the rank and file toward their regional activists. One should recall that these activists had been the leading figures in the strikes of summer 1980. They succeeded then in giving a coherent form to the workers' grievances and in overcoming the barrier to self-expression that had been erected in the past by the concrete, detailed nature of the workers' demands. During the strikes, they proved that they could operate on the same symbolic level as the ruling group; they shared the same level of semantic ability. This, in combination with the mutual solidarity of the workers, was one of the main factors in the success of the summer protest.

By the winter of 1980–81, the rank and file assumed that their leaders would be able to build structures and formulate operational goals capable of channeling all the radical dreams and instincts of the movement. But this was impossible within the limits of the trade union formula. The umbrella of charisma protecting the leadership was rapidly decaying. Radical pressures from below and the impulse to rescue their own authority caused regional leaders to over-react to the free Saturdays dis-

[8] According to the same poll, 92% of Solidarity's members identified official recognition of Rural Solidarity as the most important issue to fight for; the National Commission did not list this among its main aims.

[d] The process of legitimizing authority within the union through an electoral procedure would culminate with election of delegates for the First Congress of Solidarity in Autumn 1981.

pute in January 1981. This issue was perceived primarily in terms of self-respect and the honoring of the Gdańsk Agreement but it was also an extremely favorable area for confrontation from the point of view of the ruling group and the authorities. In this period of acute economic crisis, the union was demanding shorter working hours. This damaged the public image of the Solidarity leaders. Generally speaking, the pressure from below which built up in February for a renewed effort to put the Gdańsk Agreement into practice was the only way to burst out of this institutional corset of trade unionism. At this time the tensions within the movement were so strong, and the society was becoming so deeply politicized, that almost any problem became a political one.

SYMBOLIC POLITICS

At least some of the confrontations between the union and the ruling group during this period were model cases of falsely articulated or surrogate conflicts, which expressed only superficially the real cleavages dividing society from the ruling elite. In addition to the free Saturdays dispute, another example was the reaction to the police attack on Solidarity activists in Bydgoszcz on March 19, 1981. The real reasons for this attack were rooted in factional infighting within the ruling elite (see Chapter V). The attack was answered by a two-hour general strike in Warsaw and the threat of a general strike throughout the country.

It is worth emphasizing that the situation was not unlike that which prevailed before August 1980. The corporatist mode of articulating demands in the late 1970s made it impossible to label openly many of the workers' real needs because of the structure of negotiations and the level at which they were conducted. In this sense, what we witnessed in early 1981 was simply a dramatic increase in areas that cannot be publicly discussed and examples of false articulation. After August 1980 Poland had, on the one hand, a highly mobilized working class and, on the other hand, a situation in which the self-limitation of the revolution made any expression of needs and dreams impossible. The fundamentalist mentality of many rank and file, their inability to translate their claims into political-institutional terms as well as their characteristic ideological vagueness (see Introduction) reinforce feelings of false articulation. If we add that, in both Solidarity and in the party, the politics of status seems to be more important than politics of interests, and that the most expressive functions in the movement were monopolized by its middle-class members, we will understand the drama of the giant who weeps constantly but, in spite of that, remains mute.

These facts, together with the workers' shocked reaction to the Warsaw Agreement that ended the cultural revolution (see Chapter III) added to the rapid demobilization of the rank and file in Solidarity. The centrally conducted negotiations with the government that, after March 1981, took the place of street politics and local conflicts, in addition to the failures of the information system within Solidarity, further increased the passivity of the average union member. In a sense the tendency to organize political parties, clubs etc., so characteristic of Autumn 1981, can be explained as an escape from Solidarity toward forms promising more open articulation. Unfortunately these new creations are not mass organizations and do not have the strength of Solidarity.

In the late winter 1980–1981 the internal tensions in Solidarity plus the functional imperative of preserving the impetus of the union's movement[9] pushed regional activists at the MKZ level into symbolic politics. With amazing speed, the workers'

[9] Until now, the legal base for meeting workers' claims has been substantive rather than formal legality.

leaders were infected by the virus of playing politics through symbols, so typical of the political culture of the Polish intelligentsia. One example of this was a noticeable tendency after December 1980 for the activists to react strongly to any government decision perceived as a threat but *not* to follow the protest with any consequent course of action. This was true after the arrest of the opposition activist Leszek Moczulski and other members of the Confederation for Independent Poland (KPN). Another example was the selection by Solidarity of advisers whose names, or perhaps labels, signified radicalism both to the union rank and file and to the ruling elite. A popular variant that developed in January and February was a furious attack on problems that were really symbols of the movement's concern with justice, equality, and dignity — for instance, the question of corruption among local party and state officials.

The almost structural role assumed by symbolic politics was useful to the anti-Kania faction in the Politbureau, which welcomed any further polarization of the situation that might drive Kania's team to use unpopular measures.[10] The Bydgoszcz affair was a good example. This confrontation was provoked by the police, with some unidentified actors operating behind the scenes, and was intended to upset the new balance between the ruling group and society (i.e. Solidarity). This balance was based on the separation of the responsibilities between state and party, undertaken so that the government could emphasize its lack of control over the police. The purpose of the tactic was to avoid conflicts; but the provocation in Bydgoszcz destroyed the new balance. Popular opinion held that it was precisely the representatives of the state, Deputy Prime Minister Mach and the vice-prefect of Bydgoszcz who had ordered the police to use force. The provocation relied on the tendency of Solidarity's regional

[10] The Supreme Control Chamber, the body through which the anti-Kania faction led by Moczar operated, passed on to local Solidarity activists information about corruption among local officials or apparatus members.

leaders and rank-and-file members to over-react and to politicize every issue. This same sort of provocation was simultaneously being used as a lever in the Politbureau's factional intrigues, and as a weapon against Kania's policy of abandoning the party's old polymorphism. From the point of view of the apparatus, such abandonment would be very painful and frustrating.

The main victims of the symbolic politics that were played out in January and February 1981 were members of local and regional party and state bureaucracies. During the August 1980 strikes, this group had had a common goal with the workers' movement. Both wanted to end the semi-feudal changes overtaking the Polish system. Managers and regional party officials — especially in underprivileged regions — wanted to introduce better defined and formalized rules into the political game, as well as to negotiate methods whose impact on the legal system would be less divisive than the corporatist mode of interest representation. Solidarity's formula fit this pattern, and a part of the official apparatus favored it, especially since the protest of August 1980 was not aimed at the executive levels of the party or the administration. By January, however, the same group was being attacked by Solidarity partly as a surrogate target of confrontation. As a result it transcended its own conflicts with the Polish ruling group to ask for its protection.

DRIVE TOWARD SHOWDOWN

This change of attitude took place in several stages. During August 1980 the emancipatory interests of the working class and the anti-corporatist attitudes of the state and party bureaucracy had converged. This is why the most prominent exponents of such attitudes — Grabski, Olszowski, and Andrzej Żabiński — had been co-opted into the Politbureau at the very moment Solidarity was created. But by September 1980, the first signs of conflict between Solidarity and the apparatus had already appeared. The apparatus was being forced to act as a transmission belt for all the inconsequential and indecisive policies of the Politbureau. As a result, the authority of the apparatus (save in few cases, like that of the Gdańsk PUWP District Secretary, Fiszbach, who restored his authority by his behavior during the August strikes) seriously deteriorated.

The wage negotiations that followed the Gdańsk Agreement, which were conducted industry by industry rather than via the new territorial structure set up by Solidarity, offended the egalitarian values of the workers' movement and led to a new wave of strikes in mid-September 1980. These strikes were directed against the executive and local apparatuses of the party and administration that were now carrying out these unpopular policies. Some confrontations between workers and local officials, again, could be traced to the unclear position of the Politbureau on the scope and the legal status of the August agreement, which permitted obstacles to be raised to the organization of new unions in areas where no agreement had been signed. The rapid erosion of the apparatus's authority produced an interesting development at the beginning of October 1980. The party's executive level began to make clear that it was no longer willing to shoulder responsibility for the entire political system and to pay with its own prestige for the mistakes of the Politbureau. District party secretaries attacked the Politbureau during the Sixth Plenum of the Central Committee, demanding a clear demarcation of responsibilities between the various layers of the PUWP. It was a sign of the profound crisis of responsibility within the ruling group. This political fragmentation stood in sharp contrast to the massing of social forces around Solidarity.

During October, another interesting phenomenon emerged: the attempt by the ruling elite to transfer its legitimacy from its traditional basis — the ritualized, revolutionary legitimacy of a vanguard party — toward a quasi-legal definition based on formal techniques of problem solving embedded in the social contract concept. The significance of this shift should not be underestimated. The previous justification for the exercise of power was based on a mythical identity of interests between the state (i.e., the party) and society. The implicit assumption of any social contract is that two sides exist, with different interests. This shift in the philosophy of power, however, was not followed by any change in the system's political structure. In addition, the shift was undermined from the start both by factional infighting, which sabotaged the agreements between the government and Solidarity, and by pressures from the USSR and other East European states. The latter in particular prevented the discussion of this philosophical shift in terms that could be understood by the workers, with their lack of ideological training and imagination. In the past this "defect" of imagination had protected workers by making them less vulnerable to the ruling group's manipulations. But no[w] they did not react to the described shift.

In November 1980, symbolic politics could be seen emerging at Solidarity's regional level. All the structural dilemmas of the new union were apparent. Moreover, rank-and-file union members had been nourished on critical articles in the various union bulletins reprinted from opposition journals and publications. They were disillusioned by the extremely slow pace of change and longed for a direct confrontation with the ruling elite. At this time, nearly all negotiations were being conducted by a small group in the National Commission. The members pushed for a new showdown over more political demands. Almost all these impulses were drained away into symbolic politics: radical demands, strikes that ended only when the ruling group set a date for negotiations, and an absence of reaction when nothing actually took place and no explanation was provided by the ruling group. A good example of this was a strike that occurred in the Warsaw steel mill at the end of November 1980. Radical demands were made to disclose within two weeks a list of those responsible for the Radom/Ursus provocation in 1976.[e] The strike ended when the government agreed to the demands, but nothing happened when no such list was given.

Strong pressure from the Soviet Union, amounting to a threat of invasion, led to symbolic reconciliation at the ceremonies for the tenth anniversary of the Gdańsk massacre, on December 16. This was followed by Wałęsa's order to halt all strikes. But the period of social peace was used by the ruling group to consolidate itself, and led to a noticeable slowdown in the implementation of the Gdańsk Agreements. As a result, a new wave of strikes and symbolic political actions by regional leaders of Solidarity returned with increased force in January. Wałęsa and the National Commission were now quite unable to stop these strikes. One of the small regional centers, Bielsko Biała, conducted a general strike lasting eleven days in a region of 120,000 workers, and sent a telegram to the National Commission expressing mistrust of its decisions.

Officials of the party and the local state administration were now the main targets. A new element in the situation appeared in January and February 1981: conflicts became horizontal. Solidarity was supported by party cells at the factory level and by many rank-and-file party members against the local apparatus backed by the ruling group in Warsaw. Solidarity was even on

[e] The reference is to June 1976 workers' strikes — which were most conspicuous in the city of Radom and in the Ursus factory near Warsaw — over a government-proposed food price increase. The proposal was revoked one day after it was announced, but the authorities took savage reprisals against striking workers by beating people in the streets and in police stations and dismissing them from work, fining, and ordering arrests in summary administrative procedures. Scores of strikers were sentenced to long prison terms. In reaction to the authorities' brutalities and injustice, the Workers' Defense Committee (KOR) was established in September 1976 by a group of concerned citizens who vowed to bring "financial, legal and medical assistance" to workers, victims of government persecution.

occasion supported by regional officials of the Democratic party, a satellite formation originally set up after 1945 to "represent" self-employed and small traders. This took place in Zielona Góra in connection with Solidarity's attack on a corrupted local elite in February 1981.

POWER AND CORRUPTION

The battle lines were becoming clearer all the time. They separated those who had power from those who were powerless. The polarization peaked after the Bygdoszcz crisis. Later the situation changed: on the one hand the demobilization of the rank-and-file in Solidarity accelerated; on the other hand, Kania's regime increased pressure to block articulation and to demobilize factory-level party cells. A letter from Brezhnev,[f] as well as a clever manipulation with a "hard liners" label, changed the direction of divisions within the party from horizontal to vertical. After the Ninth Congress of the PUWP, July 1981, a new polarization appeared, but it was now a rapidly deepening polarization between Solidarity and the party as a whole, or rather its apparatus, because rank-and-file members of the party were passive, and many of them canceled their memberships. The proc-

[f] At the Eleventh Plenum of the PUWP's Central Committee (June 9–10, 1981), a letter sent to the Central Committee by the CPSU and signed by Secretary General Leonid Brezhnev had been discussed. In this letter, the leaders of the PUWP were criticized for their inability to control "counterrevolutionary forces" that were exposing Polish socialism to "mortal" dangers. First Secretary of the PUWP, Stanisław Kania, and the then Prime Minister Wojciech Jaruzelski were specifically singled out for their poor performance. Also, concerns were voiced over the preparation for the Extraordinary Ninth Congress of the PUWP, which raised doubts in the minds of Soviet comrades whether or not "a final blow to the party's Marxist-Leninist forces" may be dealt on this occasion.

ess of this new polarization, which was followed by a shift by the party Central Committee from a moderate toward a hard-line orientation, was simple: Immediately after the party congress, hunger marches took place in Łódź, Warsaw, Silesia, and Kutno. The marchers carried slogans stating "Hunger is the only outcome of the Party Congress," which antagonized already frustrated members of the Central Committee as well as the low-level apparatus. This provoked polarization, with the help of a contrived disorganization in food coupon distribution, was probably part of factional infighting.

In the early Spring 1981, as the situation polarized between those in power and the rest of society, the choice before the ruling group was not an easy one. If it protected a corrupt apparatus, it sacrificed its own very fragile legitimacy. On the other hand, if it sacrificed its executive apparatus, it not only lost potential support to a competing party faction but increased the danger that its orders would be sabotaged, which — in the long term — would also reduce its authority. This dilemma was formulated in highly dramatic terms by Andrzej Żabiński, a member of the Politbureau and first secretary of the party at Katowice. Żabiński told the seventh Plenum of the Central Committee, in February 1981, that the ruling elite could no longer rely on popular support; its efforts to construct a new relationship with society on the basis of a social contract rationale had not succeeded, and in such a situation the apparatus had become the ruling group's only supporter.

In an earlier speech to PUWP activists at Katowice in November 1980, Żabiński had defined the tactics for combatting Solidarity. He prescribed three methods: The first was to give Solidarity activists a feeling of power, for example through frequent contact with senior party and state dignitaries, and then to wait for a sign of corruption, which, in Żabiński's terms, "is naturally associated with power." The second method was to polarize Solidarity activists; for example by pushing them to react over highly controversial cases, like the arrests of people from the illegal KPN nationalistic party. The third was to exploit the tensions between the territorial and branch industrial structures of Solidarity. During August 1980, Żabiński had been an advocate of the theory of "convergence" between the interests of workers and the apparatus. Following the apparatus's change of attitude to Solidarity, however, he became one of the new union's more determined opponents.

One of the main consequences of this shift in the relationship between the party and the union was a change in the state's technique of crisis management. Three stages can be identified:

1) The government intensified efforts to demobilize the striking workers by threatening to declare a state of emergency, as in the Bielsko Biała case. In addition, new temporary strike regulations were issued in the Council of Ministers Decree of February 5, 1981, which hinted that there might be no pay after "non-statutory" strikes (i.e., when attacks on the apparatus were considered unjustified even by some members of the National Commission).

2) When these measures did not stop the general strikes in the districts of Bielsko Biała and Jelenia Góra, the next step was to ask officials of the Catholic Church to act as mediators and to offer guarantees that might allow both sides to end the conflict without losing face.[11] Such mediation made the use of more coercive measures by the ruling group unnecessary. Any use of coercion increased the danger that even the army and the police might reject orders of the ruling group. It would, also, increase popular discontent, which could be used as a lever by Mieczys-

---

[11] Bishop Dąbrowski, secretary of the Polish Episcopate, went to Bielsko Biała and signed the document guaranteeing that all corrupt officials would be progressively dismissed.

law Moczar's faction within the party, which was very active during Winter 1980–1981.[8]

3) In mid-February, a third pattern began to develop, one that was capable if necessary of stablizing the situation even without the help of the Church. (After its dispute with the government over the registration of Rural Solidarity, the Church refused to continue to act as a shock-absorber.) The first sign of the new approach was the nomination of General Wojciech Jaruzelski as prime minister. Government leaders were thus attempting to promote one "strong man" — the army commander and defense minister — to block the rise to power of another: Moczar. But this appointment also made it possible to establish a difference in the popular imagination between the images and responsibilities of party and government: Jaruzelski's uniform symbolized this. Kania and his associates had apparently given up hope of regaining popularity; they transferred the legacy of operating the social contract to Jaruzelski and the government.

Two events reinforce this interpretation. First, on February 25, 1981, at a meeting of district secretaries, Kazimierz Barcikowski, a secretary of the PUWP Central Committee and chief government negotiator of the Szczecin Agreement in August stated, "We must stop being afraid to take strong polarizing measures."[12] Second, in February a union delegation met with Stani-

[12] Józef Klasa, chairman of the press department in the Central Committee, leaked news of the meeting to the Warsaw weekly, *Kultura*, March 3, 1981.

[8] Mieczysław Moczar was Minister of the Interior (in charge of the police) in the 1960s and a principal instigator of the anti-Semitic campaign of 1968. He was later removed from power by Edward Gierek as a potential challenger and placed in charge of the politically insignificant Supreme Chamber of Control (a traditional place of exile for out-of-favor politicians) which is entrusted with periodically verifying accounts of state enterprises and institutions and tracking down corruption. Suddenly in 1980 Moczar reemerged holding many trump cards: he was not responsible for economic and political failures of the Gierek team; he acquired ample documentation about corruption, which became one of the main political liabilities of the official establishment; he had a reputation as a nationalist and a "law-and-order" man.

sław Ciosek, the government minister responsible for contact with Solidarity, to complain about police harrassment of union activists in Nowy Sącz and Białystok. Ciosek's response to the delegation stressed that the government does not control the security police and was not responsible for its activities.

This policy of separating responsibilities was probably worked out to meet pressures from the Soviet Union. It allows the regime to use tough measures against opposition groups, while at the same time maintaining fairly good relations between Solidarity and government.[13]

A very similar situation has appeared a few months later, in November 1981. The party apparatus seems even more frustrated than it was in March. The threats are also — from its point of view — more serious; they stem from Jaruzelski's efforts to rebuild the party-state into an army-state, in order to organize a strong authoritarian-bureaucratic regime that is easier to justify. The first signs of the apparatus's countermobilization, as well as the Jaruzelski government's efforts to calm the apparatus, are already visible. Can we expect a new Bydgoszcz? Will these frustrations serve as an instrument during factional fights? It is impossible to answer these questions at the time I write.

---

[13] The separation does not appear to be purely symbolic. If the pattern has not been finally demolished by the Bydogoszcz affair, we will see a gradual increase of the government's independence from day-to-day surveillance by the Politbureau. It is too early to be sure, but this may signal the end of the polymorphic type of Communist party in Poland. We could then expect the party to withdraw from economic management and, at the same time, to undergo a rapid intensification of ideology and politicization. It might evolve toward the current pattern in the German Democratic Republic.

Such a transition will probably be a new source of tensions for the apparatus, which in the mass will be neither able nor willing to exchange its present type of "leading role" for something more ambiguous. These doubts, coupled with the prospect that a withdrawal from the economy will mean a cut in the numbers of the apparatus, were the main sources of the apparatus's frustration causing factional infighting against Kania.

OTHER SOCIAL FORCES

The Catholic Church.

As I pointed out above, the Polish ruling group's change of approach toward Solidarity in February 1981 was reinforced by the Catholic Church's reluctance to play the role of buffer any longer. In spite of the deep religious feelings of the workers, the Church's influence on Solidarity weakened throughout this period, especially at regional levels. A slow but continuous trend toward secularization has occurred within Solidarity,[14] the contacts between the two institutions becoming increasingly ritualized. There are many reasons for this, including the Church's lack of neutrality in the role of negotiator, which the workers noticed. The relationship was affected as well by processes at work within the Church. For the Polish people, the charismatic leadership of the Polish Church was transferred from Cardinal Wyszyński to Pope John Paul II. This weakened the Cardinal's authority over the hierarchy, and made it all the harder for him to repress emerging internal conflicts such as the question of what are the implications of politization of the Church. These conflicts had already appeared in the late 1970s, but less openly.[15] Now they are openly expressed.[16] In addition, the position of the bishops and of the hierarchy in general is now stronger than ever, not only because the Cardinal's influence has weakened relatively but because of a great increase in the power of the Polish Episcopate as a collective body. This arose

[14] See interview with Zbigniew Bujak, the chairman of Mazowsze region, in the Solidarity bulletin *NTO*, January 1981.

[15] One could observe, for instance the pressures on these local priests who engaged in political activities (mostly on farmers' self-defense committees) which strained the delicate balance between the Church and the ruling group.

[16] See interview with Father Alojzy Orszulik (head of the Press Bureau of the Polish Episcopate) in *La Croix* (December 1980) cutting off the KOR from the Church, and the letters of Bishop Tokarczuk, criticizing him. The information about this was published in Solidarity bulletins.

when the Episcopate acquired the right to negotiate with the Polish government, conducting talks that had once been the monopoly of Cardinal Casaroli in Rome or Cardinal Wyszyński himself.[17] In this new situation, the Episcopate appeared to be more interested than before in maintaining good relations with the government, and it used its stabilizing influence on Solidarity as a bargaining chip with the government.[18] Solidarity's activists are well aware of this development and will probably seek to be as independent of the Church as they are of the party. After Cardinal Wyszyński's death on May 28, 1981, the process of secularization rapidly accelerated. A good example of the trend occurred during the Solidarity congress in September 1981, when 226 delegates voted against conducting a mass every morning, 222 voted for it, and the rest remained neutral.

Party Dissidents.

Another important actor has been the anti-apparatus movement within the PUWP. Its most rapid and promising development took place in November and December 1980, when the movement spread into seventeen districts (*województwa*) establishing links between basic party units, an organization directed against the control of the apparatus.[19] The Central Committee's rapid agreement at the Ninth Plenum in March to organize party elections above the basic cell level was not, however, an indication of the strength of these horizontal structures. Rather it was a clever move by Kania's team to cut off the old apparatus,

[17] The special joint Episcopate-Government Commission was set up in October 1980.

[18] The visit by the Soviet official Zagladin to the Vatican in December 1980 was probably to discuss the general question of the status of the Catholic Church in the Soviet Union and Eastern Europe.

[19] Unfortunately, agreements of this kind never covered an entire administrative district, so that it was impossible to conduct new elections above the level of basic party units.

serving as the lever to the opposite faction. Earlier, the Central Committee had openly rejected the right to organize such elections, and the anti-apparatus movement had slowly demobilized; the idea that a parallel party hierarchy could be organized all the way up to the district committee level seemed to be utopian. The only method of paralyzing the apparatus that now remained to the movement was to ignore it, to refuse to obey its orders. One example of this attempt was the fact that, in June, during elections to the Ninth Congress, Iwanow, a movement leader from the Towimor factory in Toruń, was still treated as the local party secretary, in spite of the fact that he had been expelled from the party in November for "factional activity." Nearly all candidates of horizontal structures were, however, cut off during elections on higher levels to the Ninth Congress. The polarizing mechanism that began to work after the Ninth Congress, and especially after the Fourth Plenum in October 1981, furthered the demobilization of this movement. Its last effort was to organize a meeting of secretaries of seventy big party cells on the 15th anniversary of "Polish October 1956" in order to make public a resolution against the polarizing pressure flowing down from the Central Committee. This initiative was, however, blocked due to "its dangerous impact on party unity." Some members of the horizontal structures such as Iwanow left the party; others, such as Witkowski in Toruń, remained in the positions to which they were elected in Spring 1981, knowing that, if they left, their places would be taken by "hard liners" from the old apparatus.

Even in the early Spring 1981 it was evident that the chances that the anti-apparatus movement would change the party's way of functioning were very bleak. The movement wanted, in the first place, to change party election rules in order to prevent members of the apparatus from being reelected to the Central Committee.[20] In principle, the Committee commands the appa-

[20] See *Wspólne Rozmowy*, the publication of the Sigma Club, Warsaw University, November 1980.

ratus, but before the Ninth Congress, 53 percent of the Committee were also members of the apparatus. Although the movement succeeded in cutting off the apparatus during elections to the Ninth Congress as well as to Central Committee, the victory was only superficial. After the Congress, Kania immediately invited nearly all unelected district secretaries as well as professional apparatchiks from the Central Committee to participate on a regular basis in all plenary meetings of the Central Committee with the right to speak. The movement's second aim was to prevent political decisions from being made by non-elected groups (i.e. the apparatus). Developments after the Congress show no progress in this matter. In September 1981 the new members of the Central Committee were already accusing their secretariat of not sending them information about the social and economic situation in Poland.[21] Third, the movement demanded the right to formulate separate "platforms" within the party. This claim was vigorously rejected during the Ninth Congress, and no arrangement was introduced to negotiate conflicts between party cells and the Politbureau (the assumption that such conflicts cannot appear works today in the same way it did during the Stalinist era).

The concept of horizontal structures had only a weak influence on the Congress Commission that prepared the emergency Ninth Congress of PUWP, in part because 83 percent of the commission's members were from the apparatus. Stefan Olszowski, the commission's vice-chairman, openly stated in March 1981 the limits of possible change, labeling all claims that overstepped the limits as "contrary to statuses" or "postulating a retreat from socialism."[22] To start with, he rejected all statements critical of the current "ideological face of the PUWP." He put the positions he was attacking into three groups:

[21] See the discussion during the Second Plenum, September 1981.
[22] Olszowski spoke at the February meeting of the commission preparing these for the emergency Congress.

1) The demand for a multi-outlook party that would attract all the social forces that were for "socialism."[23] (I personally think that this would lead — though this is not of course stated — toward a further reduction of ideology to a merely ritual role.)

2) A desire for a return to a politicized, vanguard party.[24]

3) A demand to revive the socialist tradition of the PUWP, which had been formed in 1948 out of the fusion of the Communist Polish Workers' Party and the Polish Socialist Party (PPS). The guiding role of the party should be revised and translated into the idea of a "party leadership resting on authentic authority."[25]

Olszowski rejected this last idea, emphasizing that a withdrawal of the party from the direct control over the economy would be "irresponsible, in view of the PUWP's historical responsibility." It is worth noting that he took this attitude shortly before the experiment uncoupling the responsibilities of party and state. It seems obvious that Olszowki was prepared to play the role of a leader of a new rebellion of the apparatus against Kania's team.

There were two more reasons for the growing pessimism of the activists of the anti-apparatus movement. First, the central apparatus succeeded in stealing some of the movement's arguments and slogans and set up a lack-lustre imitation of the movement in the form of "District Congress Commissions." Second, the plan to create strong links between the movement and Solidarity came to nothing. Contacts were achieved in only a few regions, like Łódź and Toruń, but then mostly at the enterprise level. In other regions, the workers' suspicion and hostility

[23] According to the party daily, *Trybuna Ludu*, this view is represented by Stefan Bratkowski, chairman of the Journalists Association and co-founder of the Experience and Future Club (DIP).

[24] This is the position of Sigma.

[25] See Wojeich Lamentowicz's articles in *Życie Warszawy*, November 1980.

toward the party as a whole prevailed over their sympathy for the dissidents' battle against the apparatus, especially in regions where the influence of opposition groups or the Catholic Church was strong. Many workers had been simultaneously members of the party and Solidarity, but nearly 600,000 of them preferred to leave the party rather than support the anti-apparatus movement.[26]

The Farmers.

Another social force on the scene at this time was the farmers' movement. The genesis of the movement lay in the "Committees of Farmers' Defense," which sprang up at Zbroża Duża and Milejów in 1978 as a response to an old age pension project and to various aspects of the situation that the farmers considered threatening. These committees, often supported by parish priests, organized a petition against the old age pension scheme in its original form and collected more than 200,000 signatures, in spite of such administrative harassments as the refusal of loans and other assistance and even the beating of some activists of the movement. Farmers' Solidarity, or rather "Rural Solidarity" because Polish farmers are rather peasants with extremely small holdings, began to organize in October 1980 and now has over 1.2 million members (farm proprietors) out of a total 3.5 million private farms in Poland. On February 10, 1981, the Supreme Court refused to register Rural Solidarity as a trade union. The legal reason was that Poland had not ratified Convention 141 of the International Labor Organization (ILO). The real reason was that the ruling elite perceived the movement as a political force that would block the present creep toward a non-violent collectivization of agriculture by way of the gradual

[26] According to *Zagadnienia i Materiały* an internal party bulletin, in February and March more than 10% of the party members (mostly workers) gave back their party cards.

pauperization of private farmers. One of the farmers' movement's main demands, for example, was fair distribution of goods and aids to production between the private, the state-owned, and the so-called "specialized" farms (or socialist "kulaks"). The specialized farms own between 3 and 6 percent of the land but receive more than 50 percent of the aid to production and machines distributed by the local authorities. It was also obvious that the Rural Solidarity, once registered, would seek to protect farmers from the arbitrary rule of local elites. It should be added that the eventual registration of Rural Solidarity in May 1981 as well as the agreements signed by the government did not prevent the recurrence of all these concerns. For instance the core of the conflict between the Rural Solidarity and the government in Autumn 1981 was the overprivileged position of large producers (who got additional incentives in the form of easier access to deficit consumer goods), on the one hand, and the lack of constitutional guarantees to private ownership of land, on the other. The latter was the main reason for the Farmers' Solidarity strike in Siedlce in November 1981.

The appearance of the farmers' movement created headaches for other institutions involved in agriculture. There was an inner split in the ZSL (United Peasants' Party, another of the satellite organizations). Some of the ZSL activists openly backed Rural Solidarity against the views of Stanisław Gucwa, the party leader. Similar events occurred in Rzeszów, during the January farmers' occupational strike, and in March 1981 in Bydgoszcz, where ZSL activists were present along with members of Rural Solidarity and the regional leader of Solidarity, Jan Rulewski, at the meeting with the district council that was broken up when the police were called in.

The government's initial refusal to register Rural Solidarity not only drastically damaged relations between the ruling group and the Church but introduced many tensions into the main Solidarity union. Small or mainly rural regions of the union accused the National Commission of not giving the farmers' cause enough support.[27] In polls undertaken by the social research center of Mazowsze, the Warsaw branch of Solidarity, nearly 90 percent of the union rank and file thought the issue of Rural Solidarity was the most important current problem. The farmers' dispute seemed also to be the reason for the rapid cooling of relations between Cardinal Wyszyński's personal adviser to the National Commission and the group of advisers linked with KOR (Workers' Defence Committee).[28]

Now, a few months after Rural Solidarity was finally registered, as food shortages increase, the first signals of hostility are appearing between workers and farmers. The workers accuse the farmers of not selling enough food and of storing it for a time when prices would be higher. In some regions arguments for the necessity of forcible requisition can be heard. On the other hand, the farmers are demanding machines and consumer goods, and they protest angrily against strikes organized by the workers' Solidarity.

The Managerial Stratum.

This map of social forces should be completed by a short description of the position of the managerial stratum. During the 1970s managers were in a typical "double-bind" — their tensions and their privileges increasing in parallel. Today the increase in prosperity has been halted. One cause of this has been Solidarity actions against corruption and special privileges; in Radom and elsewhere, in December 1980, workers' commisssions even carried out house searches. A second reason is that the faction led by Moczar, head of the Control Chamber that keeps a check on

---

[27] See the transcript of the National Commission meeting in Jelenia Góra, February 8.

[28] See the National Commission transcript published in the sixth number of the *Solidarity Weekly*.

the behavior of state officials, threatened to publish a mysterious list of corrupt officials. The main aim of this tactic, observed during Winter 1980, was to paralyze the faction's possible opponents.

Another source of frustration for managers was Decree 118, issued by the Council of Ministers in November 1980. The decree was intended to spare the ruling elite the onus of taking unpopular decisions by removing them from the field of responsibility. Regulations were introduced that linked part of an enterprise's funds to its level of productivity. At the same time, the state announced publicly that it could no longer guarantee the distribution of raw materials and production supplies except for the most socially important production. The implication was that workers would probably have to be fired, and that the dismissals would be left to the discretion of enterprise managers. The idea was to defuse conflicts over staffing policy and at the same time to implement unpopular decisions at the level where solidarity was weakest. This policy, known as the Small Reform, was, however, successfully blocked at the level of the industrial ministries, especially in the industries where the largest self-reduction of enterprises was planned. As we will see later, this development forced the Council of Ministries to draw up an unemployment policy that will be introduced through decisions taken centrally.

The next threat from the point of view of the managerial stratum was inconsistent regulation of the self-management problem. A compromise forced on Solidarity by the Sejm commission led by Adam Łopatka in September 1981, creates a very complicated system of double supervision for factory-level managers. What is more, a vision of so-called "provisorium," i.e., the government's project leading to a postponement of an introduction of economic reform, has increased the frustrations of the managerial stratum. It is no accident that many members of this stratum have reoriented themselves from looking above their heads toward an identification with their subordinates. This seems to be the safest tactic in the situation when above them exist factional infighting and a fragmented power structure.

LONG TERM TRENDS:
ECONOMIC AND SOCIAL FACTORS

I must now say something about those processes in the 1970s that caused the mobilization of the social forces active today. Five processes must be mentioned. The first is the creeping economic crisis which began in 1973–1974 and is now in full swing.

The dynamics of the present economic cycle in Poland are different from previous ones. In the past, economic crisis acted as a peculiar sort of "regulator," in a sense the only regulator possible in an economy based on artificial economic semantics and deprived of all self-regulating mechanisms.[29] Downward revisions of the plans for accumulation and investment, following the appearance of a cluster of signs that the economy had entered a stage of self-suffocation, had made it possible in the past to move into a phase that was stagnant but more balanced. A detailed description of this pattern of "regulation through crisis" will be given in Chapter VII.

These typical clusters or syndromes, which in the past led to downward revisions of plans, were already apparent in 1973–1974, but, in spite of pressure from some senior officials,[30] nothing was done. Society was quiet and relatively content; the ratio of income growth to the increase of productivity was 1.64:1. Failure to take precautions at this point can also be explained by easy access to foreign credits, the relatively high productivity of

[29] See my article in *Soviet Studies* (Glasgow University, April 1978).
[30] In 1973, Ministers Szopa, Jędrychowski, and Mitręga sharply criticized the economic policies of the Gierek team.

agriculture, and the relative social peace achieved by effective methods of buying off society after December 1970.

The signs of crisis led only to a change in these buying-off techniques. There was a move from the unselective and very expensive general pumping of money into the system toward a corporatist approach, in which only the strategically important or better-organized groups were paid off.[31] This technique created a buffer between those groups and the symptoms of crisis which remained effective until the late 1970s. During this period, 15 percent of the population had access to a "second market," the additional, internal distribution of goods in short supply. A special "fiftieth district" was created in the statistics (Poland has only 49 districts); all scarce commodities were divided into 50 parts, and the extra share was pumped into areas where social unrest appeared to be increasing. During this period of using the corporatist techniques of protest absorption there were more than 1,000 strikes.

In June 1976 another attempt was made to alter the direction of economic policy, but in different form. A political crisis instigated by the faction opposing Gierek and Jaroszewicz provoked popular unrest in Ursus, the tractor plant outside Warsaw, and Radom. The unrest arose over a change in meat prices, combined with a profoundly unfair and unequal scheme for compensation. Following the disturbances, a few minor downward revisions of accumulation and investment were made, but at the same time new, inflationary, and expensive projects were undertaken such as the Katowice Steelworks.[32] Meanwhile, the crisis spread throughout the economy and affected all social groups with cumulative force. Now the ruling group had no reserves

---

[31] Income differentials increased at this period to 1:20. Some 15% of the population had access to internal circulation of scarce goods.

[32] Recent data suggest that this plant was built not under Soviet pressure but, on the contrary, for certain Western interests promoted with the use of bribery to some Polish officials.

to create buffers around the most strategic groups. This time the shock-absorbers did not work.

Simultaneously, the economy was being increasingly overgrown by a "second economy," the black market. This not only reduced the efficiency of the national economy but diminished pressure for reform; life was bad, but for the most active groups it was still possible. Shortages of consumer goods, exacerbated by the government's decision to export additional food worth 30 billion zlotys in May 1980; a rate of inflation which reached 20 percent in 1980; lengthening breaks in production due to lack of raw materials or power supplies (these were 56 percent worse in 1980 than the year before); the freezing of a gigantic value of investment goods (worth 1,200 billion zlotys) which could not be fed into the current economy because of its high dependence on specialized imports (in 1979 nearly 60 percent of imports were cooperative goods); the increasing debts and fiscal crisis of the state; the high costs of food production and the rapidly decreasing productivity of agriculture (due to a shift of government policy toward private farms in the mid-1970s); the falling GNP (2.5 percent in 1979, 8 percent in 1980, 15–20 percent in 1981) — these were only some features of the deep crisis in the Polish economy that led to an implosion of the system and an explosion of society in the summer of 1980. None of these trends had been reversed to now.

In July 1980, the government reacted to the economic crisis with an increase in prices, and society retorted with a wave of strikes. The price increase, however, was only a pretext for the strikes, not a cause. To this very day, the higher prices decreed in July 1980 remain in force in 42 out of 49 districts. Frustrations were deep, and once people had organized Solidarity, they seemed to forget the original reason for the conflict.

The present economic situation in Poland is even worse than it was before August 1980. Only a few of the most typical signs need to be mentioned here: deep stagnation and plans to reduce employment by 10 percent (1.2 million); galloping inflation in a situation of market shortages (a miner must work nearly one hour to buy one egg in the private market; in a state-controlled market eggs cannot be bought at all due to reduced supply); a situation where every fifth zloty is uncovered by goods; only between 40 and 60 percent of productive potential is in use due to the lack of raw materials and energy (with a nearly 20 percent decrease in the extraction of coal due to the technical collapse of the mining industry, the end of compulsory work on Sundays during the Gierek era, and free Saturdays on which no more than 60 percent of miners work voluntarily). To this picture we should add six million people (one-fifth of the population) who live below the level of a "social minimum", a sixth of the state budget used to subsidize agriculture (mostly state-owned farms); and, one of the most vital factors, no prospect of a rapid and decisive economic reform. One should remember that any serious reform would have to end the second economy that helps to make life bearable; reform would cause unemployment, increase the cost of living, force the withdrawal of the party from the economy, and deliver a blow to the interests of the most powerful pressure groups in the administration and industry. A basic reform of agriculture that would favor indivdual farmers is blocked by the Soviet Union.

All this is accompanied by economic anarchy. For example, productivity in February 1981 was worse than in January. One explanation was that in February there were *fewer* strikes and, as a result, more factories at work, a worse energy shortage, and more random power cuts. This last factor in the chain-reaction caused more waste and worse disorganization than all the January strikes, which were planned in advance.

Almost all the economic elements that underlay popular discontent and the unrest of Summer 1980 still exist. It must be emphasized, however, that the social characteristics of the 1970s were an even more important cause of deep popular frustrations:

the semi-feudalization of the system, the erosion of legality, the corruption and the rapid increase in social and economic differences, the arrogance of the apparatus. These were by-products of the corporatist methods which the ruling elite employed to buy social peace.

The pattern of social protest in the 1970s, which could be perceived in terms of a "class war" between the owners of the means of production (the state and the party apparatuses) and the working class, was followed by the transformation of the methods the government used to absorb that protest. This transformation was a good illustration of the process of erosion of social forms of protest, or protest absorption. This was the second process of the 1970s that was responsible for the present mobilization of social forces. The exhaustion of techniques of protest absorption which themselves produced more and more tensions, resulted in the mobilization both of society and of the executive level of the party and state apparatus. The latter had lost status through the populist techniques used by Gierek in the early 1970s, and it had paid with uncertainty and frustration as well as prestige for the corporatist methods of protest absorption used after 1974. The corporatist methods were based on non-legalized negotiations, on exceptions that outgrew the rules. The differences in the conditions of particular regions and branches of industry deepened. In addition, the incipient negotiations between the government and the Catholic Church after 1977 led to increased tensions in the apparatus, which was trapped between greater pressures from a society whose expectations were rising and the unchanged instructions that continued to flow down through the party hierarchy. In such a situation, the apparatus became as interested as society in a change of ruling methods.[33]

[33] A few earlier waves of countermobilization in the apparatus against these ruling techniques were evident in the 1970s: Grabski's speech at the Tenth Plenum in May 1979, the Eighth party Congress in February 1980, and, in a

A third process of the 1970s that ought to be mentioned because it was responsible for mobilizing the anti-apparatus movement is connected with developments inside the PUWP. There were three parallel trends. The first arose from the peculiar crisis-oriented philosophy that flourished within the ruling elite and at the executive level after December 1970. According to this approach, crises were unavoidable, and, further, they were the only situations permitting any regulation of the system. The logical reaction to this was to introduce arrangements that would minimize the costs such a crisis would exact from the ruling elite and its apparatus. In 1972, the members of the ruling elite received a guarantee that their privileged financial position would be preserved even if they had to serve as scapegoats during the political crisis. This guarantee was formalized in Council of State Decree 49. The decree also extended these financial privileges to the children of members and ex-members of the elite! The executive level of the state administration received a guarantee of a different nature. An official list of nomenklatura posts was published in 1973, covering posts both at central and district levels, and conveying the implication that people dismissed from one nomenklatura post would be reallocated to another on the same level, or to another district. At the same time, the scope of nomenklatura was broadened, thus protecting a greater number of executive officials. The latter rule continues in effect; as recently as October 1981, a list of names of state and party officials dismissed during conflicts with Solidarity was disclosed, among them the wojewoda Przybylski from the Bydgoszcz crisis, with appointments to posts in the foreign service!

---

way, the events of August 1980, when some strikes — for instance in Cegielski in Poznań — that served as turning points in negotiations with the government were organized by the old unions with the quiet support of the district party apparatus. The district party secretary in Poznań, Jerzy Zasada, was among the seven district secretaries supporting Grabski's critique of Gierek in the late 1970s.

The second trend evident in the PUWP in the mid-1970s was the reduction in control over the party apparatus. In 1974, electoral rules were changed, permitting a majority of apparatus members to sit on the Central Committee, the body that supervises the apparatus.

Both these trends illustrate one very characteristic feature of Poland in the 1970s, namely the accelerated establishment of a legal identity for the regime. Nearly all the customary and informal practices of this regime were formalized in the 1970s. The leading role of the party was introduced into the Constitution; informal practices facilitating a blockade of interest articulation inside the party were introduced to its statutes. An obligation to vote on one list was legalized for the first time;[h] previously such voting had been guaranteed through terror, as in 1954, or by additional arrangements such as the Joint Commission of Parties in 1956–1957, or passivity and apathy of the society. This *structural Stalinism* no longer needed terror; all its rules were reinforced by law. It is characteristic that the process

---

[h] Only one list of candidates is presented to the voters at election time. It is sponsored by the Front of National Unity. One does not choose, therefore, between alternative candidates; one can, at most, reject the ones that are presented. The number of candidates presented in each electoral district is usually larger than the number of seats assigned to that district. Thus, the rudimentary choice left to the voters resides in the fact that not all candidates presented on the ballot are assured of seats in the elected body. The order of appearance on the list matters — the list is divided into mandatory positions (from which one is assured of election provided one's name is not crossed off) and non-mandatory positions (from which one can get elected only if enough candidates in mandatory positions are crossed off by the majority of the electorate). For example, in a five-seat (mandate) district where a list of seven candidates is presented to the voters, positions number six and seven are non-mandatory. This means that ballots from which no names were crossed off (and government propaganda is asking everybody to do precisely this as a show of confidence in the regime) are automatically counted as "Yes" votes for the first five candidates and "No" votes for candidates no. 6 and no. 7. Needless to say, one rarely gets elected from a non-mandatory position. Thus, to control the outcome of elections, it is enough for the government to list candidates' names on the ballot in the way it deems desirable.

was followed by the development of a pattern of repressive toleration (in which the political opposition has no legal status) of
the corporatist techniques that cannot be justified by ideology,
as well as many annexes to the regime in the form of invoked-
from-above "lame pluralism" (see Chapter IV). But all these
arrangements were outside the system, and they persist informally. In the 1970s, the system was closer than ever to its pure
form. This double logic is responsible for the present confusion
of reactions and makes it difficult to analyze this stage of the
system's evolution.

The third trend within the party of the 1970s was the buying-
off of the apparatus and the state administration by placing
them in a sort of corruption-trap: an increase in their frustration
was accompanied by increase in their income. Another buying-
off technique lay in turning a blind eye to bribery and the use
of public office for private gain. The latter was assisted by the
strong links between local elites and local private industries and
craftsmen, who operated with the help of the "second economy" and under the protection of the corrupt administration in
charge of distributing scarce goods.

These developments in the PUWP frustrated many of the
rank-and-file members of the party and led to the anti-apparatus
rebellion in the PUWP that was so prominent during the
Autumn and Winter of 1980–1981.

The fourth process, which appears to have stimulated and
mobilized the farmers' movement, was a sudden change in policy toward private agriculture in the mid-1970s. The essential
elements here were the introduction in 1974 of administrative
restrictions that limited the transfer of land into private hands;
the 1976 old-age pension scheme combined with numerous
restrictions on the inheritance of land; an administrative expansion of the basic local government unit, the *gmina*, which created chaos because titles of land ownership are kept in gmina
offices; growing difficulties in buying goods needed for agricul-

tural production (only 4 percent of industry worked for agriculture); and, last but not least, favoritism toward specialized farmers, often intimately involved with local elites, in the distribution of production supplies. All these trends led the private farmers to the conclusion that their farms were in danger and that collectivization, by means of pauperization, had become inevitable. These views accelerated the departure of young people from the land, and reduced investment by farmers. But it also persuaded some farmers to organize themselves against the threat from the state.

The last process characterizing the 1970s was a serious slowing down of the upward mobility which has always functioned as a shock-absorber in Eastern Europe and the Soviet Union, even in the Stalinist era. The slowdown was caused by economic stagnation and the fact that the expansion of managerial posts had reached the saturation point. By the mid-1970s, every eighth employee in Poland was some sort of manager. A third of the male population between the ages of 30 and 40 were managers. This method of co-optation had now reached its limit; every rational argument was against further multiplication of managerial positions. And natural replacement was very slow because of the relative youth of those co-optation into the ruling group. Most of them were even younger than the generation of the 1968 student movement activists and their opponents in the Association of Socialist Youth (ZMS).

Finally, there was the tendency of the middle-class to perpetuate itself. It became more and more difficult for outsiders from the "lower" classes to move upward because of rising social barriers. Many workers had a relatively better income than white-collar employees; thus their motivation to study decreased. These circumstances encouraged the persistence in the working class of people, who only ten years before would have become part of the frustrated and co-opted semi-intelligentsia. Now some of them have become strike leaders and Solidarity activists.

Only some of these trends were modified or reversed after August 1980. The economic situation is even worse. The future may hold either stagnation and unemployment or an invisible and uncontrollable integration with the Soviet economy through the direct cooperation of Poland's unused industrial potential with the Soviet economy, under Soviet supervision and through Soviet economic planning. A suggestion of just such a possibility is present in the Government Stabilization Plan passed by Sejm in June 1981. Such a development, if combined with a Soviet presence on the Joint International Commission supervising the rescheduling of the Polish foreign debt, would greatly increase Poland's political dependence. Some elements of this invisible intervention will be discussed in Chapter VII. If the Soviet presence were combined with the tough measures that would be used by certain domestic forces, it could even serve as a substitute for military intervention.

After the Bydgoszcz crisis, the Polish self-limiting revolution moved into a new stage of development, which I described in the Introduction. Mass strikes were replaced by centrally conducted negotiations. Within Solidarity, there was an identity crisis as well as growing demobilization of the rank and file. But the determination and despair of society are as intense as before. The frustration that has led to the politicization of every crisis and to overreaction to it, is connected with the fact that, during the period of its highest mobilization, Solidarity was infected, so to speak, by two diseases. One was detachment from reality, as when Solidarity and the ruling group collided without even touching upon their real problems. The other was the symbolic politics I have described, the malady caught from the intelligentsia. The barriers to articulation, which remained even after the creation of Solidarity, add to these frustrations. The development of the movement's consciousness, the evolution of its structures, and its methods of functioning will be described in the next chapter.

CHAPTER III

Dynamics of Working-Class

Consciousness

[Written in Autumn 1981]

IDEOLOGICAL FUNCTIONS OF
FORMS OF CONSCIOUSNESS

I have already introduced two topics that are directly linked with the problem of consciousness playing an ideological role in the movement. These were the political consequences of the fundamentalist orientation of the rank-and-file members of Solidarity and the changes in perspective during the rapid shift from narrow status groups to the supra-status of Solidarity as an organized society. This process of reorientation accelerated so quickly that it has to be interpreted in terms of cultural revolution. This chapter will describe the zigzags of this revolution, when an end of a hierarchy built on semantic competence seemed established and, later on, destroyed, and a new wave of anti-intelligentsia attitudes appeared. In Poland, nearly all turning points and revolutions have been experienced primarily in cultural and moral terms and less in terms of changes in institutions and legal regulations, as in France, or in philosophy, as in Germany. The same, dream-like way of outliving our history appeared when the gate to an authentic modernization seems to be closed—due to the "geo-political" situation.

At least some of the emotions and aspirations that were generated by the creation of Solidarity have now been transformed into a resentful wave of anti-Semitism or anti-intelligentsia feelings that recalls the darkest period of the past, with its mythical, discontinuous statuses, its lack of communication, its labels and stereotypes. The causes of this blockade of modernization seem to go deeper than the mere impossibility of changing the political regime. Is modernization possible when the leading role in the system is played by so traditional and hierarchical a body as the Polish Catholic Church? Can authoritarian personalities, with their low tolerance of ambiguity, escape from an authoritarian regime when an economic crisis is in full swing? Is it possible to build a pluralistic system based on legal guarantees supporting a fundamentalist movement like Solidarity with its strong moralistic orientation? And last but not least, can the ruling groups' reinterpretation of its own status go farther than from a totalitarian toward an authoritarian-bureaucratic regime, with an army-state taking the place of the party-state?

Three thresholds must be mentioned when talking about the development of the consciousness of working class in Poland. The first is the barrier created by the limited semantic competence of the workers, which in the past has led to articulation of interests only in restricted, situation-specific, terms. In the first part of this chapter I will try to show how this limited semantic competence made the workers' protest less efficient. This is a good example of a situation in which the structure of speech (rather than its content) plays an ideological role because it reinforces and stablizes the political system. However, this same limited competence sometimes served as an advantage by reducing the areas of possible communication during negotiations, as a result making the working class less vulnerable to manipulation and in a sense more radical. In this context, I will discuss radicalism as a problem of imagination as well as of attitude and the events of August 1980 as a type of cultural revolution.

The second threshold of working class development is the

barrier of reification,[1] in which power relations are perceived as painful but natural and without alternative. In the second part of this chapter I shall show the multidimensionality of the hierarchial order prior to August 1980 and the role of post-August working-class participation in politics (via Solidarity) in surmounting the reification of the power hierarchy.

The third threshold, which is yet to be crossed, is rooted in a peculiar self-image of Solidarity activists and in their perception of reality. Both, as I will try to show in the third part of this chapter, make it impossible for the movement to exploit fully its own potential. The characteristic features are: monistic tendencies linked with a moralistic conception of movement legitimacy, one-dimensionality in perceiving the external world ("we" versus the ruling group), an ahistoricism understood as an inability to generalize the logic of the movement's development, a lack of middle-range aims (such as, for instance, the socialization of the means of production) when the structure of Solidarity goals is a mixture of a Sorelian-type myth of a full repudiation of obedience (such as the August 1980 strikes) and a rough and tumble, mostly reactive policy.

The features of the consciousness typical of Solidarity members are reinforced by two characteristics of the movement's organizational formula: solidarism, which makes it impossible to identify and resolve conflicts inside the movement, and the fiction of its apolitical character. Maintaining this fiction creates areas of silence in the movement and makes it impossible to

---

[1] Reification, according to Gyorgy Lukacs, means the creation of a second nature of pseudo-things. Gyorgy Lukacs, "History and Class Consciousness," *History and Class Consciousness; Studies in Marxist Dialectics*, Cambridge, Mass., MIT Press, 1971, p. 98. The frozen, reified realm of objectification that affects all subjectivity was conceived by Lukacs as a becoming dynamic "objective spirit." "Just as the capitalist system continuously produces and reproduces itself economically on higher and higher levels, the structure of reification sinks more deeply more fatefully and more definitely into the consciousness of man" (p. 105).

formulate an ideology that would reflect all the aspirations of its members. This handicap is deepened by a silence rooted in the diffident character of the self-limiting revolution.

The movement's mentality combined with these features of its formula are a peculiar reflection of the PUWP, with its small tolerance for internal conflict and huge areas of silence rooted in the erosion and ritualization of ideology as well as by the contradictory status of a ruling party armed only with revolutionary rhetoric. What is more, the mentality of Solidarity activists is strongly reminiscent of the youth (in historical, not biological terms) of today's party apparatus. The moralistic legitimacy of Solidarity recalls the fundamentalist (in the sense of undebatable, based on "revealed" and unverifiable truth) legitimization of the early Polish communists. In both movements the consequences of such fundamentalism are also similar: namely a tendency to polarize social forces, a personification of politics, a contempt for formal regulation in the name of invoking substantive legality, based on a popular feelings of justice. Solidarity has difficulty making compromises because every political problem becomes doctrinal struggle between good and evil, again very similar to the early history of today's communist party. The mentality of the party apparatchiks, once built on fervent emotion, has now been frozen in everyday routines, rituals, and rationalizations; but the similarity persists. It is a likeness in the deep structure of consciousness of both sides, despite their different, even opposite, value orientations.

Members of the party apparatus recognize their own mentality in some Solidarity activists but nevertheless are unable to communicate with them, in part because both sides tend to make judgments in terms of context, rather than content. Communication has been further complicated by strong elements of status politics of both sides.[2] Following the Solidarity election to

---

[2] By status politics is meant an orientation of activity toward an improvement of one's own position (perceived in terms of prestige and a domain of power) vis-à-vis the other side.

its First Congress, it looks as if status politics, prevalent in the first few months of its existence (when the movement was trying to maintain its impetus and authority in a situation of self-limiting revolution), will revive. More people with personal status problems became members of regional authorities of Solidarity. Many dislocated, marginal, white-collar workers, their upward mobility blocked, were elected; one-fourth of the posts were kept by blue-collar workers. The similar features of both sides of the conflict not only make communications more difficult but also reinforce the mentality of both sides. That similarity is linked with some parallels of their institutional forms.

Following this short introduction I will analyze in more detail the three thresholds in the development of the working class consciousness in Poland. I will show the connections between this development and the evolution of forms of protest and techniques of protest absorption. I will also analyze Solidarity's effectiveness in overcoming these barriers.

FORM AS AN IDEOLOGY

The first threshold that must be crossed in the development of the working-class movement is the barrier of limited semantic competence. An analysis of this problem has both practical and theoretical implications. It is closely linked with a phenomenon in which a form of social consciousness rather than its substance fulfills an ideological function in regard to the system. This phenomenon results from the erosion and ritualization of ideology that is characteristic of authoritarian regimes.

By ideological functions of forms of consciousness I mean:

1) their participation in measures to stablize present social relations;

2) their influence on the opportunities of individuals, social groups, and classes in conflict situations;

3) their impact on the ability to defend against the tensions generated by the system;

4) their role in the techniques of domination and manipulation applied by the ruling group.

When I assume that the above functions of ideology are increasingly taken over by the form of consciousness, I am thinking in particular of:

1) the ideological functions of the manner of speech, i.e., structurally differentiated semantic codes;

2) the ideological functions of polarization as a way of perceiving the world;

3) the ideological functions of a segmented structure of consciousness, so typical of systems based on corporatist techniques of stabilization;

4) the ideological function of the prevailing forms of social discourse.

In the context of the development of the consciousness of working-class protest movements, the most interesting features are the ideological functions of a diversification of semantic competences. Ideological functions of other forms of consciousness will be described in footnotes.

According to Basil Bernstein, forms of speech (semantic codes) are products of social structure and act to extend its durability.[3] Bernstein was concerned chiefly with the influence of the diversification of semantic codes on the opportunities for social advancement of persons from different social classes. I am interested in the influence these forms have on political behavior.

That the forms of speech carry out such functions is obvious. As we shall see later, there are different possibilities for the speaker, depending on the code used (or rather on his class,

---

[3] Basil Bernstein, "Language and Social Class," *British Journal of Sociology* (1960), XI; "Linguistic Codes" in *Language and Speech* (1962), "Family Role Systems, Socialization and Communication," paper presented at University of Chicago conference, 1964.

because differences in codes are largely derivative of social structure) to deliver his statement from any situational context. This, in turn, not only makes it possible to articulate general interests (a precondition for acquiring class consciousness), but also, by indicating access to an alternative reality, shapes a kind of political imagination. Only the ability to think alternatively allows a group (or class) to do something more than riot, which is an isolated act of despair. In the absence of such imagination, when the categories used to define one's own social conditions are context-tied, it is difficult to argue with a definition of that situation that is externally imposed, abstract, and formulated in a different code. Such helplessness is illustratd by fragments of dialogue from a meeting between striking workers and Gierek in January 1977 in Szczecin (see appendix, p. 147). When there are no opportunities for honest discussion, what remains is silence and frustration or else aggression and total rejection of the definition of reality presented by the other side.

Before turning to the ideological functions of semantic codes, I want to show (on the basis of Bernstein's work) the differences between two types of code — restricted and elaborated. According to Bernstein, the former is encountered with statistically more frequency among the working class, while the latter predominates in the middle classes (office workers and intelligentsia). Studies carried out by Andrzej Piotrowski and Marek Ziółkowski confirm the validity of this thesis in Poland.[4] It is important to note, in this connection, that the differences in these semantic codes (or forms of speech) in no way indicate the level of the speaker's intelligence and not even the extent of his passive vocabulary. The differences are linked to different approaches to language and communication, as well as to the habits, strengthened in the course of socialization, of publicly activating the vocabulary that was passively mastered (in school

[4] Andrzej Piotrowski and Marek Ziółkowski *Zróżnicowania językowe a struktura społeczna*, Warsaw, PWN, 1976.

or via television). The basic differences between the two codes are:

1) In the elaborated code, the rules of language transformations are manifest and clearly perceived by the speaker himself. This makes it possible to maintain a distance from one's own statements (so-called "ironic speech") and also consciously to alter style and to imitate creatively. In the restricted code, these rules of transformations are not used consciously by the speaker, but are learned mechanically together with a specific phraseology. Similarly, imitation is mechanical since phrases are imitated, not the style.

2) Persons using the elaborated code assume that different points of view (or reference) exist in a dialogue as a fundamental premise. The code evolves among middle-class families in the course of socialization, where discussions and interchange-ability of roles in the process of education as well as access to differing points of view (to written matter) is more often the rule than it is (again formed in the process of socialization) among working-class families. In the latter, the distribution of roles and positions in the family are rigidly determined, and access to cultural products is more restricted. The acceptance of differences as a natural feature of a situation gives rise to the ability to present one's own argument (the culture of discourse). The opposite is true of persons using the restricted code, where the basic premise is community of context. Not only does the ability to present one's own point of view not develop, but there is less tolerance for differing opinions in general. Persons using a restricted code, as a rule, have fewer doubts in regard to interpretation; they seldom notice ambiguities of meaning, which, of course, makes any "play" on language difficult for them to understand. This habit of using language seems to create a predisposition toward the fundamentalist approach to social life.

3) Persons using the elaborated code more often employ abstract symbols, whereas those using the restricted code have a

clear preference for condensed symbols such as the first names of people who come to symbolize a situation, a feature, or group of abstract features. As a result, the latter have a tendency to personify politics.

4) An awareness of the rules of language transformations and the habit of using abstractions and ideas, freed from their situational context, give persons using the elaborated code access to the language of symbols that is a language not only of innovation and change but also of control. In contrast, those who use the restricted code and are trapped in situational context find it more difficult to use metalanguage and to make general reflections on the prevailing social order. It is, therefore, a language of resignation and of submission.

Let us review the effects of both forms of speech (codes) on political behavior and show their ideological functions, i.e., in what way they stabilize existing power relations. In Poland in the 1970s an interesting phenomenon occurred: the restricted code became more widely used by classes other than the working class. One manifestation of this tendency was the impoverishment of the symbolic content of statements. The phenomenon was, I think, the result of a characteristic feeling of linguistic shame, a conscious avoidance of symbols that had been excessively exploited in the artificial and misleading official language of propaganda. Thus, the symbols had lost their value and were regarded less as instruments of communication than as signs of identification with the Establishment. The events of August 1980 were a type of cultural revolution because they revived at least some political symbols. The inflexible structure of institutions before August 1980, reinforced by ideological myth, also made for a general climate in which one does not speak about differences or divergence of interest. Finally, an atmosphere similar to the context-tied climate of the restricted code was a result of techniques of power used in the 1970s based on stripping notions of their meaning, when the latter changed according to context. Such a tendency to evaluate attitudes and opinions by their context rather than content was the result of a peculiar ideological climate of the 1970s, when opposition groups such as the KOR used the same rhetoric as the ruling elite, underlining only that the latter lost legitimacy to use it. A similar situation had occured in the late 1960s, when the so-called revisionists formulated no different ideological proposals but argued that they, and not the official Marxists had correctly interpreted the system's ideological premise. The political practice of evaluating statements on the basis of context rather than on meaning (with arguments like: "the opinion is correct but formulated from incorrect positions" or "correct but premature") forced intellectuals, masters of the elaborated code, to adapt to a world in which a context-tied way of thinking characteristic of the restricted code had to be used. Such a voluntary limitation of their own semantic competence is an example of adaptation by regression that is characteristic of people living in totalitarian and post-totalitarian systems.

The forms of speech perform a number of ideological functions within the political system. First, the center of political power can exploit (as it did in the 1970s) the difficulties in articulation resulting from the working class's use of the restricted code, to consolidate its own position of domination. The minutes from the meeting of Edward Gierek with shipyard workers in January 1971 serve as an example (see appendix, p. 147). The meeting revealed the complete linguistic inadequacy of the workers in the face of Gierek's assessment of the situation, which was formulated in the elaborated code and employed many abstract notions not directly applicable to the context of the shipyard's problems. The workers could only keep referring to their isolated, concrete experiences (and thus gain only local concessions) or else they could remain silent. It was precisely this silence, when they realized that Gierek's diagnosis was incompatible with their own but could not express this, that

120

made the workers realize that differences in linguistic competence indicate not only dissimilarity but also hierarchy. By occasionally using stock phrases taken from the workers language, Gierek underlined the differences in competence. He was able to imitate their code, but they could not argue in the convention he imposed upon the meeting. "Could not" is perhaps the worng formulation; the workers clearly understood all the notions, but could hardly force themselves to apply them in the elaborated code that was foreign to their habits of speech. In the 1970s, all confrontations between factory management and workers were played out along similar lines.

According to a recent analysis of various Polish memoirs by Winicjusz Narojek,[5] in Polish society the differences exploited by one side with a view to building durable hierarchical relations, give rise to serious tensions. In the light of our description of protest situations, this explains the workers' aggressiveness toward bureaucratic jargon in the 1970s. Recent anti-intelligentsia sentiments may be due to this as well as to the fact that the intelligentsia had monopolized nearly all expressive roles in Solidarity. However, this aggressiveness is mixed with a peculiar fascination with others' semantic competences. A good and very characteristic example of this occurred at the beginning of the strike in the Gdańsk shipyard, the so-called "Leśniak case."[6] One of the clerks of the shipyard personnel office which had been responsible for expelling Anna Walentynowicz from her job gave a long speech, very fluent and bombastic. He underlined the workers' right to protest but, at the same time, vigorously defended Gierek's policy. He received loud applause, which slowly died when Mrs. Walentynowicz, nearly crying, said:

[5] Winicjusz Narojek, *Antropologia Awansu*, Institute of Philosophy and Sociology, Polish Academy of Sciences, Warsaw, 1979.

[6] The Leśniak case was described in the KOR monthly, *Biuletyn Informacyjny* (September 1980) by Ewa Milęwicz, as well as in *Punkt* (Gdańsk, December 1980).

"What are you doing? Do you know who he is?" The applause then changed to an aggressive attack. It was Wałęsa himself who got Leśniak safely to the shipyard's gate. When I later asked workers why they had greeted Leśniak's speech so enthusiastically, some of them answered: "He talked so well . . ." It was the form, not the content of his speech that so fascinated his listeners. The aggression that followed in a way reveals the self-hatred of workers, rooted in a depth of frustration connected with their own limited semantic competence.

Besides, the workers felt that to maintain silence when they come in contact with the elaborated code would imply that they did not understand.

The ineffectiveness of the workers' articulation when they were in conflict situations in the 1970s (especially noticeable during the corporatist-type negotiations after 1976) derived not only from the ease with which the authorities could assert their dominance by exploiting the difference in semantic capability. Another essential factor was the more difficult access of those using a restricted code to a language of symbols, which is the language of an alternative reality. This restriction of political imagination undoubtedly limited the extent of the workers' demands. The fixation of symbols, so typical of workers' protest, favored the emergence in their consciousness of an inflexbility that, in turn, reinforced their fundamentalist orientation. The restricted code led also to the phenomenon of "pseudo-articulation" that was evident in workers' protest in the 1970s. Because they have difficulty articulating their demands the workers artificially reduced all their claims (including non-economic ones) to the concrete language of wage demands.[7]

These difficulties led in the 1970s to conflict situations in

---

[7] Data from Henryk Białyszewski's research on strikes in the 1970s. Unpublished habilitation dissertation. Library of WSNS (Higher Party School), Warsaw.

which the workers failed to exploit properly their potential strength or the opportunities presented by the entanglement of the authorities in their own insistence that their legitimacy stemmed from the fact that they ruled on behalf of workers. This is also an example of the ideological function of the various forms of speech.

The events of the summer of 1980 seem to have been a turning point. The first wave of strikes in July 1980 fit the corporatist pattern of the late 1970s, with context-tied and purely economic demands. The creation of the Inter-Enterprise Strike Committee in Gdańsk on August 14, 1980, broke this pattern. Not only were the interests of the whole working class represented, but general demands for independent labor unions and the canceling of censorship were formulated.

Many factors contributed to this development (see Chapter I). Among them were: the experience some founders of MKS had obtained in unofficial Free Unions; systematic reading of the opposition monthly *Robotnik* (Worker); and the containment of upward mobility in the 1970s that left in the working class its potential leaders, some of them self-educated, who were able to overcome the barrier of limited semantic competence. It was a situation known well from history when, in the very emergence of plebeian solidarity, potential rulers also arise, with a quickness of speech rare in the working-class milieu, with instinctive perception regarding the psychology of their working-class followers, and, above all, with the ability to generalize the needs of the workers. The latter — especially when combined with a peculiar hierarchy-leveling style in contacts with representatives of official authorities — gave these individuals an immediately dominant position among workers. An interesting phenomenon was observable in that connection. Easy dominance through creative use of linguistic symbols led the leaders of the working class movement to fix quickly on a dozen symbols. This was enough for them to operate effectively, and most of the leaders who emerged in August 1980 stopped developing their semantic skills after this first step.

Being too clever could be too risky. Zbigniew Bujak, a worker from the Ursus factory and leader of Mazowsze Region, quickly caught on to the intelligentsia's style of ironic speech. After a while, however, he consciously constrained his own intellectual development (or rather any demonstration of such development) because he got the reputation of being "weak." During bargaining with the government, he, due to his capabilities, was too sensitive to the allusive style of the other side. The bargaining sphere, and thus the possibilities for compromise, was larger when he was present than when other working-class leaders participated in negotiations.

The rapid fixation and rigidity of symbolic definitions of the situation had many by-products. First of all, Solidarity leaders were not always able to perceive their own victories. One example occurred in October 1980 when Kania himself (and the mass media after him) began obsessively to use the term "social contract" as a legitimizing concept. This phrase was not picked up by Solidarity leaders in spite of the fact that it signaled a big step away from the Leninist "vanguard"-type of legitimacy. The social contract argument was in a sense of quasi-legal legitimacy with procedure serving as a justification of power. The lack of a reaction from Solidarity led to the abandonment of the social contract rhetoric.

Another consequence of the rigidity of the symbolic definition of the situation by Solidarity leaders was their conflict with the intellectual fellow travelers of the movement. The indecisiveness of the intellectuals,[8] their second thoughts, their tendency to operate on a level of pure analytical models[9] were often met with suspicion by leaders of the union. I know from my

[8] See Lech Wałęsa's interview with Oriana Fallaci.
[9] My own thesis of the "identity crisis" was presented during my lecture in Workers' University as well as in Solidarity publications.

own experience in Solidarity that such analytical models were greeted much more enthusiastically by rank-and-file members of'the movement. The reason may have been that the rank and file did not feel touched by a critical load of such models or treated them as an alternative symbolic system that could serve as a weapon against a hierarchy that was already growing within Solidarity, with those who had first conquered symbolic language on the top. The same suspicions characterized relations between Solidarity leaders and their own office staffs, a fact that accounts for the lack of efficient professional clerks at Solidarity headquarters. As a result Solidarity leaders of working class origin became bureaucrats themselves: they felt insecure, were overloaded with problems but afraid to delegate decisions to paid clerks. Because of this, they quickly developed such typical bureaucratic attitudes as an avoidance of decision making, a tendency to hide behind collective bodies, and choosing middle-of-the-road "safe" solutions. What is more, one of the most sensitive points in Solidarity—the secretariat of the National Commission—was filled with members of "Young Poland" who were not professional clerks but movement activists. Wałęsa trusts them, but they are amateurish and inefficient, and—what is more—they play their own little games.[10]

That limited semantic competence can sometimes be an advantage was seen during the Gdańsk negotiations. The inability of the workers to operate on abstract (or rather on ideological, doctrinal levels) limited the sphere of possible negotiations. The government's demand that a preamble be added to the text of the agreement thereby canceling "an ideological precedent" was not understood by the workers. Their answer was that "it will

[10] Young Poland's lasting conflict with KOR (the former was labeled by Kuroń as an *endecja* (nationalist) organization) led to the situation in which Young Poland purposely delayed sending full information on the character of the post-Bydgoszcz crisis to the National Commission in order to make possible circulation of rumors that its handling was Kuroń's way of attacking Wałęsa.

be worked out during practice." "It" was mostly a problem of a different cognitive perspective on both sides. For the workers the Inter-Enterprise Strike Committee was above all a technical creation, increasing the safety of all the enterprises and coordinating their activity. As we can see, radicalism is not only a matter of attitudes but also the product of a symbolic imagination and cognitive perspective.

As I noted in the Introduction, the events of August 1980 can be also analyzed in terms of a cultural revolution. "Newspeak" seemed to be overcome, and many words were restored to their former meanings. What was more, at least some of the working-class leaders demonstrated the ability to operate on the same level of generalization as the ruling group and intelligentsia. Many workers made a conscious effort to change their habits of speech. The hierarchy that had been built on the differentiation of semantic competence and a defenseless silence seemed to vanish.[11] Some strikes were, in fact, undertaken primarily to give the participants an opportunity to speak out, to practice their newly acquired instrument — the speech.[12]

The end of that cultural revolution was rapid and spectacular. A milestone was the Warsaw Agreement that followed the Bydgoszcz crisis on March 30, 1981 (see above, p. 19n.). A hierarchy built on semantic skills reemerged as stable as before; this time, however, its basis was more subtle — it was style, not vocabulary. As a result, the workers felt as if their own creation had been expropriated.[13]

[11] According to Maria Marody's research (Warsaw University, November–December 1980), the August events were perceived by many workers as a moment of upward mobility for the whole class.

[12] The strike in the Warsaw steel mill (December 1980) was such a strike; according to surveys, most of the workers did not know the postulates, but in spite of this wanted to continue the strike as an opportunity "to speak out" (Mazowsze Region Research Center).

[13] A. Jankowski's research, Szczecin Center of Social Research, published in *Jedność* (May 1981).

Solidarity ceased to be perceived as a vehicle of upward mobility. Faith in the reality of the cultural revolution vanished.

After this turning point, the workers grew increasingly passive. In the summer elections to the regional bodies of Solidarity and its First Congress, only one fourth of the delegates were workers. One reason for this was that the election procedure required the candidates to make short speeches; working-class delegates often resigned even before competition opened. Other factors responsible for the demobilization of the workers were the crisis of identity in Solidarity combined with an impasse of self-limiting revolution that wore down nearly all of its instruments. The impasse was intensified by the fact that people could no longer be mobilized into readiness to launch a general strike.

The different levels of radicalism between workers and the middle class were not only built on the ease with which the latter adapted to the post-totalitarian regime with its huge areas for a game with the system, and not only rooted in the differences of imagination. The conception of dignity (often the motive underlying actions) is also different in both classes. Observing workers, one gathers that the preservation of dignity in this class depends on reacting properly to the moves of the other side. This attitude closely resembles (could this be purely accidental?) the model of dignity held by prisoners, where one "loses face" by not reacting to insulting behavior by prison guards. In fact, both the insult and the retort quite often boil down to purely ritualized, symbolic gestures. For instance, one may lose dignity simply by using certain words or phrases, such as those taken from the misleading jargon used by official circles, without giving them a clear ironic slant. This phenomenon of dependent dignity (dignity that depends on the responsive behavior of another) not only had a very curious influence in shaping the tradition of protest but also made it easier to provoke and manipulate the workers. Also their adjustment to the system is more painful than is the middle class's. The dependent character of the workers' dignity was exploited by the ruling group after the Warsaw Agreement. The workers' feeling of failure caused by the lack of an effective reaction to the Bydgoszcz crisis, combined with their inability to understand the text of the agreement, was reinforced by the way the agreement was presented in the mass media. It was broadcast together with a speech by K. Barcikowski, secretary of the Central Committee of PUWP, that was criticized even by the participants of the Eleventh Central Committee Plenum. The aim of the ruling group — the demobilization of the rank-and-file members of Solidarity was, however, partly attained.

Articulation of problems is just one example of the way limited semantic competence can function as ideology. Another occurs in a situation in which the rulers exploit a specific feature of the restricted code to suit their own purpose, for instance, the regime's assertion that it requires no justification (legitimization) of the right to issue orders. This is linked with the attitude toward positional structure in most working-class families (in whose socialization the restricted code originates), and to the superior status of the "speaker" peculiar to that code.

A third manifestation of the ideological function of forms of speech is their influence on differentiating the opportunities for a political career available to persons from different classes. Under the conditions of the ritualization of ideology in the 1970s, those who mastered the elaborated code found it much easier to imitate the required style of expression, while at the same time preserving an appearance of neutrality and calm. The best example of such an ability is the "ironic speech" that was typically used by the Polish middle class in the 1970s. This type of speech abounded with quotations, parenthetical insertions, and turns of phrase that clearly indicated the speaker's distance from his own statements. On the surface, this appears to be a very good mechanism of adaptation. The misleading statement addressed to the Establishment was sufficiently "recognizable" to enable the speaker to function and even be promoted in the official hierarchy. On the other hand, the "distance-indicating" part of the sentence, recognizable by the speaker's own group (which as a rule was critical of "officialdom") allowed him to save face and preserve a feeling of identification with the group. Thus, for the middle class there was no question of the disintegration of personality that was often the case with the workers, whose limited semantic ability prevented them from resorting to mechanisms of self-defense based on language decomposition. It was difficult for workers to construct phrases with an internal structure that would indicate their distance from their own statements. On the other hand the misleading official language was more tangible to them, because of their respectful attitude to the spoken word. As we have seen, during strikes of summer 1980, this attitude resulted in a global rejection of everything that was said by the government sources and the creation of Solidarity's own sources of information.

To return to the 1970s, one wonders about the cost of adaptation through decomposition of the language and the use of this particular ironic speech. In my opinion, the cost was very heavy indeed. It was a regressive adaptation for it hindered and made more difficult both the articulation of one's own interests and one's contact with reality. Ironic speech, with its built-in distance from its pronouncements, was in fact nothing more than a peculiar example of the phenomenon known as "negative freedom of speech," which leads to speech devoid of inner dynamics. This kind of speech constitutes one of the more typical mechanisms of regression known to psychoanalysts. The limitation of this speech form stems from the fact that its misleading and distance-indicating elements can fulfill their intended function only when they are recognizable to others as being mere window-dressing and irony. The elements, thus, must acquire the form of a more or less permanent ritual. Therefore, this kind of speech, though it does perform its adaptive role and facilitates

129

functioning in the schizoid society (at the same time it preserves the feeling of being "internally correct"), loses its value as a flexible instrument of communication.

An impoverished, ritualized language was indeed a high price for adaptation in the 1970s. The half-conscious recognition of this was one of the reasons for the workers' determination during the Summer 1980 strikes and their characteristic espousal of "truth" as well as moral commitment.

Another indication of the ideological function of the forms of speech is the ruling group's exploitation of tensions and frustrations caused by the differentiation of these forms. Anti-intelligentsia sentiments, for instance, were exploited in recruiting the party apparatus and also as a force with which to drive the political machine in crisis situations (especially within the lower echelons of power). Anti-intelligentsia slogans were also used by the ruling group to mobilize workers against the student movement in 1968.

THE BARRIER OF REIFICATION

In totalitarian and post-totalitarian systems, reification plays the same ideological role as, according to Marx, commodity fetishism plays in a capitalistic system. It masks the structure of power by illuminating only its appearances and by underlining its objective character and unchangeability. Both the relations between commodities in capitalism (where labor is also perceived as a commodity) and the relations of power in socialism are shown as the results of objective social laws (respectively, the laws of market and the laws of dialectics) and not as an effect of a struggle and conflict of interests. The main function of both ideological constructions is to darken the origin and the nature of the domination and to display it as perhaps painful, but the only possible system.

The barrier of reification was the second threshold in the development of working-class consciousness. It is difficult to describe the process of overcoming this barrier. First of all, the concept itself is a badge rather than a technical term. It combines the maximum of emotional resonance with the minimum of precision. Second, empathy and commitment are not enough to recapture a lived experience of common man. Broad research is necessary, and I have at my disposal very fragmentary data.

According to the data collected by Narojek at the end of the 1970s, the hierarchy of power and prestige was frustrating to the workers but legitimated by the lack of any imaginable alternative.[14] The hierarchy was accepted as long as those who held high positions did not exploit their status more than normal expectations allowed.

The acceptance of the power structure as part of the natural order of things (in other words, its reification) made possible the populist techniques of the early 1970s. Even at the beginning of Solidarity's existence, a majority of its members did not believe it was possible to change the power structure. All they wanted was to divorce themselves from that structure and to organize independently as many social functions as possible — information, education, shifts in cooperation in industry, etc. Their goals echoed the KOR doctrine of a society independent of the state. When I observed the workers' reaction to the Fourth Plenum of the Central Committee held on August 22, 1980, I was surprised by their lack of interest; for the workers, the power structure was out of reach, untouchable, and invariable.[15]

Four factors seem to be crucial in overcoming the barrier of reification. Two of them appeared during the August 1980 strikes. First was the workers' realization that part of the ruling

[14] Narojek, *Antropalogia Awansu*.

[15] In spite of this, an argument about alleged "workers' pressure for personnel changes in the Politbureau" was used by Gdańsk District Secretary Fiszbach during the very same plenum.

group's power depends on the obedience to its orders of those governed and that mass refusal to obey can paralyze even the most powerful elite. The second factor was linked with the workers' spontaneous attempts to restore (or rather to create a substitute for) some of the same functions of state administration, an attempt that was disorganized and which, in a sense, imploded.[16] This activity, poorly coordinated and quickly abandoned (in a process of self-limiting revolution that began at the moment when the negotiations were undertaken), left, however, an important realization. If one is recognized as the center of power, that is sufficient to become such center in reality. This was a practical (and not even articulated) lesson of legitimacy.

Two other factors that helped to overcome the feeling of reification were generated by the experience of Solidarity. In the institutionalization of the movement, the important roles of manipulation, competition, and even chance in building a hierarchy became obvious. In other words, it becomes clear that the hierarchy was not part of the natural order of things. Even more crucial for transcending the barrier of power-structure reification were the conclusions drawn from the few clashes with the government. Especially important in this respect was the January–Febraury 1981 conflict in a few regions over the dismissal of some corrupt members of local administration. This conflict ended with the recall of Prime Minister Pieńkowski for "not being able to communicate with Solidarity." During these clashes the workers felt themselves to be actors in the game and, for the first time, watched attentively the changes in the ruling group. They recognized that the power structure was not set objectively and forever, but was changeable and could be affected by their own activity. The workers understood that the

---

[16] For instance, Wałęsa himself began to direct the city transporation system or arranged to sell food from warehouses to shops, and his orders were obeyed.

power structure was itself the result of conflict and that its concrete form was a sign of the relative strength of particular political forces.

However, these attitudes, learned by the Polish working class
during its political practice in August 1980 and after, did not
last. The freshly acquired awareness that the power structure
could be de-reified, were quickly dislodged by new experiences
and, in a way, forgotten. On the other hand, it was not possible
for the workers to return to their former acceptance of the existing order. What we observe today is rather the post-Bydgoszcz
demobilization combined with a radicalism that avoids political
categories and does not transpose its dreams into power relations.
These attitudes are not only the result of the fundamentalist
orientation of the movement but comprise the ambiguity of a
"coopted revolution," as Solidarity appears increasingly to be the
trammeled giant. The latter is the consequence of the identity
crisis described earlier.

The experience of watching, in the mass media, the Ninth
Congress of the PUWP in July 1981 contributed to the renewal
of the reification of power. This populist Congress left surreal
feelings. I will say more about it in Chapter V, but here a few
remarks on its connection to the reification problem are pertinent. After the election of new members to the Central Committee, Polish society faced new power holders who mirrored
the popular, fragmented, non-ideological mentality. The new
PUWP elite consisted of ordinary people, uncorrupted, and
elected through relatively democratic procedures. They were as
blank vis-à-vis crisis as the rest of the society. During the following weeks, however, the polarizing mechanism revealed its
whole potential. On the one hand, a delegitimization of power
deeper than ever before was observed: the democratic procedure
stripped the power holders of a "demonic" aura that had served
in the past as an important part of the pattern of power legiti-

mated mostly by a lack of alternatives. The newly elected Central Committee members from big factories felt rejected by their communities: Zofia Grzyb, the only Solidarity member in the Politbureau was rebuked by Solidarity's factory organization for her critical remarks about this organization. What was more, factional games, now conducted on the district committee level (because Kania's opponents were not elected to the Central Committee) led to a few provoked conflicts just after the Ninth Congress. A mix-up with rationing coupons in Katowice and Łódź and a disorganization of the rationing system prompted "hunger marches" in both towns. This pattern was picked up in Kutno on July 26 and on August 3–5, 1981. Tensions heightened when the route to the Warsaw march was blocked, and demonstraters themselves blocked a central crossroads in Warsaw for three days. The main slogan of all these events was "Hunger—the only outcome of the Ninth Congress."

The new Central Committee members were thus immediately confronted with popular anger blaming them for mistakes of their predecessors, of which they themselves were critical. Frustrations abounded on both sides: Central Committee members who elaborated no new proposals during the Congress (the party program was a copy of the government stabilization plan), and Solidarity members who felt increasing despair and were involved in the union's own crisis of identity. The mutual hostility between the two groups deepened, reinforced by the similarity of mentality and status of both. As a result we observe in Poland two unanticipated circumstances. On the one hand the new, democratically elected Central Committee has a more "hard-line" orientation than does the Politbureau with its few professional apparatchiks. On the other hand, the feeling of reification has returned; now it is even deeper. The public feels that the system itself is out of the control of both society and power holders. It is no accident that a politics of despair has been recently evident, for instance a trial of party committee arson in

Świnoujście on June 23, 1981, or racial incidents in Konin[a] — with local gypsies — (August 20), and more talks among young workers about terrorism.

THE "ANTIPOLITICAL" POLITICAL CULTURE OF SOLIDARITY

The third threshold on the way to the development of mature political consciousness by the Polish working class organized in Solidarity concerns its distinctive mentality. I use the term "mentality" as a synonym for a framework of cognitive forms actually operative in political life that is action-oriented and loaded with emotions. This term seems more useful in our case than the concept of ideology.[17] One of the reasons for this mentality is a ritualization of ideology typical of post-totalitarian systems, with their search for such values and rules of game that would possess a minimal constraining power on political actions. The second reason is a peculiarly non-ideological climate in Poland. Communism was brought to Poland on Soviet tanks, and a leftist ideology was never very lively here, except in the tradition of the farmers' movement. As a result, even anti-communist attitudes have a very weak ideological component: ideological counterrevolution is impossible without an authentic revolution preceding it. Polish Catholicism, very broad in its

[17] Compare Linz's analysis of "mentality" and "ideology" in authoritarian regimes, in Greenstein and Polsby *Handbook of Political Science*, Reading, Mass., Addison-Wesley, 1975.

[a] A small gypsy population living in the town of Konin was repeatedly assaulted by local inhabitants in a series of episodes of racial violence. The August 20 episode was notable for its scale, property damage, and the inability of the local police to restrain the angry mob of Poles. The event was reported in the national press, both in Solidarity-sponsored and in government-sponsored media, and made an important symbolic impact because of its implicit analogy to anti-Jewish pogroms in which the Polish population had participated in the past.

social scope, is mostly a culture and a way of life, with minimal metaphysical or intellectual baggage.[18] This eases the Church's coexistence with both the ritualized communist ideology and secular rationalism.

The style typical of political opposition in Poland is also non-ideological. Revisionists of the 1960s simply reinterpreted official ideology and denied the ruling group's right to use leftist rhetoric. KOR, which organized in the late 1970s, was a loose coalition of the system's opponents from different origins, from the ex-orthodox left through moderate socialists to the ex-right. In recent surveys concerning political attitudes of the Polish working class,[19] more than 55.5 percent of workers surveyed could not label their political positions (among workers who were PUWP members, 37.1 percent responded similarly); 11.7 percent described themselves as democrat and 4.4 percent as social-democrat (among members of PUWP the number was 8.6 percent), 8.7 percent as socialist (in PUWP 23 percent), 1.5 percent as communist (in the PUWP 1 person!) and 0.7 percent as patriot. This ideological under-determination was also revealed by answers to a question on the need for a legal opposition party. Sixty-five percent of the answering workers, and 54 percent of the worker-members of the PUWP answered positively, but their rationale was also non-ideological. They justified the need for a new party mostly in organizational terms, as a necessary element of competition in the political system. On the other hand most of the 36.5 percent of workers who declared support for opposition groups (mostly KOR) could not give an ideological or political reason for their attitude, or even any ideological

[18] Kawecki's research (Institute of Marxism, Warsaw, 1979) indicated that more people declared that they regularly attended church than labeled themselves as "believers in God." Other functions of the Church in Poland (political, cultural) are responsible for this phenomenon.

[19] Research of Anna Odrobińska and Bolesław Stąporek from Gdańsk Shipyard Research Group data (June 1981) presented at the sixth Sociological Conference in Łódź (September 1981).

interpretation of the KOR position. More careful examination, however, reveals that the situation was not so simple. This superficial ideological underdetermination, using *ideology* in its traditional sense, can as well be interpreted as ideological over-determination, when we take into account the fact that in Poland the role of ideology is played by a peculiar mentality on the one hand and status-orientation on the other. Four elements of this mentality will be discussed below: its ahistoricism, its moralism, its one-dimensionality, and its strong status orientation. Some conclusions will be drawn about the genesis of these features as well as their relationship to the movement's political practice.

Ahistoricism

The perception of a movement's past as a series of discrete events, rather than as a process in which events affect each other and establish general tendencies, is typical of Solidarity members as well as activists. Two factors are responsible for this ahistorical perspective. First is the common inability of the workers to generalize from their own experiences, which is rooted in limited semantic competence. The second factor is a conceptual framework that, due to the movement's solidarism, excludes all dialectical concepts like "conflict" or "contradiction." In a sense, the static cognitive perspective through which Solidarity generates guilt and suspicion. Such a perspective makes it impossible to accumulate and record knowledge of the movement's dynamics as a development of its internal contradictions and conflicts. As I show in Chapter II, the first stage of Solidarity's history was marked by the development of two conflict-generating processes: self-limiting revolution and hierarchy building. Both increased intra-organizational tensions and led to the eruption of the symbolic politics so characteristic of that stage. The latter helped the middle-level activists of Solidarity

137

retain their status. The second stage of Solidarity's development was characterized by crisis of identity. That crisis appeared in many forms: one of them was the increasing gap between Solidarity's political power and its lack of economic power, or even its role in reinforcing state ownership of the means of production. Another aspect of the identity crisis was the more and more obvious impasse of self-limiting revolution. The concept of "social enterprise," worked out by a self-government-oriented movement in Solidarity was aimed at reducing the crisis of identity. For a long time this tendency was opposed by the regional and national leaders of Solidarity, who, due to their ahistorical perspective, were unable to perceive the necessity of such a development. As we see, ahistoricism had serious practical consequences.

The inability to generalize the movement's experience and to put it into an abstract formula created a barrier to the accumulation of knowledge and social learning in Solidarity. In such a situation the personal experience of the movement's leaders has a double value; the fact that the knowledge gained by the movement's activists cannot be transferred is a useful rationalization and a half-conscious self-justification for leaders who want to retain their positions as long as possible.

Another political consequence of an ahistorical perspective on the movement's past is the ease with which the strings of the movement can be pulled from outside. Within such an ahistorical framework the movement's past is encapsulated within its present. This can be very dangerous, especially if a moment of the movement's development is perceived by its members as a failure, as was the case of the Warsaw Agreement on March 30, 1981. This feeling of failure can be reinforced by the ruling group's manipulations. In such a situation all previous victories can be forgotten, and, what is more, the feeling of failure can become a self-fulfilling prophecy. The tendency to generalize the feeling of defeat is further reinforced by the concept of "dependent dignity" so characteristic of workers' culture. Those who have lost "face" and have moved to the category of "losers" must then operate according to different rules. To get back to the category of winners is not so easy; one must earn it. These elements add to the mechanism of the self-fulfilling prophecy of the generalized attitude of failure. This attitude is clearly very convenient for the ruling group.

Another aspect that serves the interests of the rulers is the fact that the feeling of failure is often followed by the phenomenon of social amnesia. Psychiatrists studying social amnesia with elements of aphasia, point out that one tends to push into the subconscious those situations in which one has failed to preserve one's personal dignity, the memory of which invokes a feeling of shame and bitterness. This feeling molds the image of the past that remains imprinted in one's mind. The experience seems to be similar for social groups. If we examine the process in which traditions of protest among the Polish working class were being formed in the 1970s, we notice two characteristic moments. Prior to August 1980, the events of December 1970 were remembered and had become an element of spoken tradition, but the similar events of June 1976 had been driven into the subconsciousness, even though in both cases the protesters achieved their objective (the cancellation of announced increases in food prices). In December 1970, however, the protesting workers managed to preserve their dignity; in June 1976 they did not. Both situations are directly tied to the "dependent" concept of dignity. In 1970, the most massive strike broke out when the party press printed information that a group of workers, on behalf of all the workers, had promised to work harder in order to make good the losses in production sustained by the state as a result of the events in Gdańsk and Szczecin (during which many workers had been killed). The resort to strike as a reply to this press statement, which the workers saw as a violation of their dignity, was aimed at restoring that dignity. In

June 1976, just a few days after the strikes, a group of workers appeared on television with "spontaneous" apologies addressed personally to First Secretary Gierek. The same show was repeated, on a mass scale, on a few sports fields in industrial towns. Although conversations with workers show that they saw it as infringing upon their dignity, this incident did not provoke a reaction. It created social amnesia, and the events of 1976 somehow disappeared from the spoken traditions of protest and became non-events to which the workers most unwillingly return in their recollections. After the August 1980 strikes, the situation changed, and the strikes were perceived as a revenge for the symbolic defeat of June 1976. After August, workers spoke more freely about the — demystified — events of 1976.

Political Moralism

The strong moralistic current in the events of August 1980 and after, with its values of solidarism and concern for dignity, was a reaction to the moral ambiguity of the corporatist techniques of the 1970s and the increasing segmentation of the society that followed them. Solidarity, as the social movement, had the character not only of a cultural revolution but of a moral crusade as well. To retain that quality has been one of the movement's visible imperatives.[20] From the beginning, the ruling group's tactic has been to strip Solidarity of its moral legitimacy.[21]

---

[20] Compare the data on the conflict in Silesian mines, where, as stated previously, miners refused higher pay for work on free Saturdays because they did not want to be "treated as something special and again as in the 1970s be cut off from the rest of society."

[21] For instance, the so-called Żabiński doctrine (first party secretary in Katowice district) that underlined three tactics of fighting with Solidarity: through polarizing the movement, through over-stressing particular interests that would decrease the moral legitimacy of the movement, and through "giving them a taste of power and affluency that should corrupt them in a very short time" (speech delivered in Katowice to PUWP activists, December 1980).

The movement's political moralism has a strong impact on the way it functions. It is worth recalling Lipset's remark that "the application of any fundamental truth to the political scene, being undebatable, makes impossible the open market place of ideas and powers."[22] Another consequence of the movement's political moralism is that every compromise is perceived by the movement's members as very painful: to compromise is not only a tactical defeat but a sacrifice of some basic values.[23] What is more, in Solidarity as in every movement that operates according to the rules of a moral crusade, the democratic process is perceived as the triumph of a majority of those who know the "truth" over devious others. This is the opposite of a liberal concept of democracy as a procedure for obtaining compromise.

Another result of this political moralism is a tendency to see politics in black and white terms. This is strikingly similar to an old communist rule according to which: "he who is not with us is against us." In a way the fundamentalism of the prehistory of the communist party (with its faith in the absolute rightness of "dialectical laws") had a very similar effect to that of political moralism.

Three additional consequences of Solidarity's moralistic attitude should be mentioned here. First of all, it creates a deep disinclination to disclose differences and conflicts inside the movement because to do so would weaken its moral rightness. For instance, conflicts that appeared in the National Commission of Solidarity after the Bydgoszcz crisis ended with the recall of the National Commission Secretary Celiński, accused of manipulation, and the resignation of Karol Modzelewski, who described the National Commission as "Wałęsa's feudal kingdom." For

[22] Compare Seymour Lipset and Earl Rabb *The Politics of Unreason; Right Wing Extremism in America, 1790-1970,* New York, Harper and Row, 1970, for an excellent description of the moralistic orientation in politics.

[23] For instance the compromise on the free Saturdays problem was seen by the workers as a sign "that they did not treat us seriously . . ." (research of Mazowsze Center, January 1981).

outside use, however, these conflicts were labeled a conspiracy of extremists who want to destroy the movement's unity."[24] In such an atmosphere, when the revelation of internal differences generates guilt feelings, it is impossible to build into the movement the mechanisms for internal negotiation and problem solving. On the contrary, informal techniques for suppressing dissent are developing, for instance movement censorship of union bulletins, which led to strikes by their staffs in Lublin and Gdańsk. Lack of tolerance for internal differences sometimes has a distorting effect. During Solidarity elections, when some differences had to be mentioned as a part of the selection mechanism, coalitions were built in a very mechanical way, for instance, small enterprises against big.

One extremely dangerous effect of political moralism has occurred in the autumn of 1981 in the form of a strong wave of anti-Semitic and anti-intelligentsia sentiments. A Solidarity factory commission at one of the large Warsaw enterprises wrote to Solidarity authorities asking who was responsible for the graphic design of the Solidarity First Congress plaque that, in their opinion, "reminds one of a zionist star." This and similar attacks on some Solidarity experts and activists can be interpreted as a type of surrogate conflict.

An accumulation of tensions rooted in the movement's oligarchization and in conflicts that could not be solved because the movement contains no mechanism to negotiate differences led to a situation in which the first opportunity to criticize some officials of Solidarity — without, however, threatening the union formula — was immediately exploited. The absence of ways to negotiate (or even name) internal conflicts was caused by an ethos of solidarism. The penetration of Solidarity by small groups of so-called "true Poles" (a nationalistic branch of political opposition) as well as by the "Grunwald" organization (spon-

[24] National Commission meeting, April 4, 1981.

sored by one of the ruling group's factions) furnished ready scapegoats and a rhetoric that helped to canalize deep frustrations without injuring the idealized image of Solidarity. These features, together with the low tolerance of ambiguity that is rooted in the difficulties of generalizing individual experience, remain well known from the historical shifts of progressive movements into obscure ones. If we add to this description an increase of hostility toward farmers, we can see how the deepening of the economic crisis has been followed by rapidly increasing irrationality of attitudes and actions.

Another consequence of political moralism is the belief one need only be right in order to win. This belief leads to an underestimation of the tactical elements in politics and to neglect in publicizing one's own case. This attitude corresponds with the fundamentalist assumption that politics are unnecessary to win. During strikes the argument that the demand for "right" things was the substance of victory was often linked with a conviction in the universality of one's own way of thinking. According to such point of view, those who oppose one's ideas are motivated by bad will or conspiracy. This position was further reinforced by a cognitive framework typical of those with limited semantic competence: the inability to take into account a variety of possible meanings and their relativistic character. A cultural (cognitive) uniformization of the world is taken for granted and, as a consequence, the need to make one's own meaning explicit is not so strong. In July 1981, I was, for instance, surprised at the indifference of the strike committee within Polish Airlines to the suggestion that they organize a press conference to explain their demands (the right to elect a director). They were so sure of their moral and political correctness that they did not bother with the additional publicity of their case.

To conclude this analysis of the consequences of the political moralism of Solidarity members, I want to address another aspect of the problem, namely a peculiar attitude toward the legal system. Typical of this attitude are a contempt for laws (even the union's own statutes)[25] and a readiness to manipulate them, the resistance to the creation of an institution inside Solidarity to control the correspondence of activity with statute. The situation recalls the beginning of the so-called "socialist state" when a mythological "will of the people" was quickly replaced with a "will of the vanguard" that took precedence over law. The contempt for laws within Solidarity is accompanied by a characteristic lack of interest in the formulation of the laws. Until quite recently, the Solidarity leaders who participated in the Joint Commission preparing a new union law were quite passive. Wałęsa's remark on television on July 25, 1981 — "If the new regulations do not satisfy us, we will go our own way . . ." — is characteristic. Such an attitude is slowly beginning to change; the ruling group has begun to prosecute cases of breaking the formal law by union functionaries. In September 1981 more than 200 such cases were in the courts.

One-Dimensionality

The constellation of forces and political pressures in Poland after August 1980 was very complicated. In spite of this, the image of the political situation shared by Solidarity members is simplified and takes into account only two forces: "us" and "them." In such a conceptual framework some significant political phenomena (for instance the "horizontal structures" inside the PUWP) went unnoticed. Also the situation today, whereby the "pragmatists" (or pseudo-pragmatists) in Solidarity and those in the party are closer to each other than to the fundamentalists in

[25] For instance Bujak justified an overconcentration on the National Commission level of competences that in the statute were reserved for regional-level activists by the argument "Let's forget for a while that we are the National Commission and treat ourselves as a meeting of regional leaders" (February 1981 meeting of the National Commission).

both institutions seems to be too complex to be perceived by movement members. This one-dimensional perspective is in part a heritage from the KOR (i.e., society versus state). Such a perspective, which does not take into account that the society was for years marbled with the state's agendas, was a good slogan during momentary eruptions of discontent, but it is very misleading in more or less normal situations. This historical simplification was linked with the political moralism that regards structural differences, cleavages, ambiguity, and pluralism of ideas and aims as illegitimate.

It may sound like heresy, but Polish political life and especially the flow of ideas after August 1980 and the creation of Solidarity has been improverished as a result of the impact of the populist and solidarist perspective pressed upon society by Solidarity. This view contrasts with the segmented, often morally ambiguous but nevertheless less uniform and less aggregated course of society in the 1970s. The earlier atomization of PUWP led to the pluralization of positions and ideas. They varied from totalitarian utopians from the Sigma Club at Warsaw University, with their abstract, dialectical imagination (see Chapter IV), to the primitive demonstrations of a need to dominate, that were often fed by personal frustrations and rationalized in terms of "class dictatorship," of the Club Warsaw 80. Varied reactions to the ritualization of ideology were observed, from the Karl Marx Club, which gathered a few dozen tired party intellectuals (and semi-intellectuals) to the much more primitive and populist Katowice Forum.

Status Orientation

The status-elevating feature of Solidarity explains the predominance of status politics over interest politics in its activity. It must be remembered that the origin of Solidarity was perceived by many of its members as a lever for the upward mobility of the whole working class and as an instrument of cultural revolution. A tendency to see society in terms of status, not functions, which is typical of a political culture of authoritarian regimes, reinforces the strong status orientation of Solidarity. Socialization in such regimes teaches people that the sphere of domination is the most crucial dimension of social life. Such socialization develops also a special instinct for weakness and strength. The main consequences of the strong status orientation of Solidarity are: a tendency to personalize politics, an inability (or unwillingness) to formulate institutional safeguards against an overuse of power, and the belief that to change people is more important than to change structures. A last consequence is a tension between strong competition for status on the one hand and egalitarian values on the other hand. Such collision erodes the feeling of moral rightness. This is quite dangerous for a movement that has taken on itself an obligation of the moral crusade.

This account of the mentality characteristic of most Solidarity members of the working-class origin is not meant to introduce analytic concept but rather as a description. My aim has been, first of all, to expose the three thresholds on the way to developing an efficient and emancipatory political consciousness. They are: the limited semantic competence, reification of the power structure, the mentality characterized by ahistoricism, political moralism, one-dimensionality, and status orientation.

Appendix to Chapter III

As an illustration of the workers' semantic problems in articulating their protest, and the populist mode of that protest described above, I present fragments from the transcript of original tapes of a meeting between the First Secretary of the PUWP, Edward Gierek and the Szczecin Shipyard workers in January 1971. The meeting took place at the time of the so-called "Strike for Truth." The cause of that strike was a report by a Szczecin newspaper that one of the shipyard's departments had promised greater output, to show support for the policy of the PUWP. The report was false, and the department workers went on strike again, taking 2,000 of the yard's 12,000 workers with them.

The meeting was recorded by workers, and the tapes were subsequently smuggled out of Poland.

> GIEREK: Point five. "We demand that Prime Minister Jaroszewicz and the First Secretary of the Polish United Workers' Party . . ." we're here! Point six. "We demand honest information on political and economic situation . . ." — well is that sufficient, what I've already told you?
>
> CROWD: No! Comrades! No. Comrades! He's suppressed the point! The point is that your camera has done nothing but point at *you*! Your press has done nothing but publish . . .
>
> ULFIK (Strike leader):
> False information! It's false information!

GIEREK: Now wait a second! False? False, comrades? I'm not talking about falsehoods! I'm talking about what we made available. Is that false, what we make available?

CROWD: Yes! Yes! . . . It applies to the local press!

GIEREK: Wait, we'll come to that too. Please. . . . You mean . . . I see what you mean, comrades. You mean you want information about what is happening here, in your city and in your shipyard? Well we are all for keeping people informed, but not, you know, not about every detail that just anybody might want to publish. There are certain rules, comrades, that must be strictly observed. Don't ask for the same sort of democracy for everybody, for friends and enemies! Don't demand that kind of democracy!

CROWD: We want information! We want . . .

GIEREK: Ah, you say you want honest information; then you go on to deal with that report, the tube section's undertaking about extra production. And now, your next request . . . What do you mean? The whole list?

CROWD: Yes! No! . . . Yes!

GIEREK: Yes? No? Part of it? What part? What?

ADAMCZUK: We'd like this point published in the local media.

GIEREK: Oh, I see! Just this one point. Well of course, you mean simply a note about these undertakings. Certainly, most certainly. And so we're on to point ten . . .

The next fragment shows the populist character of the protest:

JARCZEWSKI: We haven't been fighting to overthrow those in power, or anything else. But actually we've been fighting about a bit of gravy. We haven't got that bit of gravy, because so far Comrade Gierek has promised us nothing. Thank you.

STRIKER 4: People are inquisitive here. They'll check the cemeteries, they'll check everything, and they'll work it out. People will not let it drop. I believe that Comrade Edward Gierek should take this matter into his own hands and find the guilty ones who let this happen, and they should get the severest punishment possible. Thank you ... that's all.

STRIKER 5: We would like to know—what the earnings of directors and ministers are like? Please answer. Now, if they are more than double what a highly skilled worker can earn, on the average about 5,000, we believe such income should be cut and frozen.

STRIKER 7: Well, a controversial matter, but I was told to put it in—do away with excessive luxuries in the offices and cut out the number of office cars. Comrade Gierek, you have our full and unreserved support. Furthermore, if there's any messing about, any plots at the top, if you get into trouble, we'll stand behind you.

STRIKER 8: Those who are against Gierek and the People's Republic of Poland—they're all at home, asleep! ... Workers, workers! I am a Pole, a man, a Communist and a shipyard worker. Let me put a question: does our member of Parliament, General Jaruzelski, know that until today all food, water and other things have been cut off from us?

Detotalization From Above, the 1970s

PITFALLS OF TOTALITARIANISM

The evolution of the Polish political system in the 1970s from a totalitarian to an authoritarian-bureaucratic regime was more responsible for the events of August 1980 than was the worsening economic situation. The dynamics of the political system in Poland in the last decade was marked by the appearance of new elements not encountered on such scale in other East European countries. These were a limited, non-responsible, "lame" pluralism with a characteristic pattern of repressive toleration (in which political opposition had a peculiar, a-legal status but possessed no institutional channels to reach the mass of the population); well-developed corporatist techniques of interest articulation and protest absorption including the highly political Catholic Church; and, last but not least, a peculiar crisis-oriented philosophy of ruling. The latter led to a risky, but—until the August 1980 crisis—efficient, technique of using or even provoking crisis as a regulatory mechanism.

This evolution of the political system produced tensions throughout society as well as in the power structure itself. Increasing social differentiation and rapid segmentation of society combined with moral ambiguity were the consequences of corporatist techniques. The very same techniques generated serious status problems and uncertainty within the executive stratum of the power hierachy. The great efficiency of the mechanisms of protest absorption, combined with the ease of securing financial credits, postponed until too late the necessary downward revisions of the investment plan and the slowing of an accelerated and, at the same time, suffocating economic growth. The techniques used by the ruling group to cut off its political opposition did not work, and the opposition's influence grew. What was more, a part of the PUWP apparatus that was interested in overthrowing the Gierek–Babiuch team, too greatly trusted their ability to demobilize popular protest after they had used it as an instrument of factional games and a lever of a palace revolution.

The controlled evolution of the political system went out of control at the end of the 1970s. The deep frustrations of the security police[1] and party apparatus,[2] rooted in the repressive tol-

[1] The first signal of the apparent dissatisfaction of the security forces with Gierek's policy was the Pyjas case (Kraków, summer 1978). The death of Stanisław Pyjas, a student-supporter of KOR who according to evidence, was beaten by the police was intended to polarize social forces and end Gierek's repressive toleration policy. When this tactic did not bring the expected results, the internal security forces changed their approach and began to misinform the Gierek-Babiuch team about the extent and forms of oppositional activities, in order to use these activities to provoke a crisis that would overthrow Gierek.

[2] Several waves of a countermobilization were observed: In 1974 a letter was sent by Ministers Mitręga, Jędrychowski, and Szopa to the Central Committee criticizing the economic policy of the Gierek-Jaroszewicz team. This letter was followed by a serious warning sent the same year to Deputy Minister Kaim by Minister of Finance Kisiel about fast-growing market disequilibrium. In 1976 street riots occurred in Radom and Ursus after a provoked crisis caused by changes of food prices, followed by unjust system of recompensation also aimed at overthrowing the Gierek-Jaroszewicz team. (The decision to increase prices in 1976 was signed by the same official in the PUWP Central Committee who signed a similar decision in July 1980, Manfred Gorywoda.) Political countermobilization occurred at the end of the 1970s, with a letter from seven district secretaries criticizing Gierek's detotalization policy; Grabski, who delivered a critical speech at the Tenth Plenum, May 1979, was left alone during discussion by the other secretaries who had signed the letter and was dismissed from his position of First Secretary in Konin. The last element of this countermobilization was Olszowski's speech at the Eighth Congress of the PUWP, February 1980, which sent him to "exile" as ambassador in East Germany.

eration pattern and corporatist techniques of protest absorption, undercut the Gierek regime's ability to manage the system and led to the collapse of the state even before August 1980. The economic crisis that began in 1974 and was in full swing after 1978 seemed to be not only deeper than ever but indifferent to routine techniques of control used by the government during the previous crises (see Chapter VII). A nearly mystical need for social unity (in order to overcome the dangerous social atomization and corporatist segmentation) found expression in the wave of solidarity strikes in summer 1980.

In this chapter I will describe the interrelationship of two processes characteristic of the 1970s: the detotalization from above, that can be seen as the ruling group's attempt to escape from traps it had itself created and the simultaneous continuation of nearly all totalitarian techniques of the past.

The totalitarian tendencies characterized by a high degree of centralization and concentration of power, total penetration of all realms of life by the state, and the elimination of independent self-regulators (e.g., the market) have dynamic and logic of their own and pass through various stages. At least in their initial phase in Poland, they were an attempt to actualize a specific, totalitarian utopia. The basis for the implementation of this utopia promising equality, as well as state-led, accelerated, industrialization and modernization, was to be full mobilization of all resources and their subsequent allocation by a central authority. Any independent expression of social preferences (including the market) was seen as a hindrance to mobilization and also as favoring a revival of the old production structure and social differentiation. According to Lenin's famous thesis, it was the Communist party which was to undertake "the historical task of capitalism" following revolution in underdeveloped countries. It was the task not only of industralization but also of culture modernization to overcome a perspective characteristic of traditional status-oriented society. This outlook was based on a generalization of local, status-group perspectives, not on abstract roles or functions of the system as a whole. Its perception of social hierarchy was built on a mythologized discontinuity of discrete features not on gradual change. Social life was analyzed in terms of communities not institutions. The imagination characteristic of this perspective could not cope with diversity and ambiguity; in addition, it was based on condensed (personalized) symbols, not on abstract symbols.

According to Ken Jowitt,[3] only a political party that possessed the legitimacy of a collective hero (in other words, an institution with charisma), and was able to exploit this peculiar ontology for its own sake, could have gotten in touch with such traditional society as Russia. At least some features of the Bolshevik party corresponded with the imagination typical of the status-oriented society: the party's super-status built on a mythologized discontinuity (the "vanguard" versus the rest of society).

The third group of factors responsible for the way the Communist party was organized were ideological assumptions taken from the "classics." The notion that conflict between an individual and society would end once private ownership of means of production had been liquidated was the most important among these assumptions. The second centered on the "objective" character of class interests that should be discovered by the "vanguard," and not negotiated through a political process. This position justified the cancellation of all forms of parliamentary politics and all mechanisms of compromise-building. It also encouraged the reduction of spheres beyond the control of totalitarian authorities to a minimum. An additional feature of this totalitarian utopia was full mobilization, even coercion, of the entire population for participation in public life, guided by one party and one ideology. Any sign of indifference was suspect.

---

[3] Kenneth Jowitt, *The Leninist Response to National Dependency*. Research series No. 37, Institute of International Studies, University of California, Berkeley, Calif., 1978.

The utopia was also characterized by the belief that the differences between the rulers and the ruled could be eliminated by a strong emphasis on the principle of equality,[4] and by breaking up the old social-status structure. The latter was part of the process of modernization.[5] Other features of this utopia were: political control over the economy and its subordination to goals outlined by politicians and ideology, and a strong emphasis on the need for a new culture, personality, and morality.[6]

The party—according to the concept of totalitarian utopia—should be a highly politicized movement, guided by a mission. The state, which is a set of institutions based on the ideological assumption of the unity of interests, was unable to deal with social conflicts not only due to the lack of mechanisms for compromise building but also due to serious barriers to the verbal expression of diversity or conflict within official (and monopolistic) ideological rhetoric. This dilemma was especially obvious in the the concept of the polymorphic party.[7] The communist party, with its "leading role," quickly became an arena of competition of interests and was unable to cope with the situation. The structure based on a myth of unity was defenseless when

[4] One of the first revolutionary decrees in Russia was the "party minimum" decree, December 24, 1917, limiting income of party apparatus and administration to the level of the average wage in industry.

[5] All prerevolutionary titles and formal statuses were liquidated by a revolutionary decree of November 23, 1917.

[6] Compare Sergei Eisenstein, *Film Form: Essays in Film Theory and the Film Sense*, New York, Meridian Books, 1960, or Victor Erlich, *Russian Formalism: History, Doctrine*, The Hague, Mouton, 1965. Also Boris Tomashevsky, "La Nouvelle école d'historie litteraire en Russie," *Révue des études slaves* (1928) vol. VIII, and Lev Trotskii, *Literature and Revolution*, New York, Russell and Russell, 1957.

[7] The idea of a polymorphic party, incorporating itself into all other institutions with the help of transmission belts was first formulated by Lenin in his book published in 1920, *The Childish Disease of "Leftism" in Communism*, and developed during his speech on the meeting of Pro-Soviets, November 1920, when he underlined the necessity of "building and organizing all spheres of social life according to one line," quoted from Polish edition, *Dzieła*, Warsaw, 1950, vol. 31, p. 375.

facing a conflict. Even after the events of August 1980, and in spite of a change in official outlook and an obvious lack of unity, the absence of mechanisms to negotiate and solve conflicts in the party still exists. For instance the new statutes of the PUWP do not take into account a situation of a conflict between a local party unit and its authorities. Within the party only individuals can appeal the judgment of a higher level; but even here there is no formal procedure for dealing with such conflict. An efficient barrier to the articulation of conflict is an article in the party statutes underlining that the privilege of a party member to defend his opinion cannot be "over-used and exploited against an interest of the party." When open discussion of differences is impossible and no mechanism exists to deal with inner conflicts, the only way to assure the party's unity is to build into the party (and the institutional system in general) such barriers to articulation, or to demobilize party members to such an extent that they would refrain from formulating their own positions. The whole evolution of the political system in Eastern Europe and Soviet Union can be interpreted in terms of improving and formalizing organizational mechanisms that demobilize party members and prevent free articulation. Both the high mobilization and free articulation could destroy the institutional system by formulating problems unsolvable in a structure built on the myth of unity.

A short phase of party mobilization did appear in Poland, in spite of the fact that the "revolution" in 1944–1945 was introduced mainly from above and through foreign forces. This phase ended quickly.[8] The next phase, consisting of efforts to demobilize party members (and the working class), was signaled

[8] Workers' councils, created in liberated areas in spring 1944 were already demobilized by 1946. The Polish Workers Party's decision to undertake such demobilization was made already in 1945, see PPR, VIII 1944 — XII 1945, Documents, Warsaw, 1969, pp. 145–152. *PPR: rezolucje, odezwy, instrukcje i okólniki Komitetu Centralnego*, Warsaw, Książka i Wiedza, 3 vols., 1959–1973, vol. I.

by the liquidation in 1946 of the self-management councils in factories that had originally been promoted by the Communist party.[9] After 1949 one could also observe a policy to demobilize the left-wing party intellectuals who were demanding a new culture and criticizing the tendency of the party bureaucracy to compromise with the Catholic Church and the traditional culture.[10] The anti-bureaucratic orthodox Marxist adherents of a totalitarian utopia raised their heads once more in 1953, after Stalin's death, at which time and due to their pressure more repressive policies toward the Catholic Church began in Poland. One possible explanation for this could be that Stalin's death ended the integration based on a mixture of terror and emotional involvement with a charismatic leader, and that a need for ideology as a mechanism of integration reemerged. After forming a temporary coalition with the liberal intelligentsia in October 1956, this group of "true believers" was again broken by the party bureaucracy in 1957–1958 (see Chapter VI).

The second half of the 1970s was the stage for a new generation of totalitarian utopians[11] reminiscent in many ways of the earlier group and mobilizing itself around a similar concern — the corporatist techniques of protest absorption based on the ruling group's flirtation with the Catholic Church. This group was also demobilized and partly coopted.

A third wave of anti-bureaucratic mobilization within the party based on ideological premises is apparent now in 1981, taking the form of so-called "Marxist-Leninist seminars." The reac-

[9] "Over-radicalization" of the workers councils was already perceived by the ruling group as a threat in 1945, but its efforts to demobilize councils met some resistances when a few officials met with the representatives of the councils, September 1945, see Władysław Gomułka, *Artykuły i przemówienia*, 2 vols., Warsaw, Książka i Wiedza, 1962–1964, pp. 360–367.

[10] Note a 1950 agreement with Catholic Church that was based on the Church's promise not to "act against the state's interests and to punish priests who will agitate against the state. . . ."

[11] Typical was the Sigma Club at Warsaw University, which will be described in more detail below.

tion of the party leaders to the first signs of ideological mobilization has been the same as in the past: the activity was labeled "unstatutory," and organizational mechanisms blocking articulation were introduced. It is noteworthy that one main object of attack by today's totalitarian utopians is the group of liberal intelligentsia who served as the "public" during the 1956 and 1968 crises. The irony of this situation is that some of today's liberals (or opposition) were the totalitarian utopians of the 1950s, having shifted in the intervening years through a revisionist phase toward social democratic or even conservative positions.

The technique most frequently used to demobilize party members perceived by the ruling elite as "trouble-makers" was to block them from the only channel of communication, the elected part of the party apparatus. The best way to do this was to elect people fully dependent on the higher authorities, without prestige of their own. A variety of methods were employed: from limiting the number of candidates proposed as a result of open discussion (usually no more than 25 percent), through strengthening the position of incumbent authorities (who in 1958 got the privilege of proposing a list of candidates), to detailed instructions from the Central Committee as to what topics should be discussed during party meetings.[12] These rules were rigorously controlled. The information gap between the elected and professional apparatus[13] reinforced the passivity of the former. Different methods of punishing "trouble-makers" also had a demobilizing effect. The labels have changed: from

[12] See the instructions sent from the Central Committee to local party officials, *Uchwały KC PZPR między V a VI Zjazdem*, Warsaw, 1971, pp. 225, 528, on "special political brigades sent to local party authorities to help during elections," or, on p. 268, the obligation of the party secretary to organize propaganda campaigns during elections for local councils.

[13] Compare Barbara Zawadzka *Przedstawicielstwo w państwie socjalistycznym: Problemy teorii w świetle praktykci Rad Narodowych*, Ossolineum, 1976.

"class enemy" in the 1950s through "revisionist" of the 1960s to a "person with good intentions but acting objectively against the party's unity" in 1980. Recently a label has also been formulated for those criticizing the party from the orthodox Marxist position; they are called "dogmatists."

Two recurring patterns emerge in the party's history. First of all, organizational pressure to maintain party unity increased during all periods of relative pragmatism of the ruling elite. We must remember that such pragmatism was usually connected with an undertaking that could not be legitimated in terms of official ideology. One good example is the New Economic Policy (NEP) in Russia, which was a step backward from a form of state legitimized by its analogy with the Paris Commune. Another example occurred in Poland in the 1970s, when not only did corporatist technqiues flourish but ideology was more deeply ritualized than ever. In both these situations, pressure on the unity of the communist party was followed by the development of mechanisms that blocked free articulation.

Second, customary and routine, but not legalized, mechanisms for blocking points of view different from the official view were usually formalized in two situations: either when society was highly mobilized and politicized or when it was extremely passive. We must remember that the system never loses an opportunity to reinforce its legal identity. A good example is election procedures. Even in 1954, multi-list elections were formally possible. One paragraph of the election regulations even asked that no more names than mandated be put on one list, which suggests a necessity for several lists. In practice, however, one list was used, containing a few more names than mandated. But the practice was not legalized. In 1956, when society was highly mobilized following the October "renewal," a new paragraph was introduced to the regulations: should the central authorities of particular parties and organizations decide not to formulate lists of their own, but one common list, all local efforts to formulate separate lists would be invalid. What was more, the Joint Commission of Parties with Gomułka, Ignar, and Kulczyński,[a] removed some names that were introduced on the common list by some "irresponsible local groups." This happened in January 12, 1957, a few weeks after the peak of the "renewal" (Seventh Plenum). One more change was introduced: the ruling group, expecting a boycott of elections to the Sejm, decided to cancel the paragraph stating that only candidates who received more than 50 percent of eligible votes could be elected. The formalization of the one-list election took place in 1973; it occurred not from the need to block the activization of the society. On the contrary, society was demobilized and seemed to have been bought off. Consumer aspirations served as ideology and helped to stabilize the regime. The passivity was indicated by the results of elections conducted the same year: no one was elected from the places on the list that was not supported by the National Unity Front (FJN). This meant that the number of people who crossed out the FJN candidates was very small (in the 1957 elections, 15 percent of those elected were from non-mandatory places). This passivity made possible not only the formalization of practices that previously were informal and habitual but, unnoticed by the general public, led to the rapid centralization of the youth movement, further limitation of intraparty democracy, excessive centralization of the council system (making it more difficult to contact an office), and changes in the Constitution. The process was similar to that called "structural Stalinism" in which Stalinist practices, informal and based upon terror, received legal justification and no

[a] The leaders of the PUWP, the Peasant party, and the Democratic party. Ignar and Kulczyński were ostensibly representatives of the peasantry and the "working intelligentsia" — presumably two social classes that exist in socialism alongside the working class. The latter is, of course, represented by the PUWP.

longer needed to be reinforced through terror. Thus, a very important step in building the system's legal identity was made. The system was able to adapt its institutions to its practices.

At the same time, however, a contrary process was occurring. Paradoxically, this process was also rooted in a functional imperative of the system. The blockade of interest articulation that was built into the political system led to a situation in which informal competition and negotiations in the economy became the only form of interest articulation left. This further deepened the disorganization of the economic system: a process of plan-building served as a substitute for formal negotiations over wages; an investment policy became a "game" aimed at the development of local social facilities and housing. Status politics took the place of economic rationality. The conflicts latent in structures based on a myth of unity became more and more dysfunctional. Furthermore, the functional imperative to stabilize the system in the long run led to the necessity of introducing some changes and reforms. This action was very difficult for a system based on the myth of infallibility. Any process of change (or reform) from above in an authoritarian-bureaucratic regime is complicated, and at some stage it is necessary to invoke (or even reconstruct) a "public" (see Chapter VII). Of course such ritual drama, and regulation through crises in general, was also in a sense a case of blocked, unauthentic articulation. The ruling elite, through provoked conflicts, marked out areas of confrontations that were the most convenient and safest from its point of view. Such more or less ritualized political drama also helped to channelize and to lower social frustrations.

Another activity characteristic of the political process of the 1970s was an effort of the ruling group to build a structure characterized by "lame," irresponsible pluralism. This was an answer to the full blockade of interest articulation caused by the constantly active, totalitarian tendencies. The dysfunctional impact of the blockade made it necessary to reconstruct from above at least some points of view that were blocked, however without representing concrete interest groups. "Lame" pluralism was simulated from above; it was not free articulation from below.

These detotalizing tendencies, operating simultaneously with their opposites, were followed by a gradual slackening of social mobility, an ever-decreasing openness of the structure, and efforts to make more pragmatic the functioning of the economy. It is evident that in the long run, the organizational mechanisms created in the name of the totalitarian utopia in fact have impeded its realization. They resulted in the systematic waste of ill-placed capital, eliminated the motive for production at the level of the only producers, the enterprises, and absorbed more and more social energy to cover the gap between utopia and reality. The organizational blockade of interest articulation as well as the ruling group's efforts to demobilize party members could not stop the process of gradual distintegration of the communist party. All the traps created in the course of proceeding toward totalitarianism became clearly visible, even to the ruling group itself.

The difficulties of rationally allocating capital and the means of production after elimination of the market or an automatic bank control through credit-risk evaluation, and the purely artificial categories of economic semantics, have reduced the regime's economic effectiveness despite its vast outlays and high accumulation (high, that is, only in the distribution of the national income and not in its production). The difficulties in verifying the demands of enterprises and the unhindered reproduction of an unbalanced structure have resulted in a cyclical repetition of economic self-strangulation and made it necessary to take decisions outside the usual framework of planning and allocation concerning the transfer of resources and even the halting of certain investment projects. Such periodically made decisions may temporarily alleviate economic tensions, but they also cause considerable losses.

The dogmatizing power of a strong authority and the myth of its infallibility make it very difficult for the ruling group to introduce any changes, and these weaknesses are freely used against it by lower executive levels. A personnel policy that gives preference to individuals holding conformist attitudes has destroyed any possibility of obtaining corrective feedback within the party and the administration. Any such opportunities for feedback from society as a whole, if only in the form of a free press, were disrupted in the first stage of the totalitarian process. Accurate measures of the economy were non-existent due to the completely artificial economic indicators (including indices of effectiveness), which were themselves the effect of bargaining between the lower and higher echelons. The centralization of decision making made it necessary to expand the sphere of transmission, i.e., the medium-level rungs of administration. This was costly and required the additional transfer of resources from the productive to the non-productive sphere. The expansion of the administrative apparatus was accompanied by continued disintegration of the instruments of regulation and of the system of executive rules. These rules, frequently created on the basis of exceptional or purely local situtations and then extended to the entire economy, were often mutually contradictory and constantly broken both by the executive rungs and the ruling group itself, as it applied the principle of ruling by exceptions and continually tried to improve its status vis-à-vis the executives. The very detailed rules and directives governing the activities of the state and economic administration created a situation in which so many participants in the system had an interest in breaking the laws that no meaningful sanctions could be applied against any of them. This, in turn, only accelerated the erosion of the law and the devaluation of the instruments of leadership at the disposal of the center. The elimination of economic mechanisms and self-regulators (often carried out in order to subordinate the entire economy to a political center) had effects contrary to those intended, and even helped the economy escape from the control of the ruling group. In particular, the inability to assess objectively the effects of economic activity and expended outlays, as well as the artificiality of economic semantics, made the control of the economy a mere illusion.[14]

A similar collision between attempts at modernization and the systematic hindering of capital accumulation has been evident historically in stituations in which politics has prevailed over economics, for instance in the imperial states. Such a contradiction appeared forcefully during the modernizing efforts of Peter the Great in Imperial Russia. There the mode of activity of the highly centralized state administration and the traditional type of legitimization of authority greatly hindered the emergence of an independent basis of authority (accumulated capital) and of an economic mechanism (the market) independent of the emperor. The permission granted by the czar to foreign merchants to pursue their activity (and to accumulate capital) was an attempt to find a way out of the trap set by the state itself. Nevertheless, the merchants had not been given the "privilege" of participating in the totalitarian utopia (conceived as a national unity), and consequently they were not subject to restrictions imposed by this utopia. They were treated as elements not belonging to the system; their acquisition of wealth posed no threat of the emergence of an independent foundation of economic power. What was more, they could always be expelled.[15]

In Poland in the 1970s one could observe attempts to find a

[14] For example, in 1973 every 1% increase in efficiency was followed by a simultaneous increase of wages of 1.64%.

[15] Compare Robert G. Wesson, *The Imperial Order*, Berkeley, University of California Press, 1967.

way out of the traps authority had set for itself on its course toward totalitarianism, as well as the simultaneous renewal of totalitarian tendencies rooted in tensions generated by the process of detotalization. The former manifested themselves in selective, centrally guided, informal steps without legitimization (for the ideology remained unchanged, only ritualized). It was characteristic that the object of both processes — detotalization and a simultaneous totalization — was the same: maintenance of the apparatus of power. The coexistence of these two tendencies was, in my opinion, one of the intrinsic elements of the Polish political system in 1970s.

DETOTALIZATION

Lame Pluralism

In the mid-1970s, the ruling group attempted to correct the irrationality of the decision-making process (linked, as we recall, with over-centralization and with the artificial character of economic semantics) by ever greater segmentation and specialization in the institutions of transmission. Their aim was — first of all — to decentralize decision making with deconcentration of competence to make decisions. This lame pluralization was intended to simulate the different points of view indispensable for reaching rational decisions, while, at the same time, not weakening the mobilizing role of the state. It was not, thus, intended to transmit the interests of the society. The point was, and this must be very strongly emphasized, to simulate but not represent points of view. Using Juan Linz's phrase, it was irresponsible pluralism.[16]

This simulation constitutes the main difference between

[16] Juan Linz in Greenstein and Polsby, *Handbook of Political Sciences*, Reading, Mass., Addison-Wesley, 1975.

lame pluralism and the corporatist structure of interest representation. The positions of the institutions (commissions, committees, etc.) that make up the system of lame pluralism should, in
accord with the purpose of the ruling group, reflect its power
through personal connections or the delegation of authority
from above, and not the authority and support provided by society. These institutions incidentally, were not controlled by the
society nor were they responsible to it. An interesting phenomenon is worth noting in this connection. The system of institutions for transmission of society's interests consists of branch
industry authorities (industrial ministries and associations) and
functional authorities (functional ministries, such as the Ministry of Finance or the Committee for Labor and Wages). Only
an increase in the number of functional ministries is linked
with what I call the phenomenon of lame pluralism. Any
increase in the number of industrial ministries and associations
indicates the opposite tendency — greater centralization and
totalization — and is an attempt to prevent collision between the
growing number of centrally made decisions and limits the
range of guidance.

The purpose of the functional bodies is to represent the logic
of system functioning, e.g., financial or market balance, without, the essential point, actually representing society. Hence,
the Committee for Market Affairs established after 1978 when
economic disequilibrium was deepening rapidly was not established by consumers but reflected efforts by the ruling group to
simulate artificially a point of view whose other possibilities and
mechanisms of self-assertion it had eliminated during the process of totalization. The same situation was true of the Council
for Family Affairs.

In order to make it impossible for the institutions constituting
the system of lame pluralism to take firm root in society, the
leadership widely applied a kind of "merry-go-round of positions," i.e., frequent transfers of personnel. This duality of

intentions (to reproduce differences of opinion but not to transmit interests) which was behind the ruling group's strategy of lame pluralism not only failed in its aim to enhance rationality of the decision-making process but also resulted in the further disintegration of the instruments of steering (wages, prices, credits, political appeals). The decomposition of the intermediate sphere, and even decentralization within the framework of a broad ruling group—when certain rights were transferred to lower regulatory levels, though not to production enterprises— replaced real decentralization. No wonder, therefore, that the strategy did not meet the expectations of the ruling elite, since it failed to eliminate the real causes of inefficiency.

Analogous politically to the creation of the system of lame pluralism was the introduction of a pattern of repressive toleration, in which informal political opposition is tolerated. Two examples of such opposition are the Workers' Defense Committee (KOR) created in 1976 and the Movement for the Defense of Civil and Human Rights (ROPCIO).[17] As we will see, repressive toleration had far-reaching consequences for Polish society and its political development. Gierek's team hoped that the social and political costs of permitting the existence of such opposition would be outweighed by the advantages. Among the latter was the image of "the most liberal ruling elite in Eastern Europe," which increased Poland's access to foreign credits. What was more, the non-ideological character of KOR made possible its coexistence with the ritualized ideology; its "workers' defense" rhetoric of opposition especially made it a very difficult object to attack. The confidence of Gierek's team that they were playing it safe was reinforced by the absence of institutional channels that would allow the opposition to reach the mass of

---

[17] Both groups published samizdat journals, bulletins, and books and organized centers for financial and legal aid for all who needed it. Unofficial lecturing and more and more frequent contacts with workers at the end of the 1970s flourished in common activities during the August wave of strikes.

the population. That feeling was increased by the efficiency of the corporatist techniques of protest absorption that in the late 1970s helped to pacify nearly 1,000 strikes and to keep them out of the opposition's reach.

Even the creation of the Free Labor Unions in 1978 at Katowice and Gdańsk did not change the policy. Factional fights within the party were already in full swing, and the security police misinformed the ruling group about the scope of opposition activities; the security police seemed determined to use the opposition as an instrument of the already prepared palace revolution against Gierek's team. The latter continued to believe in the isolating impact of repressive toleration, in which sanctions were disproportionate to real involvement, to create a climate of moral ambiguity about the opposition's status and to undercut social trust in it. The selective sanctions, which grew more severe as the distance from the capital increased, were aimed at isolating the opposition. The attainment of this effect was certainly furthered by the political climate that prevailed in a society brought up in a totalitarian system, in which nonenforcement of sanctions was an immediate cause for suspicion, and gave the opposition group the appearance of yet another rival elite.

Stability in the 1970s seemed to be guaranteed less by the absence of frustrated (and even articulated) groups and communities than by the prevention of communication between such groups in the different sectors of the system (e.g., the party apparatus and the society). The lack of such communication led to the separation (and often alternation) of crises within the PUWP and between the ruling group and society. The polarization tactics used by the KOR (under the slogan of defending society against the state) also hindered communication. The sensitivity of the ruling group to potential intercommunity lines of communication was demonstrated in its reaction to the origin of the debating club "Experience and Future" (DIP) in September 1978. This club was closed down in December 1978, even though the program of its meetings was much more moderate than that advanced by the factions in the party itself or by the KOR. The DIP did not stop work, however, and by September 1981 had published three reports on the political and economic situation in Poland, as well as many "open letters" to the ruling elite, particularly during August 1980.

Repressive toleration was sometimes accompanied by the authorities' attempts to borrow legitimacy from institutions that in the eyes of society were traditionally linked with critical groups (such as the Church) as well as by the official mass media's practice of taking over the symbols (but not the content) from the opposition (for instance the national republican tradition of *Rzeczpospolita*). For naive observers, this created the impression of convergence between party and opposition that was further enhanced by the haste with which opposition publications had to be read and by the great interchangeability of the language used by both sides (the main changes being the context and the grammatical fine points). This process hastened the devaluation of those symbols uttered as means of communication and reduced the emotional load they bore.

Parallel with the lame pluralization and the development of repressive toleration was a further de-ideologization of state activity; ideology acted mainly as the lowest denominator of the coalition and had little impact on its choices and decisions. It was also very seldom used by the ruling group to rationalize decisions (i.e., to avoid future commitments). During the 1970s, during Gierek's tenure, principles of totalitarian utopia no longer guided the society, becoming instead a mere verbal façade. The principles were used to name phenomena that did not exist outside Marxist ideological terminology (e.g., proletarian internationalism) and also as a language for excommunication, incantation, and labeling. But now the strength of these labels stemmed not so much from the emotions they aroused as from the power of the authority behind them. Fear created an empty space around a labeled person and thus had the power of a self-fulfilling prophecy. Symbols derived from the ideological façade were also successfully manipulated by rival factions to force through particular interests in situations when, under the pretext of upholding fundamental principles, controversies within the ruling group were skillfully exploited. For instance in the early 1970s, anti-market pronouncements by representatives of industries opposed to the introduction of the principle of "selective development" (which demanded the liquidation of some industries and introduced more risky conditions for most) recalled the formulations used by the ruling group in its struggle against so-called "economic revisionists" during the March 1968 crisis.

In the cultural sphere, this period was marked by stronger and even more frequent references to such traditional values as the nation and the family; a departure from the concept of a separate, socialist culture; and the growing role of elements of mass culture and a pattern of consumption following more developed Western countries.

Horizontal and Vertical Segmentation

Another manifestation of detotalizing efforts was the attempt to loosen the cohesion of the state's system of activity. The attempt was aimed at decreasing the centralization of that system. The techniques used included, first of all, an effort to disconnect the spheres of internal, external, and economic policies. This idea, which had been successfully applied in the Soviet Union, was intended to prevent a rapid and spontaneous spread of changes (or liberalization) introduced in one sphere of activity to other spheres.

A similar fragmentation of the system of activity took place along horizontal lines; the principles and methods of, for instance, cultural or personnel policies applied in the capital city differed from those applied in small provincial towns, far from the center of authority. The criteria used in the capital, where the regime's image was created for external use, were usually slightly more liberal.

Another effort by the ruling group to limit itself was the selective use of the sanctions and rules it had created in the past. This technique played a very important role in the strategy of repressive toleration.

The next sign of detotalization characteristic of the 1970s, was a segmentation of the regime, which was used by the ruling elite as an instrument to stabilize the political status quo. The objects and methods of such segmentation were extremely varied. For instance, different social demands were kept distinct and played off against each other by, say, dealing with economic crises separately from political ones (see Chapter VII) or with the help of corporatist techniques of protest absorption. In this regard, the segmentation of the party hierarchy helped to provide an alibi for its lower-level officials. In the 1970s the PUWP Central Committee, and only the Central Committee (or even the Politbureau), had real power to make policy decisions. The Central Committee was, however, represented by a lower-level committee in every factory and state enterprise. Ironically enough, the secretary of this local party committee was ex-officio (from 1967) the head of the workers' self-management body. Thus we have the strange phenomenon of the lower-level party secretary fighting the enterprise administration as it tried to carry out socially unpopular decisions that originated within the party's Central Committee. The segment of the ruling party that was visible to the workers had an alibi: it was fighting or was going to fight for their interests.

The increasing segmentation of the economy was also used by the ruling group to escape the traps it had earlier created. For instance, in the period 1978–1980 there was considerable growth of small, private industry and trade in Poland. The private economy functioned as a safety valve for the economic system as a whole. It fulfilled needs of social groups with higher income for such consumer items as fashionable clothes, and created the illusion of market equilibrium. This technique, as well as the corporatist forms of protest absorption were intended to remove the results of a creeping economic crisis on the periphery of the social system. On the one hand, the needs of lower income groups for durable, cheap, and good products were as unfulfilled as before. On the other hand, the stronger consumer demand of higher-income groups apparently gave the rulers a chance to stop the pattern of production for production's sake in the state-owned economy. But this chance was lost by the creation of a private, profit-seeking sector as a substitute for rationalizing the state-owned part of industry. Such a move was in agreement with the ruling group's interests: it not only minimized tensions of the executive strata of the power apparatus (and so decreased the risk that they would withdraw their support for the ruling elite) but made possible personal alliances of some higher officials with the private craftmen and tradesmen that met the financial appetites of the former.

What was more, the situation of a dual economy led to increased wage differences and standards of living. Wages in the private sector was higher than in the stagnant, anarchic, and inefficient state economy. In the late 1970s, highly qualified labor was drained from the state sector to private industry. This reduced to some extent the pressure on wages in state industry, but at the same time created a shortage of qualified labor and serious problems for the managers of the state-owned firms.

Elements of Corporatist Structure

An important tactic of detotalization used by the Polish ruling elite in the 1970s was exploitation of the corporatist network of interest articulation. Characteristic features of corporatist techniques of protest absorption were analyzed in Chapter I. Another important element of this pattern was an attempt by the ruling group to borrow legitimacy from the Catholic Church. These attempts began in October 1977, with the first meeting between Cardinal Wyszyński and Edward Gierek. In the following years, the power elite tried to enlist the support of the Church hierarchy for unpopular decisions and for maintaining peace and public order. The price paid by the state administration was the creation of a more tolerant environment for religious practices and the Catholic press. For instance, in 1979 the main bargaining points were the Pope's visit to Poland and the legalization of a youth educational organization, "Oaza," that had developed around parishes and had more than 100,000 members. The approach taken by the Gierek team after 1977 exploited the authority of the Church in order to stabilize the system, in contrast to the former policy of destroying that authority by disrupting the Catholic community with help for example, of government-inspired activists of the "patriotic priests" association created in 1951, or the Association of Atheists in 1954.

This new policy was based on the premise that actions which shore up the central power are the more valuable and better serve the system's legitimacy, the more independent of the regime are their initiators. Thus the Gierek team valued more the post-December 1970 expressions of support coming from the independent Catholic weekly publication, *Tygodnik Powszechny* (January 3, 1971) than declarations of loyalty formulated by the splinter group led by Catholic deputy Zabłocki from the Church organization "Znak." The former was regarded by public opinion as being consistently independent. A similar approach had been taken in 1956, when support for the "post-October" Gomułka team by Cardinal Wyszyński (released from prison where he had been held since 1953) in the form of urging believers to vote in the forthcoming general elections, carried a greater weight for the rulers than did declarations made by "PAX,"[b] which had collaborated with state authorities from the outset. The twofold price the government paid for that support was, first, the annulment of the decree of February 9, 1953, stipulating government consent to appointments to Church posts and, second, the extension of voluntary religious instruction in the schools.

An interesting light on the evolution of the policy toward the Catholic Church in Poland, from the initial efforts to undermine its prestige and role (such as the show trial of Bishop Kaczmarek during the Stalinist period)[c] to the attempts to exploit the Church in order to consolidate the system, is shed by a comment in 1953, quoted by Andrzej Micewski, made to the Catholic writer Antoni Gołubiew, representing *Tygodnik Powszechny*, by Franciszek Mazur, secretary of the PUWP Central Committee, which was responsible, among other things, for relations with the Church.[18] Mazur said: "Mr. Gołubiew, this is revolution, and we are not concerned with any subtleties or

[18] Their meeting took place in 1953, shortly before the authorities removed the paper's editorial board. Interestingly enough, this occurred in the wake of the publication, for the first time ever in the history of this weekly, of an article that more or less gave the official party line in reporting the show trial of priests from the Kraków curia charged with espionage (*Tygodnik Powszechny* 4/410, 1953). Andrzej Micewski, *Współrządzić czy nie kłamać. PAX i znak w Polsce, 1945–1976*, Paris, Libella, 1978, p. 174.

[b] A lay Catholic organization, formally registered in February 1947.

[c] Bishop Kaczmarek, of Kielce, was tried before the Warsaw Military Tribunal in September 1953. Together with three other priests and a nun, he was accused of spying for the United States, assisting the Ukrainian nationalist underground, and collaborating with the Nazi Gestapo during the Second World War. He was jailed for two years before his case was brought to trial. In court he "confessed" and pleaded guilty to all accusations. On September 22, 1953, he was sentenced to 12 years in prison. Kaczmarek was the highest Church official ever brought to trial. Barely a week after he was sentenced, the Primate of Poland, Cardinal Wyszyński, was put under house arrest. September 1953 thus stands out as the peak of the communist government's assault on the Catholic Church in Poland.

moralities. . . . You are decent people, so why do you stick your necks out, what has all this got to do with you . . . ?'' Could it be that even at this time party authorities recognized the value of keeping the image of the Catholic Church community untarnished for the future? Did they think so early of the possibility of exploiting this image in the future for the benefit of the regime?

An analogous situation, in which a ruling group borrowed legitimacy from its opponents in order to smooth a transition, occurred in the Soviet Union in the early 1950s. At the Congress of the Communist party, Darya Lawkina, who had been imprisoned by Stalin for nearly twenty years, announced that, during a spiritual conversation with Lenin, he told her "It is unpleasant for me to be alongside Stalin who did so much damage to the party." The statement was widely publicized in the Soviet Union at that time, and the body of Stalin was removed from a mausoleum he shared with Lenin.[19]

The policy of borrowing legitimacy from the Catholic Church has from the outset, however, encountered opposition from the left wing of the party. It is interesting that the arrest of the Primate of Poland, Cardinal Wyszyński, took place in 1953, *after* the death of Stalin and at the same time the first signs of a "thaw" were appearing in other areas of life, such as agricultural policy and the cultural sphere. The thaw originated with the anti-bureaucratic wing in the party, chiefly party intellectuals, whose outlook was similar to today's totalitarian utopians in Poland. Yet this group was even more steadfast in its orthodoxy and militantly secular.[20]

---

[19] Quoted from journal of Mircea Eliade, *No Souvenirs*, New York, Harper and Row, 1977, p. 145; also *Christianity Today*, (1961), vol. VI, no. 4, p. 31.

[20] See the discussion on secularization and the church in *Nowa Kultura* 57/1957, the weekly that expounded the views of party intellectuals and was quickly closed down by the centrist and non-ideologically oriented Władysław Gomułka.

COUNTERMOBILIZATION

A similar phenomenon occurred in Poland in the late 1970s. The countermobilization against Gierek's detotalizing techniques had three motives: tactical, ideological, and organizational. A good example of the *tactical* countermobilization against Gierek's policy was the activity of the Olszowski-Grabski faction in the late 1970s. Grabski decided to attack Gierek's policy at the Tenth Plenum of the PUWP Central Committee in May 1978. He chose as a relatively safe line of argument two elements of that policy, the relations with the Catholic Church (he accused Gierek of being "clerical") and the pattern of "window dressing" liberalization characterized by selective use of sanctions (a kind of repressive toleration). Both policies (together with the populist pattern of absorption of working-class protest introduced in the early 1970s) were a source of tension for the lower echelons of the party apparatus. Stefan Olszowski wanted to use the frustration of this level in the PUWP hierarchy as a political lever during the Eighth Party Congress in February 1980, and this, together with safety, was the main reason for his tactical choice of the direction of attack. I labeled it a semantic choice because in a situation where factional intrigues are forbidden, a potential ally may be recognized not in open discussion but by the use of some key words; unfortunately for Olszowski, the word "clericalism" became such a sign. "Unfortunately" because his choice of this tactic in early 1980 diminished his chances to get the post of first party secretary after August 1980. The negative reaction to his candidacy by the Catholic Church hierarchy (through unofficial bargaining conducted in the Sejm in September 1980, with Zabłocki representing the Church) ruined his chances. The Catholic Church was at that time desperately needed as a shock-absorber by the ruling group and could not be antagonized.

Much more complex and interesting was the *ideological*

countermobilization against Gierek's policy in the 1970s. The activity of the Sigma Club at Warsaw University was characteristic of this movement. At the base of this activity was not so much a strong faith in totalitarian utopia as deep disillusionment with the prevailing corrupt, bureaucratized, and ritualized system, which was even compelled to borrow legitimacy from the Catholic Church. Sigma Club members wanted to return to the purity and equality (mythicized by them) of the early postrevolutionary years. An excellent example of their thinking was their thesis about the cleansing function of dictatorship and terror. Advocates of the thesis, writing in Sigma's quarterly publication *Colloquia Communae* (Spring 1979), invoked Marx's "Private Property and Communism" and underlined that the accumulative phase of state capitalism, in which Poland found itself in the late 1970s, was conducive to the development of a consumer ideology that had affected even the working class. According to them, a real danger facing all social classes (including the workers) in view of the omnipotence of the state bureaucracy was a permanent loss of dignity. This could bring about the situation that, when the time was ripe for implementing "true" communism (a community of producers) there would be no one left to do it. The Sigma people recognized that reintroducing the dictatorship of the proletariat could not change the accumulative logic of the system, but it would, at least, allow the working class to preserve its dignity by purification through violence and by giving them the illusion of power and strength. Dictatorship of the proletariat, aimed both at the bureaucracy and at the intellectuals who, the authors claimed, were in the service of the bureaucracy, would also put an end to the widespread corruption and willfulness of the ruling elite.

The advocates of the purification thesis had only a vague idea what concrete form such a dictatorship should assume. They were mostly young people between 25 and 35, who had no memories of Stalinism in Poland. Yet they created several myths about that period, among them that industrial management's function was to serve the workers. Management's job was to insure an uninterrupted and smooth production process, in which the workers were the principal actors as well as the politically dominant group in the factory. These young people had other illusions and emotions about the situation in the 1950s; for instance, they longed for firmer political control over the economy; they criticized "technocrats" and believed in the myth of egalitarianism. Some of them had experienced the cultural and social barriers to advancement and rejection by the circles of children of old intelligentsia. Hence, they were a fertile ground for emotions and aggressions stemming from cultural differences, and they understood the longing for the status-leveling policy that had been characteristic of the early 1950s. They prefered a return to "class" criteria for advancement. For them it was a very practical problem. In the 1970s the conditions of a ritualized ideology held out much better prospects for a career in the party and state machine to young middle-class people, whose semantic ability enabled them to deal much more freely with the misleading jargon that was employed by those in power. Most of the Sigma Club members were of worker origin.

The evolution of the Sigma Club shows the strength of the polarizing tendencies in Poland in the late 1970s, and the difficulty of overcoming them. In the spring of 1979, some members and followers of this totalitarian utopian group, together with some career-seeking young apparatchiks, were used as a fighting squad against the students and lecturers of the underground Flying University (TKN). The latter was linked with so-called "liberal opposition." Sigma Club members became pawns in a move by one faction of the ruling elite against the Gierek faction. The former was the Grabski-Olszowski faction, which for tactical reasons had criticized Gierek's policy of repressive toleration making possible the continued existence of the liberal opposition. Any move against this liberal opposition, which could increase polarization, was an indirect move against Gierek.

Ironically, it was the argument used by the totalitarian utopians to back their demands for intraparty democracy that made it possible for them to be used in the interfactional struggle. They argued that a communist party that is undemocratic becomes ritualized and lacks genuine political functions. In this condition it is weak and less able to hold its own against attacks by the liberal opposition. In order to strengthen their argument, the totalitarian utopians demonized the liberal opposition, making it appear more numerous and more effective than it actually was in 1979. Few from the Sigma Club believed that the liberal opposition posed a genuine threat to the ruling elite; others wanted to avoid being labeled "objectve oppositionists," which in ordinary language means being unwitting supporters of liberal opposition due to "weakening the party with their criticism." These complex rationalizations became a sword that was turned against the totalitarian utopians rather than against the liberal opposition.

First of all, their position as the fighting squad was the source of very bad feelings about themselves. After March 1968, the Sigma group spent 10 years trying to understand and express the falsity of their role when they were used to fight a genuine student movement. Nevertheless, some elements of that earlier situation recurred in the spring of 1979.

The second effect was the disintegration of the Sigma group, and, as an antidote, its strong tendency to ritualize in order to create the illusion of a "community." As we know, ritualization is fatal for genuine intellectual development. The intellectual regress of this group was the cost paid for its involvement in factional rivalry. Its members were conscious of all this cost. Some of them left the group; others were over-aggressive, seeking justifications for their previous involvement. More and more they saw everything in the social surroundings in black-and-white terms. All these factors — the tendencies toward polarization, guilt, aggression, and ritualization — could, as we know from recent history, signal a pre-fascist situation. These factors were also very important elements of the return of totalization tendencies. The breaking up and demoralization of the totalitarian utopian group was one effect, and a minor one, of using fighting squads against the Flying University. The second effect, unintended by the organizers of provocation, was to give the Flying University more publicity in the West.

Most of the aims of the Grabski-Olszowski faction that had organized the confrontation were not realized. Its members wanted, first, to discredit Gierek. Their move was violent and could have signaled a new wave of terror. If terror occurred, Gierek would be blamed both by Polish society and Western observers. Gierek could not protest that the terror was unleashed not by him but by an opposing faction because any exposure of lack of unity in the Polish ruling elite was taboo. Gierek, however, was strong enough to put a stop to the use of the fighting squads and furthermore to do so without publicity.

The second aim of the Grabski-Olszowski faction was to end the present semi-official status of the liberal opposition by creating a spiral of drastic moves and countermoves that would force the opposition to take actions that were clearly illegal. The liberal opposition, however, stayed calm and took care not to break the law.

Their third aim was to prevent various frustrated social groups from joining in common action. In this aim, and this only, the faction succeeded by placing off the totalitarian utopian group against the liberal opposition.

A dramatic dimension of the ideological countermobilization against the Gierek regime was the reaction of Sigma Club members to the wave of strikes in the August 1980. In spite of the fact that this protest was something they had dreamed about, they stayed apart from it, due to party discipline. Later on, trying to rationalize their position and to reduce bad feelings about themselves, they articulated their reaction to the Gdańsk events in very orthodox terms. During a discussion of the strikes at the Sigma on September 3, 1980, one of their leading theorists, Professor Balcerek, said "It was not a working-class liberation movement. The workers, by emphasizing that they wanted to keep watch over administration, accepted its existence and the bureaucratic, Stalinist formula of the social system. They are not revolutionary, they do not want to liquidate the division of labor. They accepted their own role as workers and wanted only to make it easier." Such disappointment with the working class as "not revolutionary enough," typical of the orthodox Marxist, deepened as nearly all expressive functions in Solidarity were monopolized by people from the liberal opposition, or by members of the same "public" that had been active in the 1950s and 1960s. Later on, the Sigma Club tried to create links with the horizontal structures in the PUWP that originated in October 1980, but here again their orthodoxy and ideological rigidity made them suspicious (see Chapter V). They are now largely demobilized; some of them were coopted after August 1980 into minor positions in the party apparatus.

In the late 1970s, the longing for a totalitarian utopia appeared not only in the political but also in the cultural sphere. Activists inspired an anti-bureaucratic, anti-"cosmopolitan," and anti-liberal letter signed by 24 writers, film directors, and actors that circulated in December 1979 in the form of an "Open Letter to the PUWP Central Committee." This activity was probably inspired by the same party faction that was responsible for the fighting squads. Its social base was people with problems of upward mobility, unsuccessful artists and frustrated writers who were unable to understand and accept Gierek's tactics of repressive toleration which would have made it possible for them to have "clean hands" while simultaneously making a professional career. But one could also detect in this movement a longing for the atmosphere of the first, post-revolutionary phase of the totalizing process in Russia. The longing boils down to nostalgia for a myth, and an ambiguous myth at that. Because of the character of the revolution in Poland, social mobilization was not guided from above, but from the outside. The postwar enthusiasm was mainly an enthusiasm for rebuilding and not for revolution. In the area of culture, however, an element of mechanical imitation predominated. For in Russia, the appearance of socialist realism in the late 1920s and the reversion to national traditions was an expression of the logic of the state's development and of the abandonment of the idea of a new revolutionary morality, law, and culture, which proved too anarchical in view of the need for discipline and order. It was also in Russia, a period of attacks (mainly in the theory of psychology, law, and history) on orthodox Marxism, characteristic of the cultural revolution of the early 1920s.

In Poland things took a different turn: socialist realism appeared nearly simultaneously with orthodox Marxism, both imported from the U.S.S.R. and mechanically blended without the internal dialectics and tensions that had occurred in Russia. In Autumn 1945, at Poznań, the young communists from the Academic Association of Fighting Youth (AZWM, organized at Łódź University) were holding discussions with young Catholics and criticized the Young Socialist publication *Płomienie* (edited by Jan Strzelecki) for "concentrating on the luxury of a clean conscience, instead of making revolution." In 1947, activists of the AZWM argued that "one must be ready to take on himself a burden of using violence in order to defend the working class's interests." This position was based on an assumption of a relativity of all values and on the concept of the "creative terror."[21] During this and similar discussions, democracy was labeled as "an aesthetic abstraction, useless in a situation where it was necessary to break the old order."

[21] Compare A. Leśniewski, *Łódzka organizacja AZWM*, Łódź, 1963, as well as the unpublished manuscript by Tadeusz Drewnowski.

The ideological orientation of the AZWM members in the mid-1940s often took the form of scientific dispute. Examples of this were a dispute over a romantic orientation in culture and politics (the young communists preferred the Enlightenment tradition), or a dispute over "method" (when many of the AZWM members discovered Marxism and Russian Formalism for the first time). They also discussed the "utopian" and "moralistic" implications of the humanistic tradition. Among the members of AZWM were Leszek Kołakowski, Ignacy Wald, and Ryszard Herczyński, who were to be accused of "revisionism" in 1968; Józef Kępa, who would be first secretary of the Warsaw Committee of PUWP at the very time the "revisionists" were expelled from the party; Irena Moczarowa, who would become wife of General Moczar, the leader of the nationalist faction in the 1960s; Kazimierz Kąkol, in the 1960s the main ideologist of the nationalist orientation; Antoni Rajkiewicz, who would serve as one of the government's experts during negotiations in Gdańsk shipyard in August 1980 and was an actual Minister of Labor. This list illustrates a dramatic dimension of the contemporary history of Poland. Characteristically, the former friends of the so-called "revisionists" used their 1940s arguments against them in 1968.

These ideological disputes of the 1940s ended quickly, and administered socialist realism took their place. The turning point was the Nieborów Seminar of Young Writers in 1949 and the Szczecin Congress of young intelligentsia the same year. During these meetings the texts of leading young, left-oriented writers (W. Woroszylski's "Batalia o Majakowskiego," J. Andrzejewski's "Wyznania i rozmyślania," and T. Borowski's "Rozmowy") were criticized for "attacking the middle class from the very same class point of view." Following these disputes, a meeting in the Council of State in 1950 introduced some bureaucratic guarantees of the "socialistic character of art"; compulsory "scholarships" in collective farms and factories were arranged. Apathy and frustration among writers and young "totalitarian utopians" increased. Some of them (for instance Borowski) committed suicide. But most of them eventually adjusted to the new situation. The material privileges for members of the Writers' Association (inexpensive housing, cheap lunches, and occasional access to "forbidden" Western films at special screenings closed to the normal public) made life boring but possible.

The longing for the "revolutionary culture" formulated in the late 1970s was built on a mythologized conception of the cultural life of both postrevolutionary Russia and postwar Poland. First of all, its popular and egalitarian elements were overestimated: in both countries the "revolutionary culture" was an elitist one. The authoritarian temptations present in the late 1970s were more the results of personal resentments and frustration than faith in the "creative implications of terror." In a sense this wave of totalitarian utopianism, with its hidden consumer appetites and professional resentments against more talented colleagues, was a caricature of the earlier AZWM activists.

The proponents of a totalitarian utopia in cultural life forget that it was never realized, in its pure form, in Russia either. The mobilization was rather dubious in Russia, and the old patterns of petit bourgeois culture very soon regained their attractiveness (formal artistic experiments, even though publicly presented in the form of street posters, remained the art of the elite). The authorities' tendency to make pragmatic compromises with traditional values and with the Church became apparent immediately after the revolution, and again in the early 1930s at the time of the party purges. As early as 1918, Alexander Blok made a note in his diary under the date March 22nd: ". . . horrifying symptoms: the district Soviet wants gradually to 'mould' the public with the help of a 'light comedy' repertoire, because there are 'some 80 people who are worker aristocrats' in the district," and further down ". . . yet another telling symptom: the authorities are not prepared to celebrate May Day in the new style just because it falls in the seventh week of Lent."[22]

Blok notes that, even in that early postrevolutionary phase, differences arose between the ruling group and the executive rungs of the party apparatus. He wrote "Who is going to win this time? Total anarchy (the provinces reproach the Commissariat for publishing the classics instead of political pamphlets), or a new 'cultural system'? I don't know (January 6th, 1919)." That same year, he called attention to disagreements between those members of the postrevolutionary ruling group and the executive rungs who came from the intelligentsia-aristocracy and those of working-class origin. In Blok's words, they differed in "social consciousness." Furthermore, leaders from working-class backgrounds viewed those from other social classes with suspicion, even if the latter declared themselves on the side of the Bolsheviks. According to Blok, they felt "A master will always weather the storm, and will remain master."

A similar suspiciousness has been evident in the hostility toward the intelligentsia of some totalitarian utopians in Poland. This has been true especially when the longing for this utopia expressed the mounting tension regarding social status among those who owed their social advancement to the breaking-up of former status groups, and reflected the difficulties encountered by those representatives of the working class who were trying to make a career in the party. In the presence of a ritualized ideology, one's social origin is less important than the skill with which one imitates the ostentatious verbal façade; and members of the middle classes are more skillful at doing this.

While reviewing the mechanisms and pressures in Poland in the late 1970s that enhanced the trend toward totalization of social life, we should also mention a specific attitude that

[22] Alexander Blok, *Diaries, 1901–1920*, Polish edition, Warsaw, 1963.

evolved at the middle levels of state, economic, and party administration. The totalitarian temptations had—in this case—mostly *organizationl* roots. These middle-level administrators were deeply frustrated, on the one hand, by the inescapable necessity of listening to expressions of the society's dissatisfaction about the prevailing market difficulties and budget cuts, and, on the other hand, by the growing uncertainty and risks involved in transmitting the center's policy. These risks were caused by the unofficial tendencies to detotalize that had not been legitimitized by any changes in ideology.

An additional risk (or even, as some officials claim, a violation of an unwritten contract) lay in the fact that the administrator himself had to interpret the signs from above to guess what "style" (and which faction) currently predominated in the party. He could not retreat behind a convenient screen of clear instructions and rules. The risk was enhanced by the lack of a uniform policy at different levels (for example, criticism uttered in the capital was tolerated to a greater extent than criticism in the rest of the country), as well as the wide range of centrally initiated symbolic actions (in order to create a favorable image for external use), which were obviously not conceived as signaling a new internal policy. The ruling group's methods of absorbing social protests at the end of the 1970s (e.g., by engaging in official talks with striking workers even though work stoppages were regarded as illegal) were applied over the heads of the executive levels and most often at the expense of their positions and prestige. We must remember that between 1976 and 1980 there were more than 1,000 strikes in Poland. The frustration at the executive level was mainly linked with the way the detotalization policy was pursued and not, as is generally thought, with the policy itself. It was a case of a collision between a bureaucratic culture (regulations, rules, legality) and an autocratic culture (guided by exceptions and informal actions). Yet, this frustration was used by those factions within

the ruling group that were interested in promoting the totalitarian process, either because of their yearnings for a totalitarian
utopia or because they sought to strengthen political control
over the economy. Attempts have also been made to exploit this
feeling of frustration in conflicts, as evidenced by theses about
"irresponsible leadership and irresponsible society" formulated
in circles close to the Kraków Club *Kuźnica* and in *Życie Li-
terackie* (October–December 1978).

The peculiar situation of the Catholic Church in Poland after
1977 also provoked the apparatus's countermobilization and its
yearnings for a totalitarian utopia. The motives in this connection were not ideological or tactical but organizational. The
apparatus perceived the new policy of the ruling group toward
the Catholic Church as a serious threat to its status and prestige
and as a hindrance to its, after all, unchanged instruction in the
sphere of propaganda and everyday contacts with the clergy (on
such matters as the building of new churches or religious teach-
ing in the schools).

This description of the various social groups that, for widely differing reasons, advocated a totalitarian utopia and tried to organize the countermobilization against the limited detotalization
policy of Gierek in the late 1970s is intended to make supporters
of the idea of pluralism and democracy realize that such ideals
are not as universal as we used to think. This problem is as true
today, after the events of August 1980 and the creation of Solidarity, as it was in the 1970s.

Believing in the attractiveness of the ideals of democracy and
their superiority over other ideals and utopias, one tends to forget that, in confrontation situations, the idea of democracy is not
juxtaposed to a similarly attractive ideology, open to discussion
and arguments, but to a rationalization on which activities of a
very different nature are based. It also tends to be forgotten that
extremist movements are not usually founded by extremists but

by ordinary men, driven by personal frustrations and individual interests. The problem democrats often have in understanding ideologies other than their own (such as the totalitarian utopia) is the result of transposing their own way of perceiving their own ideology to other ideologies. If they conceive their ideology in the category of a myth (as understood by Sorel) — as an unitary structure without any internal tensions, indivisible into separate elements — similarly, they view a totalitarian utopia in its entirety, but as an antimyth. Yet in fact, totalitarian utopia does have quite a number of different aspects, which leads to the emergence of a coalition and mobilization of widely different interests around it. This aspect is readily grasped by those who manipulate society in that utopia's name. They know that their strength lies in gaining the selective support of various social groups for individual parts of their programs, and also that only a combination of supporting actions of which the individual backers are often not aware, will be decisive for eventual success.

The main aim of this chapter has been to analyze the peculiar inter-relationship of two contradictory tendencies characteristic of Poland in the 1970s. One of these was Gierek's policy of limited detotalization (combined, however, with strong pressure for unity inside the party); the other was the totalitarian temptations and the countermobilization of the opponents of Gierek's policy. It is noteworthy that the corporatist practices of the mid-1970s were responsible for an increase of tension not only within the executive stratum in the power apparatus but within the Catholic Church hierarchy as well. The lower levels in the Church hierarchy seemed to be much more radical than the higher echelons, often exceeding the role of "loyal opposition." Some priests became the leaders of oppositional activity, for instance Father Małkowski in Warsaw, who published a samizdat journal in the late 1970s, or the priest from Zbroża Wielka who organized the Independent Peasant Union in 1978. Both had difficulties with the Episcopate and were treated as trouble-makers; Father Małkowski even lost his position in his parish and became a full-time oppositionist. The delicate balance between the Catholic Church and the Gierek team, built on mutual concessions, helped to stabilize the situation in spite of the creeping economic crisis; but, as we shall see, it generated tensions of its own.

CHAPTER V

Dynamics of the Political System

after August 1980

[*Written in November 1981*]

The evolution of the Polish political system following the wave of strikes in summer 1980 was more the result of a web of spontaneous processes and uncontrolled political forces than the effect of purposeful, reform-oriented action. The most characteristic element of this evolution was the transformation of the polymorphic status of the party, which attempted in February to withdraw from the economy as well as from the government. This transformation was more a desperate ad hoc effort to divide responsibility, in order to avoid a confrontation with Solidarity, than the realization of a long-term policy of building a new type of communist party. Also, Kania's surprising agreement to a democratic election of the party apparatus was less a turn toward democratization or the result of the activity of the so-called horizontal structures in the PUWP, than a method to weaken or even cut off the old apparatus supporting the Olszowski-Grabski faction. These and other tactics of Kania's team vis-à-vis a frustrated and organized society were responsible for sweeping changes in the party that at first glance appeared to be deep and lasting political reforms.

A second array of forces leading to the transformation of the Polish political system in general, and the party status in particular, was linked with structural tensions inside the PUWP. These tensions were generated by the two features characteristic of the party: its polymorphic status and its traditional formula legitimatizing power. The polymorphic status of the party led to a situation in which the polarization of society between those who ruled and those who were ruled also polarized the party between its leaders and the powerless masses. The lower levels of the party fully identified with the powerless rest of the society. An indication of this was the nearly full participation of rank-and-file party members in the March 1981 warning strike that followed the Bydgoszcz crisis. Nearly one million PUWP members (mostly workers) became members of Solidarity. Many of them left the party, which now, in November 1981, numbers no more than 1.8 million members. Increasing polarization within the PUWP was one of the main costs of its polymorphic status; its existence as a viable, ruling, unified organization seemed less and less possible.

Another factor generating structural tensions in the PUWP was the "vanguard" legitimation of power. This type of legitimacy not only accounted for the poor formalization of prerogatives and responsibilities inside the party and in its relations with the government but also forced the executive level of the power structure (the apparatus) to pay with its own authority and prestige for mistakes and the unpopular policy of the narrow elite. This was one consequence of the myth of party unity and infallibility rooted in its legitimacy as a vanguard. The situation grew especially painful during the few months following the events of August 1980, when the erosion of the apparatus's status accelerated as a result of the Politbureau's indecisivness and its lack of a policy vis-à-vis Solidarity. The apparatus reacted with open rebellion. During the Sixth Plenum of the Central Committee on October 4–5, 1980, the apparatus asked for a formalization of responsibilities inside the party; in other words, it demanded the party's structural modernization. Several circumstances blocked this rebellion. One was the growth of the anti-apparatus, horizontal structures within the PUWP (which were partly invoked from below in order to check the apparatus). The horizontal structures demanded the party's democratization as well as control by the party masses over the professional apparatus.

Energetic attacks by regional functionaries of Solidarity on the party and state administration also made it easier for the party elite to pacify the apparatus. These attacks were part of the symbolic politics engaged in by Solidarity during Autumn 1980 and Winter 1981.

A final element blocking the open rebellion of the party apparatus was the channeling of its frustrations through factional intrigues, with Andrzej Żabiński's slogan "we must before all defend our cadres."[1]

However, some efforts were made to change the PUWP's legitimacy. In October and November 1980 the mass media were filled with "social contract" rhetoric. This signalled that the ruling group was building a new, quasi-legal legitimacy based on problem-solving procedures. As I have noted earlier, this major step ("major" in ideological terms, because it meant that conflicts were accepted as normal elements of social life) has gone unnoticed by Polish society.

In Chapter II, I underlined the relation between the dilemmas of the development of Solidarity and the multistaged factional activity and the evolution of the horizontal structures in the PUWP. In this chapter I want to analyze some features of the political system's transformations. I will concentrate above all on the evolution of the polymorphic formula of the Communist party as well as on the deepening crisis of its identity and functioning. The former illustrates the thesis that the ruling group's self-limitation (in other words, its detotalization effort) was generated not by its love of democracy but by its pragmatic orientation. Also notable is the non-ideological char-

[1] Speech delivered at the meeting of the party apparatus, Katowice, November 1980.

acter of this process; it is analogous to the ideological underdetermination characteristic of Solidarity. The fate of two ideologically orientated groups in the party, the Sigma Club and the Katowice Forum, which evaded this rule will be instructive; it not only supports the thesis that the party transformations were non-ideological but illustrates the power elite's policy to demobilize party members.

This demobilizing policy (combined with the prevention of free articulation inside the party) became more and more visible as the crisis in the PUWP deepened and its functional problems seemed unsolvable. Efforts to demobilize party members as well as the apparatus were followed by attempts to integrate the party. This integration was especially obvious during Autumn 1981, when the crisis in the PUWP was in full swing. The techniques used were, first, polarization (the party versus the rest of society) and pressure on the executive apparatus to undertake unpopular tasks. The latter eroded the authority of the elected party secretaries and made them more dependent on the party elite. A good example of the policy was the situation in which the PUWP secretaries from big factories were made watchdogs of self-management (against the radical concepts of Solidarity's Network). The second instrument of artificial integration was the creation of feelings of menace among party apparatus; rumors spread that Solidarity had created a mysterious list of 50,000 names of future victims. An obsessive underlining of the similarity of the Polish situation to that in Budapest in 1956 and an overemphasis on the role of "street politics" in Solidarity's tactics also served as the instrument of this artificial integration.

All of these activities were followed by promises of "protection" and "loyalty" given by the party elite to its executive level. This was a general policy aimed at demobilizing the whole party. The first wave of this policy was observed immediately after the August 1980 strikes when party committees on the factory level were instructed to slow down and ritualize their activity in order to prevent transmission of the prevailing atmosphere of politicization into the party. The second wave of the policy appeared more than one year later, after the Fourth Plenum of the PUWP in October 1981, when the crisis of the PUWP's formula seems unsolvable. This policy has two goals: to maintain the party's unity on the one hand and to redefine the political system on the other hand. The tasks are linked; as we remember, the pressures to build the party's unity always increased when the ruling group undertook a pragmatic policy that could not be justified by ideology.

The first objects of this new wave of demobilization were two groups in the PUWP characterized by a strong ideological orientation: the Sigma Club and the Katowice Forum. The former, with its orthodoxy and dialectical imagination was unacceptable to both the party apparatus and to the workers. The workers could not understand Sigma rhetoric and were offended by its assertion that the August events were "not revolutionary but, on the contrary, a bureaucratic, Stalinist phenomenon." The Sigma Club contended that the strikes "had not eliminated a division of work and the state's ownership of means of production but had stabilized this ownership by canalizing and institutionalizing the workers' frustrations."[2] Sigma members were also never fully absorbed or trusted by the horizontal structures in the PUWP. The activists of these structures were typical products of the 1970s, they were suspicious of all ideological programs, avoided ideological rhetoric themselves, and, during their fight for intraparty democracy, used only organizational arguments. For a while they exploited the printing facilities of the Sigma Club but never gave its members leading positions in their movement. In such a situation of relative isolation, pressure brought to bear by the ruling group using a mixture of cooptation and threat was especially efficient.

[2] Sigma Club meetings on September 3 and 18, 1980.

Another strongly ideological movement in the PUWP was the so-called Forum of Communists, the most famous of which was the Katowice Forum. This group was much more aggressive and primitive than the Sigma Club in its attacks on Solidarity, the intelligentsia, the mass media, and Kania's policy. Part of this aggressiveness was probably rooted in frustrations at blocked upward mobility as well as real indignation at the depoliticization and de-ideologization of the polymorphic party. These frustrations were later reinforced as Jaruzelski began a series of delicate maneuvers aimed at redefining the political system. Signs appeared that the Communist party was being removed as an active part of that system and that an effort was being made to rebuild the regime around the state instead the party.[3] However, the aggressiveness of the Forum of Communists also served as an instrument of factional fights within the party. For instance, the accusation by the Katowice Forum that the Polish mass media were "too liberal" helped to erase the "hard liner" label from Olszowski (who was responsible for propaganda in the Politbureau). This made possible Olszowski's election to the Central Committee during the Ninth Congress of the PUWP. After that Congress, all Forum groups were warned of party sanctions if they continued their activities.[4] The Forum, with its orthodox (and at the same time radical)

[3] The first sign of this shift were the military operational groups sent by Prime Minister Jaruzelski to take control of the local authorities in October 1981. After two months, these groups were reallocated on the level of the regional authorities. This could be the beginning of the creation of an army-state, to take the place of the previous party-state. The army-state formula seems easier to legitimate and can be based on the broader coalition of social forces due to its a-ideological character. Efforts to demobilize party apparatus are taking many forms: from ostentatious signs of loyalty and promises of protection in the future, through meetings with the most active groups in the party, such as the political club Warsaw 80 or the Karl Marx Club, to more noisy propaganda against political opposition combined with the interruption of a political meeting in Jacek Kuroń's house on November 21, 1981.

[4] Speech by Central Committee Secretary Kazimierz Barcikowski at the First Plenum (July 1981).

"class" rhetoric played the role of a semi-loyal opposition, in Juan Linz's terms.[5] It not only took seriously the rhetorical pronouncements of the regime but was able to use radical measures to defend them. A good example of the latter was the occupation by the Forum people of the party committee in Katowice steel-mill, where they wanted to create the center of "revolutionary" (to use their own rhetoric) activity directed against both Solidarity and the government. If we label Solidarity as a "self-limiting revolution" and Jaruzelski's government as "antirevolutionary," we have to label the Katowice Forum as a "counterrevolution." Its political doctrine is a violent reaction to the revolutionary challenge, and it borrows the methods of revolution to save the old position of the communist party. The Forum's most characteristic activity has been its break with the politics of compromise and concession of Jaruzelski's government. Like the Forum, this regime is against Solidarity, but it has tried to adjust to the new situation without violence. The existence of the Forum is even more dangerous for the government than it is for Solidarity. Accusations made by the Forum play the role of denunciations, repeated later by the GDR and other East European countries. It is very characteristic that now, when the Jaruzelski regime is redefining the system; the Forum is looking for help to the GDR rather than to the Soviet Union.[6] One would assume that such a serious operation cannot be undertaken without the previous agreement of Moscow.

TRANSFORMATIONS OF THE POLYMORPHIC PARTY

The beginning of the transformation of the polymorphic status of the PUWP occurred in mid-January and early February 1981.

[5] Juan Linz in Greenstein and Polsby, eds., *Handbook of Political Science*, Reading, Mass., Addison-Wesley, 1975.

[6] Marxist-Leninist seminar sent greetings to Erich Honnecker, GDR leader, on November 1981.

The political situation took on a few new features. First the danger of a confrontation with society was rapidly growing. The symbolic politics of Solidarity were in full swing, the attacked apparatus was demanding protection, and its frustration served as a lever for the anti-Kania faction in the PUWP. What was more, the party's only shock-absorber (the Catholic Church) refused to continue this role due to its own conflicts with Kania's team over the registration of Rural Solidarity. The polymorphic status of the party (both the government and the Sejm being perceived as the party's pupils) led to deepening polarization, cutting through all hierarchies. The social climate in Poland was similar to the atmosphere in Italy before Mussolini.[7]

During this period, all the elements that could lead to the emergence of a strong, authoritarian political system were present. In the first place a power deflation occurred, with the characteristic fragmentation of political forces, the polarized and factionalized PUWP facing Solidarity divided in terms of political versus strictly syndicalist practices. Another feature of power deflation was a visible loss of autonomy of the political system due to broadening of the political arena, politization of the populace and in political mobilization of originally non-political institutions such as the Catholic Church and professional associations. The latter development was a continuation of the corporatist practices of the 1970s, but it now took a more open, ostentatious form, with more general political demands. The gap between the formal organization of the political system and civil society was increasing; the "social contract" rhetoric changed the style but not the structure of the Sejm and other elements of the political system. The PUWP functionaries seemed unable to find a new formula for their relations with

[7] Compare Paolo Farneti, "Social Conflict, Parlimentary Fragmentation, Institutional Shift, and the Rise of Fascism: Italy" in Juan Linz and Alfred Stepan, eds., *The Breakdown of Democratic Regimes*, Baltimore, Md., Johns Hopkins University Press, 1978, part II, pp. 3–33.

society; they escaped into ritualized activity, trying in this way to erect a glass wall between themselves and the society.

A political stalemate was obvious. Social forces were tending to neutralize each other. The politics of status seemed to be more important to both sides than the politics of interests and problem solving. Issues had divisive rather than aggregating functions inside the constituencies of both the main political actors.

The economic crisis continued to deepen early in 1981. The government, accustomed in the past to servicing clients rather than to dealing with organized society, to group patronage rather than mass politics, appeared increasingly paralyzed. Both sides longed for order and feared increasing social anarchy. The situation provided fertile ground for Mieczysław Moczar, Kania's rival, who used a mixture of authoritarian-populist rhetoric and played the role of "strong man." The factional fights in the ruling elite exploited the confused reactions to the process of democratization in the same way that Mussolini had done in Italy in the early 1920s. One tactic used by anti-Kania factions was especially similar: an appeal to the need for "order" and at the same time an indirect attack on the very same order as the NIK (the Supreme Chamber of Control led by Moczar) fed the symbolic politics of Solidarity with materials it had collected during the Bielsko-Biała and Jelenia Góra strikes in February 1981. Another tactic was the practice of local violence on the grounds of provocation. The aim here was to exhaust the legitimacy of Kania's team by creating a situation in which it would be obliged to use methods that would destroy the social contract rationale. This tactic exploited existing constraints on Kania's freedom of maneuver, the most important among which was the myth of unity. Kania was also unable to talk openly about his successes in restoring order (for instance, through secret negotiations with some Solidarity leaders or by an effective cooptation and demobilization of some union activists), as such disclosures would only remobilize the workers. The tactical obligation of Kania's team to maintain a symbolic impression of Solidarity's impetus and unity made the disloyal opposition's attacks especially easy. This again was very similar to the situation of the Italian government in the 1920s, acting in a triangle of Socialists, Fascists and Labor Unions.

A third element of the situation that was exploited by opponents of Kania's regime in the December–February period was the fact that the coalition of social forces around Kania was deteriorating rather than maturing, with the visible withdrawal of the most important force, the Catholic Church.

The psychological climate of the Polish society during the December 1980–February 1981 period was strikingly similar to the social mood in pre-fascist Italy. The ease with which the legal system could be breached in the name of a material legality, characteristic of both sides of the conflict, is especially notable.[8] The deep frustration of Solidarity members, rooted in the painful process of the movement's institutionalization, led to a series of surrogate conflicts, an overreaction to some minor problems, and an accumulation of unsolved or even unlabeled problems. A longing for profound changes was mixed with a longing for order, neither of which could find political expression.[9] Both were exploited by the anti-Kania faction, who appealed to the

[8] An instrumental treatment of formal rules is characteristic of Solidarity leaders as well as the Polish ruling group. The latter recently broke the statutory rules of the PUWP, which had been voted upon only two months earlier, by permitting General Jaruzelski to retain three posts: defense minister, prime minister, and first secretary of the Central Committee. The invitation to the party apparatus to participate in plenary meetings the Central Committee also violated the formal rules voted during the Ninth Party Congress. On the other hand, similar manipulations with its own legal base can be observed in the actions of Solidarity; a good example here is the nomination by Wałęsa of the Presidium of the National Commission in October 1981.

[9] Results of sociological research conducted by Professor Adamski at the Institute of Sociology and Philosophy, Polish Academy of Sciences, December 1980.

populist emotions of society and tried to unify nearly all resentments — for instance a strong hatred of "liberals" within the party apparatus and anti-intelligentsia attitudes in Solidarity. These feelings were linked to a hostility aroused by a characteristic of the Polish intelligentsia, a ready adaptation to the repressive toleration of 1970s on the one hand and the tendency to exploit its own "moral rightness," to judge and moralize, on the other hand. Strong anti-middle class political culture accents were present in "Forum" documents, and the weekly *Rzeczywistość* was linked with this orientation, as were some Solidarity publications.

This situation in the winter of 1980–1981 combined with increasing pressure from the Soviet Union and more and more obvious traps set by the polymorphic status of the party. The only workable alternative for the Kania regime was to try the three following steps. First, to weaken the network of social forces acting against Kania by decomposing the political system in a manner different from its actual fragmentation. Kania's method was to introduce new polarizing criteria dividing both the party and Solidarity into "extremists" and "reasonable elements." Second, he tried to avoid confrontation with society by dividing the responsibilities of the party and the government in such a way that the party took on itself the responsibility for all unpopular actions (and thus met the Soviet Union's expectations) while the government continued negotiations with Solidarity, capturing all the credit of social contract legitimacy. This step meant the virtual end of the polymorphic status of the party; the consequence should be a gradual withdrawal of the PUWP from the state administration as well as from the economy, or at least the appearance of such withdrawal. Kania's third tactic was to satisfy the popular longing for a "strong man" in order to prevent one of his opponents (for instance, Moczar) from seizing the role. For this position Kania selected General Wojciech Jaruzelski. It was an unusual situation; a man with a

199

not very strong personality was selected to play the role of a "strong man." Jaruzelski's association with the army helped, as did the myth of the leader in a uniform (by association with Piłsudski.) The connection with this myth was skillfully fed with publications circulated unofficially by the government highlighting Jaruzelski's strong links with General Berling.[a] It was also publicized that during World War II he had opposed a group of pro-Stalinist communists called the Association of Polish Patriots, who had been indifferent to the future autonomy of Poland. Rumors circulated underlining Jaruzelski's declaration to defend Poland "against any aggression," made at the time when the Soviet intervention seemed very probable (December 1980). Society's longing for authority was so strong that the positive image of Jaruzelski survived his quickly revealed inability to deal with a paralysis of the state administration and to halt the economic crisis.

This discussion of the tactical alternatives open to Kania's team is of course a hypothetical reconstruction, but much evidence supports my thesis. Early in February 1981 one of the leading men on Kania's team, Kazimierz Barcikowski, delivered a speech at a meeting with the PUWP activists that included a characteristic remark: "don't be afraid to use unpopular, polarizing measures . . ." Another leading Kania supporter, Andrzej

---

[a] Józef Piłsudski (1866–1935) was a legendary, charismatic figure in Polish politics of the interwar years, who is credited with winning back Polish independence in 1918 and saving the newly reestablished state in 1920 by fighting back Bolshevik armies at the outskirts of Warsaw. He was a soldier and a politician, who executed a military coup (the so-called May Coup of 1926) against a duly elected Polish government in order to "sanitize" politics. Hence, the name of the regime that followed — Sanacja. Zygmunt Berling was taken POW by the Red Army in 1939. Released from imprisonment after the Soviet-Nazi War broke out, he served in the Polish Army in the East, formed in the U.S.S.R. When the army was evacuated to Iran, he chose to stay in the U.S.S.R. to form a Polish army under Soviet auspices. Eventually, promoted to the rank of general, he became its commander and fought the Nazis until their surrender in Berlin.

Żabiński, in a speech at the February 1981 Plenum of the Central Committee, stated his opinion that the PUWP had no chance for an authentic legitimacy. From the whole context of his speech, this remark can be understood as an argument for the following thesis: even the use of a hard line cannot further undermine the PUWP position in society; it is as bad as it ever can be. Such pessimism was a good opening for Kania's tactics.

Another sign of this development was a statement made by Józef Klasa, chairman of the Central Committee's Press Department, during a meeting with the staff of the Warsaw weekly *Kultura* on March 3, 1981. He informed them that Kania's relations with the Episcopate were rapidly worsening and added: "now we (the ruling group) are alone vis-à-vis society, and we must get along without the Catholic Church as a shock-absorber."

Shortly before his nomination to the post of prime minister, General Jaruzelski made a spectacular entry on the political stage. He sent his own "independent" observers to Bielsko-Biała during the regional general strike in early February. Rumors circulating at that time emphasized that Jaruzelski prevented the introduction in that region of a state of emergency. After his nomination, and the creation of a special position in the government for contacts with Solidarity, Jaruzelski at once started to build an image of a government that was independent and strong, although at the same time, he lacked influence over some tension-generating areas of state activity, particularly police and episodes of local violence against Solidarity activists.[10] However, after a short time, this image-building operation became something more. Jaruzelski began to change personnel in less visible but crucial positions, for instance in the legislative section of the Council of Ministry Office. The need to formalize the "leading role of the party" and for the party to withdraw

[10] Incidents of beating at Białystok, and a suicide after the interrogation of Solidarity functionaries at Nowy Sącz were reported in January and Febraury.

from the economy were publicized in party newspapers and government publications.[11]

The opinion began to circulate within the party apparatus that an evolution of the PUWP toward the East German type of the communist party should be expected, followed by the reduction of the party apparatus to half its size, a withdrawal of the party from the economy, and its future involvement mainly in ideological and cultural matters. At the end of February the signs of the party apparatus's frustration increased.[12] The anti-Kania faction decided to use these frustrations as a political lever. Olszowski took the first step in a speech during the meeting of the pre-Congress Commission when he announced that the party's withdrawal from the economy in a moment of crisis was a sign of irresponsibility. Kania responded indirectly: he not only participated (and presided) at the next meetings of this commission but managed to organize these meetings in the big enterprises with the smallest possible participation by the apparatus. For Olszowski and Grabski (with their poor relations with the Catholic Church) the political situation was ideal to start a fight against Kania, because the latter was also having difficulties with the Episcopate due to Rural Solidarity. It was a very rare moment when the maintenance of relations with the Church did not matter.

The aim of the anti-Kania faction was, first of all, to halt the changes in the polymorphic status of the party. The best way to attain this aim was to destroy (or rather to demystify) the Kania regime's image-building operation, to demonstrate the Jaruzelski government's involvement in unpopular activities, and to provoke a confrontation with Solidarity that would end the social contract legitimacy of the ruling group. The Bydgoszcz crisis on

[11] Compare the conceptions of economic reform published at that time by L. Balcerowicz, vice-president of the Polish Economic Association, or Albinowski's articles in *Trybuna Ludu*.

[12] Compare critical speeches at the Tenth Plenum, May 1979, or the Seventh Congress of the PUWP, February 1980 in *Nowe Drogi*.

March 19, 1981, was exactly such an attempt. A number of circumstances convenient for the anti-Kania faction coincided: Jan Rulewski, the leader of Bydgoszcz Solidarity, was known as an extremist, an important government (not party) official, Deputy Prime Minister Mach was on the spot when a decision to use force was made. Finally, Deputy Prime Minister Rakowski, and probably Jaruzelski himself, agreed to the use of police force in Bydgoszcz to clean up City Hall; they were probably misinformed that the possibility of an occupational strike was high. Of course they (Jaruzelski, Rakowski, etc.) wanted a peaceful operation, as at Nowy Sącz a few days before. But in the situation when they probably prefered to keep their involvement secret (for the fear of destroying the image Jaruzelski's government had previously established) a guarantee existed that another secret would be kept as well, namely a phone call from one of the highest officials connected with the anti-Kania faction suggesting that a small brutality would teach the "extremist" Rulewski a pinch of wisdom. The same tactic was followed by the anti-Kania faction during the following Ninth Plenum; its threat to make public the contents of an agreement signed by Kania, and Jaruzelski, in Moscow a few weeks earlier also served to dispel the illusion of differences between the party and government positions.

It should be stressed that these events were not merely a struggle for power. This was also an ideological confrontation, in spite of the fact that the word "ideology" sounds incongruous in connection with such a brutal plot. The ideological conflict lay in the different conceptions held by each side of the party's role in the political system and of its relations with the government.

The Bydgoszcz crisis was only a partial success for the anti-Kania faction. The myths of an independent policy and the "clean hands" of the Jaruzelski government were destroyed. Jaruzelski's personal prestige, however, remained intact. Society's need to believe in somebody was very strong and, in a way, blind. The Bydgoszcz maneuver did stop the transformation of the polymorphic structure of the PUWP. This transformation had not been a conscious policy but rather a half-instinctive, tactical step to avoid a confrontation with Solidarity. The step was probably made without taking all its implications into account. When the tactic ceased to work, or rather met strong obstacles, it was simply abandoned, and a new repertoire of instruments was introduced. Kania's defense was a very clever one. It was based on two simple devices: he labeled his opponents "hard liners" (and himself "moderate") and, he contracted a coalition with the anti-apparatus movement in the PUWP. Kania's unexpected agreement to new, democratic elections of the party apparatus destroyed the social base of his opponents.[13] Kania retained his position, but the opportunity to elaborate a new model of the party, based on different relations with the government, was gone. The coalition with the anti-apparatus movement was only temporary; one month later, "observers" from that group did not get access to the Plenum meeting, in spite of promises made earlier by Secretary of Central Committee Zdzisław Kurowski.

Later, events moved swiftly: only 400 delegates to the Ninth Party Congress were elected directly in the big enterprises. Twice as many were elected at District Conferences with Kania's "recomendations" for those apparatus members that would not be elected otherwise. The effectiveness of Kania's persuasion increased rapidly after word spread about Brezhniev's letter to the Eleventh Plenum in June 1981 and Kania's "brave" defense of a "renewal." Increasingly, populist techniques took the place of democratic procedures. The same was true during the Ninth

[13] The most characteristic was a speech by Skrzypczak, first district secretary in Poznań, who stressed that the elections on the lower levels of the PUWP apparatus were conducted in more democratic ways than those to Central Committee, which were preceded by Kania's populist "recommendations."

Congress with its pre-elections and, following it, when radicals of all kinds were cut out. As a result, the Central Committee was composed of "people from the street," most of them unknown, without any experience in politics, and extremely vulnerable to manipulation by the professional apparatus. In Chapter II I described how this new Central Committee comprising "average men" caught in the cogs of the polarizing political machine, drifted toward a hard line orientation. Kania apparently has won the Ninth Congress: he was elected, and the appearance of party unity was not broken. At the same time the opportunity to transform the PUWP so that it could better adjust to the new social situation was gone. Kania's team vigorously rejected the alternative of politicizing and ideologizing the party, in order to avoid the polarization that would unavoidably ensue. Open withdrawl of the party from the economy, linked with an end of the nomenklatura mechanism and radical economic reform, was also dropped due to fear of losing power. A conception of the party as an institution, or rather a movement, fighting with the state bureaucracy, formulated by some ideologically oriented groups inside the party, was also rejected. On the contrary, the Ninth Congress accepted as its program the stabilization plan formulated by the government experts that specified no particular role for the party. It was characteristic that, at the Second Plenum of the Central Committee held after the Congress, the only role for Central Committee members formulated by Kania was to "persuade people not to go on strike."

The traditional ways in which the district party committees had functioned no longer worked. In the past they had been mostly a parallel economic administration or had played the role of the broker in negotiations or conflicts between enterprises. Now, as both horizontal and vertical links in the economy atrophied, and the natural economy and direct exchange between enterprises took the place of the competition and pressures traditionally conducted via the regulatory bodies, the administration as well as the party lost their traditional functions. Now, raw materials and investment goods (the main objects of bargaining in the past) were out of reach of the district-level authorities. These goods were either centrally divided or unofficially reallocated by barter. All these elements led to a deep crisis of identity and function of the party, which increased after the Ninth Congress. Before I analyze the mechanisms and inner dynamics of this crisis I want to look once more at the political system as a whole.

THE INNER DYNAMICS OF THE POLITICAL SYSTEM

In the late 1970s, the Polish political system could be described as a typical authoritarian-bureaucratic regime. It contained limited, not-responsible political pluralism, without an elaborated and guiding ideology but with dinstinctive mentalities. There was the characteristic melting together of party and state administration and the segmentation typical of corporatist forms of interest articulation. This system was very unstable. The most interesting endogenous processes affecting its dynamics were the exhaustion of forms of social protest and techniques of protest absorption on the one hand and a dialectical relationship of detotalizing and totalizing tendencies, rooted in tensions produced by a process of reforms, on the other hand.

August 1980 marked a move toward the next phase of the transformation of the political system. The lame pluralism of the 1970s became an almost-responsible pluralism. The PUWP's monopoly of power was challenged not only by society (coordinated by 40,000 elected and paid functionaries of Solidarity) but also by some legislative initiatives (for instance, self-management regulation). The leading role of the PUWP was seriously limited. A major change also occurred in the status of the political opposition. Its existence was, as before, a-legal, but now it was able, through Solidarity, to reach the mass of the population. These changes were not formalized and were possible due to the legal underdetermination typical of the bureaucratic-authoritarian regime.

A second new element in the political system after August 1980 was the regime's partial overcoming of one of the main weaknesses of all authoritarian-bureaucratic regimes, namely the lack of a distinctive formula of legitimacy. A quasi-legal social contract formula took the place of the eroded legitimacy based on the myth of a vanguard party and the unity of interests of state and society.

The third characteristic of the post-August 1980 development was a new stage of the system's feudalization. The depth of the economic crisis led to the rapid weakening of the central government. One year after August 1980 the unmanageability of the system is obvious. Both the money supply and the command instruments at the Government's disposal are out of control. What is more, a natural, exchange, barter-type economy, beyond the reach of the ruling group, has swiftly developed. This group has nothing to exchange, divide, or offer: special privileges have been canceled, investment funds have been cut off. The security of managerial posts depends more upon good relations with Solidarity than on obedience to orders from above. The economic crisis has had a peculiar detotalizing impact on the system. One industrial administration ministry tried to prolong the existence of bargaining spheres (and its power) by keeping secret as long as possible a list of canceled investment projects. A second cause of the unmanageability of the economy (and the weakening of central power, characteristic of this new stage of the system's feudalization) is the tendency to close regional borders and to defend by all means the regional (district) state of possession. Such a tendency seriously damages any ability to plan. Examples of this tendency are a District Head's order forbidding the "export" of food produced in one district to other regions, or not selling out of the region cooperative goods produced by local craftsmen until regional needs were fulfilled. In this connection local authorities cooperate with local branches of Solidarity. Local party apparatuses, elected with the help of democratic procedures feel more independent and demonstrate it openly. The segmentation of the system has been deepened by the different styles used to deal with Solidarity in every district, due to the decentralization of regional administration-level responsibilities to solve local conflicts.[14] Decentralization was undertaken to divide responsibility and to avoid an accumulation of tensions. Such dispersion of power, however, makes control from the center impossible and facilitates provocations (especially now, when factional activities are conducted outside of the Central Committee, mostly on the district level). The collapse of central authority recalls the situation in China during the first stage of revolution, before 1911, when for the sake of stabilization additional administrative responsibilities were decentralized to the level of provincial authorities. This not only made some necessary central decisions impossible but weakened the central authority to such an extent that it was unable to absorb the tensions caused by the reforms it began. In a sense, the reforms destroyed the reformers. Furthermore, the weakness of the state made the rebellion possible.

Poland at present is a classical case of a weak absolutist state, able to control only the processes it has itself generated (such as passport procedures, nominations, etc.) and not real life. Even a system of repression does not seem to be fully under control due to factional fights and resentments. According to Theda Skočpol, the collapse of the state is a main element of every pre-revolutionary situation.[15] Perhaps Poland has yet to have its revolution?

[14] The main aim of this manuever was to avoid an accumulation of tensions by fragmenting responsibilities.

[15] Compare Theda Skočpol, *States and Social Revolution*, New York and Cambridge, Eng., Cambridge University Press, 1979, Chapter 2.

Another feature of the Polish political system after August 1980, probably characteristic of the second stage of every detotalization process, is the emergence of some — not very strong — ideological elements, which contrasts to the previous ritualization of ideology characteristic of the first stage of detotalization in the 1970s. The totalitarian period of system development had been characterized by a melding of society and state. This was a result of the politicization of everyday life and an atmosphere of mobilization. But in spite of such melding of everyday life and politics, the language of ideology was very definite and contrasted to the way common men thought and spoke. The next phase of system development in the authoritarian-bureaucratic regime of the 1970s was characterized by a reprivatization of everyday life and an end of mobilization. These features were, however, followed by the blending of ideological language and everyday language. This was not simply the result of a development of ironic speech, built on a ritualized ideology. The regime shifted toward values of family life and consumerism as a source of legitimacy and ideology. During this stage of its development, the gap between state and society continued to grow, and strategies for dealing with it also changed. Now these were mainly corporatist techniques, not direct pressure or control. The blending of ideology and everyday language was possible not only due to the ritualization of the former but also due to a peculiar non-ideological style of opposition in Poland as well as the non-metaphysical style of Polish religiosity. The lack of ideological debates in the 1970s made it possible for these tendencies to coexist in everyday life. In the 1970s general orientations [?], often mixed with complexes and attitudes that could be explained only in psychoanalytical terms, took the place of ideological programs. Forms of consciousness — polarized images of social reality, semantic competences — played the role of ideologies by making difficult or easy the articulation of interests. In the 1970s, incidents of ideological mobilization were very limited and isolated.

The events of August 1980 were also characterized by a lack of open ideological articulation. In Chapter I I described the peculiar, non-ideological imagination of the striking workers. Later on, due to the self-limiting character of the Polish revolution, huge areas of silence developed, when various activities of the union could not be called for what they were. A similar silence existed on the part of the party, which also tried to limit itself and similarly avoided the labeling of its own activity in order to make it less visible to hard liners. After a few months, however, new accents appeared on both sides. Ideological countermobilization appeared within the party criticizing Kania's "pragmatic" policy. Two opposing orientations were openly formulated within Solidarity: fundamentalism and the pragmatism. The line of division in both the party and the union was similar: the fundamentalists in Solidarity resemble the ideological extremists in the PUWP not only in terms of how they think and argue but also by the ease with which they have adopted violent, "revolutionary" instruments and underestimated the efficiency of legal means. They are similar in the way that revolution and counterrevolution are similar. The pragmatists, or pseudo-pragmatists, of both sides are also similar. Both are much more clever than their institutional opponents in political activities understood in terms of compromise and institutional games. Both have similar problems in understanding extremists within their own organizations due to differences in political imagination.

The most interesting new phenomenon observed after August 1980 has been the transformation of the PUWP. The principal elements of this transformation have been an unsuccessful attempt to change the party's polymorphic mode, and later on, the Ninth Congress of the PUWP, when populism was mistaken for democracy and the superficial victory over the party apparatus ended with a visible increase in the strength of this apparatus. During this Congress, nearly all chances to elaborate a new model of party functions were cut off. This accounts for the deep crisis of identity now evident in the PUWP; the continuation of its old polymorphic status and traditional function is no longer possible, but no new roles have been elaborated. The signs of this crisis were evident during Kania's visit to Cegielski factory in Poznań on August 25, 1981, when many newly elected party secretaries from large factories from the Wielkopolska demanded that the Politbureau (and the Central Committee) adopt a more energetic policy toward government. The slogan "you have to beat them to work" was often used during this meeting. This atmosphere was repeated during the meeting of the first party secretaries from the 205 largest factories in Poland on August 26, 1981. Nearly all of them talked about the lack of a clear pattern of PUWP functions in the new social and economic situation. Characteristically, factory-level party secretaries were not against administration of their own level; the pressure seemed to be rather an expression of status politics. It was not accidental that these pressures were formulated in Poznań, where a very active "true communists' forum" operates. As Hannah Arendt stressed, totalitarian movements cannot be understood without reference to their hostility to the state.

CRISIS OF IDENTITY WITHIN THE PUWP

To analyze the crisis of identity of the Polish Communist party, I will list the functions of the party during the totalitarian phase of development and describe the decline of these functions in the 1970s and its acceleration after the events of August 1980.

Five roles were characteristic of the Communist party during the totalitarian phase of the development of the political system. These were the politicization of the masses, the creation of transmission belts for communication, the recruitment and

211

training of a new political elite, influencing the economy, and, above all, a "guiding and leading" function understood as the continuous presence of the party in many sponsored organizations (and those that had been taken over). Today each of these roles has changed dramatically or has been seriously reduced.

The politicization of the masses involved efforts to mobilize and desocialize members of society as well as to detach them from all independent bonds. In Poland this aim was never fully realized. The scope of autonomy within society was large even during the Stalinist era. For instance, only 10 percent of land was collectivized. Also, the Polish Catholic Church very early found a modus vivendi with the state. The exception was the 1953–1955 period, when the already bureaucratized terror machine received strong encouragement from the totalitarian utopians to fight with the Church. In the 1970s the PUWP's monopoly on politicization as well as its penetrability was still seriously limited. The tactic of repressive toleration used by Gierek facilitated the functioning of the extra-legal political opposition, with a limited but slowly increasing influence on public opinion. Parallel to that process was the increasing bureaucratization of the party itself and the ritualization of its ideology due to two factors: the corporatist techniques of interset representation and the full development of the polymorphic party that led not only to its depoliticization but also to a loss of ideological specificity. For pragmatic reasons (payments for a legitimacy borrowed from the Catholic Church) Gierek tolerated an increase of the Church's impact on the educational process.

The limitation of the party's monopoly on politicization accelerated after August 1980. First of all, against the demobilized and disintegrated party Solidarity set its own powerful abilities to mobilize and politicize its own members. Even if the politicization of Solidarity members was characterized by ideological underdetermination it definitely affected the party's option to execute one of its more important roles. As we noted, after August, the political opposition in Poland (KOR, ROPCIO, KPN) obtained broad access to the masses via Solidarity, although its extralegal status did not change, and it could not formally compete for power. The role of the Catholic Church (and its bargaining power) also increased after August 1980.

The second function of the Communist party in the totalitarian phase of system development was to create a structure of fully controlled and subordinated transmission belts: labor unions, window-dressing parties, professional associations, the Sejm, etc. In the 1970s this function was increasingly limited. Most of the transmission belts became fully ritualized and some independent channels of articulation were constructed from above out of the old transmission-belt structure (see previous chapter). However, until August 1980, the party kept full control over the ritualized structure of transmission belts. Only in the Sejm were individual cases of dissent evident in the 1970s, but their impact was mostly symbolic. Such traces of dissent appeared especially in the mid-1970s, when a rapid shift toward political centralization took place, followed by efforts to build a legal identity for the system — for instance the introduction of a "leading role of the communist party" formula to the Constitution or the formalization in 1973 of an obligation to one-list voting.

The change after August 1980 was dramatic. The creation of the Independent Self-governing Labor Union Solidarity seriously breached the transmission-belt structure. In the following months not only some new independent associations were created but old ones demonstrated their independence. The Polish Economic Association openly supported the "social enterprise" project formulated by Solidarity's Network, which was criticized by the government and Kania himself during the Ninth Congress of the PUWP. One of the most important transmission belts, the Association of Polish Journalists, not only openly criticized the ruling group's policy in the mass media (especially the manipulations after the broken negotiations between the Government Commission with Rakowski and the National Coordinating Commission on August 6, 1981), but also supported Stefan Bratkowski, chairman of the Association, who sent a critical letter to the Politbureau and was expelled from the party in October 1981.

The window-dressing parties also made serious efforts to formulate an independent policy. Peasant party (ZSL) activists, remembering that the PUWP apparatus lost its authority when executing unpopular policies of the Politbureau toward Solidarity, decided to change nearly all the leading figures of the old central committee of their party. The Democratic party (SD) not only strongly supported demands of the private sector of the economy but formulated its own political program demanding the organization of a state tribunal as well as a constitutional tribunal in order to control the law-making process.

The Sejm also became more independent. It not only played the role of arbiter or negotiator between the PUWP and Solidarity but became slightly more autonomous in fulfilling its regular functions. However, the discussion and later rejection by the Sejm of the first version of the government's stabilization plan in May 1981 reveals how precarious was its new autonomy. The real reasons for the government paralysis were not even touched upon; the concessions given to Poland's partners in Comecon (RWPG) were not discussed; the increasing doctrinal rigidity of the succeeding stabilization plans was not questioned.[16]

One of the most efficient and subordinated transmission belts was the system of People's Councils (Rady Narodowe). Methods

[16] Successive governmental "plans of stablization" were characterized by the increasing doctrinal rigidity in the treatment of individual farmers and by a decreased willingness to close heavy industry and some steel mills. In the last version, the U.S.S.R. was openly invited to exploit Poland's unused economic potential, and its interest was mainly in these enterprises that were listed to be closed as energy-intensive type of production.

varied from direct intervention of party committees, through the more subtle technique of suggesting (through party members in the presidium of council) which outcome of a decision-making process would be optimal from the point of view of the party committee, to joint meetings of council and district party committee commissions. All these forms were extralegal and very rarely formalized. But until August or until the shock of the Bydgoszcz crisis, when the members of the district council were directly involved and pushed to revise their relations with wojewoda, the process worked.[17]

The third role of the Communist party during the totalitarian phase of the system development was the selection, testing, and training of the political elite. The main mechanism was the practice of nomenklatura. In the 1970s this role was continued with some, largely symbolic, concessions to institutionalized Catholic groups (Znak, PAX). Due to the nomenklatura mechanism, more than 80 percent of factory-level managers were party members; 64 percent of them participated in regional committees of the PUWP that served as instruments of horizontal coordination. More than 90 percent of the higher-level officials were party members. Their nomination and recall fully depended on the initiative of the PUWP. In 1972 a list of nomenklatura positions was formalized, for the first time in Eastern Europe, in order to guarantee that people in these positions would not lose their status during recurring crises but would be reallocated to similar positions. This was the first sign of the development of a crisis-oriented philosophy among the ruling group.

After August 1980, this function of the PUWP was seriously limited. First, some evidence of pluralization of the ruling elite

---

[17] Compare Barbara Zawadzka *Przedstawicielstwo w państwie socjalisty-cznym* (Ossolineum, 1976); also W. Sokolewicz and S. Zawadzki "Wyniki badań uchwał rad narodowych i ich prezydiów" in *Problemy Rad Narodowych* (March 1965).

could be observed, as well as increasing autonomy of leaders of other parties.[18] Second, although the PUWP formally retained its monopoly over recruitment to important positions in industry and administration, in practice this monopoly was seriously limited by democratic elections inside the PUWP up to the level of district secretary in May–June 1980 and by Solidarity's influence on the dismissal of many corrupt high officials of the party and administration (the best-known cases are Bielsko-Biała and Jelenia Góra in February 1981, Olsztyn in April 1981, and Nowy Sącz in May 1981). In addition in a situation where the power structure resembles a layer cake (with factional anti-Kania/Jaruzelski groups existing on a district level), the best survival tactic, from a managerial point of view, was to keep good relations with subordinates, not with supervisors.

The end of the reification of the power structure in social consciousness added to the reorientation of lower-level managers. In October 1981 Sejm passed a new regulation of enterprise and self-management status; this further limited the PUWP's influence on personnel policy by giving some workers' councils the right to elect themselves managers of their factories.

The next role of the party in the totalitarian phase was its direct influence on economic planning and on the functioning of industry. During this period, structure of dual controls was created that slowly merged following bureaucratization of the party. In the 1970s some changes to this pattern were introduced from above. There were moments when party and administration kept distant from one another for tactical reasons. This was one result of the crisis-oriented philosophy of management.

---

[18] The chairman of ZSL contacted Rural Solidarity and supported its case against the opinion of the Politbureau. Reiff, chairman of the Catholic association PAX, served as a negotiator between Sejm and Solidarity's National Commission in the matter of self-management regulations, promoting solutions that varied from the position of the Third Plenum of the Central Committee (October 1981).

During every period of serious economic troubles, the party press received instructions to attack "technocrats," in order to create an alibi for the party apparatus. To attain the same goal, a peculiar organizational arrangement was introduced in the mid-1970s. The first secretaries of factory-level party committees became, ex officio, the chairmen of the so-called Conferences of Workers' Self-Management (KSR). This was the beginning of the unusual situation in which the average party secretary spent most of his time contending with the implications of the economic policy formulated by the Politbureau and executed by factory managers. The repeated economic crises stimulated the division of roles between the government and Politbureau. In the middle of every 5-year plan the latter routinely undertook decisions leading to downward revisions of the investment plan formulated by the government two to three years earlier. It should be noted that the development of such a dual regulation technique (normal by the government, and extraordinary by the Politbureau) was inflicted on the party's unchanged (although loosely formalized) pattern of doubling functions of state and economic administration. This pattern was one of the most important elements of the polymorphic status of the PUWP that did not change in the 1970s. After August 1980, direct party control over the economy was seriously limited. The main reason was the rapid deepening of the economic crisis, which decreased the manageability of the economic system.

During the Ninth Party Congress, a new formula for the leading role of the PUWP was articulated. This formula stated precisely the "guiding role" of party leadership as executed through party members elected to the representative bodies (the Sejm, city and district councils, self-management bodies at the factory level). In spite of the fact that after two months (at the Third Plenum, September 2–3, 1981) the Politbureau returned to the old interpretation of its guiding role ("we cannot give up the nomenklatura mechanism"), some activities of Solidarity executed the formula articulated during the Ninth Congress of the PUWP. In Szczecin shipyard a battle began to stop informal interferences by party committees in the distribution of bonuses and, generally, in personnel policy. The slogan "Get the PUWP out of factory" became more and more popular.[19] In July 1981 the Szczecin district party committee, responding to these pressures, sent a letter to all factories in the district arguing that the attack by Solidarity was an action against the "constitutional role of the PUWP." The letter contained a curious statement underlining that the informal character of the PUWP's interference "reinforces its leading role." The conflict at Szczecin demonstrates that the consequent execution of the Ninth Congress formula could serve as an instrument further limiting the PUWP's role. Another factor limiting the role of the party in the economic system is the recent turn of Solidarity toward organizing a self-management structure on the one hand and the new tactic of an "active strike" on the other hand.[20]

The last (and the main) function of the party in the totalitar-

[19] See the speeches of the chairman of Szczecin's Solidarity, Jurczyk, delivered in Trzebiatów on October 21, 1981, where he concluded, speaking about the PUWP: "Let them sit in their marble building and multiply their ideology — but it will be we who will have the power." Very similar in tone was the position of the factory commission of Solidarity in the Bielsko Biała auto industry: "One day we have to take their [the PUWP's] furniture and reallocate it to the District Committee building; they have no tasks here in the factory." In the same direction was the resolution of Warski's Shipyard, Szczecin, voted in mid-November 1981. Also the recent referendum in Kraśnik Machine Factory "Ponar" was linked with a problem of the party role on factory level: 92% of workers answered "No" to the question whether they saw the need for the party on the factory level. All these developments led to the publication by Central Committee Secretary Woźniak of a furious letter claiming that "the party will never leave the workshop" (November 24, 1981).

[20] The concept of "active strike" was formulated by Z. Kowalewski (of MKS Łódź). It is based, first, on taking control of both management and the distribution of products by the strike committees and, second, on arranging direct links between factory and farmers in order to obtain food and service (an exchange economy).

ian phase of political system development was to penetrate (or rather to flow into) other government and economic organizations. The polymorphic status of the PUWP was the reason for the extensive bureaucratization of the party, its depoliticization, as well as the ritualization of its ideology. However the principal cost of this polymorphic status was the conflict between those in power and those who were powerless, which polarized the PUWP hierarchy. The peak of the split inside the party occurred during the March 1981 warning strike, when a majority of party members among the workers (as well as many local party organizations) supported Solidarity in spite of the interdiction of the Politbureau. Even some working-class members of the Central Committee went on strike.[21] Kania prevented a lasting split in the party by a strategic and momentary coalition with the horizontal structures inside the PUWP.[22] His agreement to democratic elections in the PUWP up to the level of district secretaries both reinforced his own position by keeping intact the unity of the party and weakened seriously the faction opposing him.

The idea of changing the polymorphic status of the party was never taken up again; instead, the Ninth Congress of the PUWP took as its program the government's plan of stabilization that listed only the tasks for the agenda of the state, not even touching the role of the PUWP in the whole operation. This created tensions within the party apparatus (especially among its newly elected local secretaries, who longed for more active roles in order to preserve their authority and prestige). The ruling elite's efforts to demobilize troublemakers, by pushing them to con-

[21] Comapre the speeches of Central Committee members during the Ninth Plenum in March 1981, which stressed that "the party has to be with the working class, not the apparatus. . . ."

[22] The coalition of Kania and the "horizontal structures" was not a lasting one; the delegates of the latter were not permitted to participate in the Tenth Plenum in April 1981, in spite of the previous promises of Central Committee Secretary Kurowski.

duct unpopular policies (for instance, preventing the radical workers councils supported by Solidarity) seems to have worked out; the local secretaries have grown increasingly passive. Some of them were close to withdrawing from the party. As one newly elected secretary told me recently, the only argument for staying in the party was the knowledge that his place in apparatus would be taken by somebody with a hard-line orientation.

Thus, the old party model was gone, and no new model was elaborated. The limits of its power were visible to the apparatus itself. Confused reactions to this identity crisis have disintegrated the PUWP; it was no longer unified. The effort to reformulate the role of the party from one of "guidance" (based on the polymorphic status) to "political leadership" (based on authentic authority), did not work. Not only were efforts to alter the legitimacy of power unsuccessful but the horizontal structures were destroyed. The latter, the only body that could have prevented the alienation of the party apparatus, was able to generate new ideas and to mobilize at least some party members, not through "ethos of fight" as the Fourth Party Plenum tried to do in October 1981, but through a popularizing attractive, anti-hierarchical orientation.

All these possibilities were lost in Ninth Congress discussions stylized on an "average man mentality." Kania's populist recommendations seriously limited the democratic nature of the elections to the Central Committee, the "extremists" (hard liners as well as liberals such as Tadeusz Fiszbach or Krystyn Dąbrowa) were cut off by not getting reelected to the Central Committee. The role of the apparatus apparently increased: secretaries at the district level who had not been reelected were invited to participate in plenary meetings of the Central Committee. The decisions of the ensuing plenary meetings seemed to be much closer to the opinions of the apparatus than of elected members of the Central Committee. This was evident at the Second Plenum discussions of self-management.

In such a situation, the PUWP's crisis of identity seemed to be more and more unsolvable. The artificial integration of the party, with the help of polarizing techniques that cut off the PUWP from society, were not sufficient to stop the party's desintegration and collapse. To redefine the political regime as whole and give up the efforts to rebuild the "guiding role" of the party seemed to be the only way left to stabilize the system. Jaruzelski's efforts to build a strong authoritarian bureaucratic regime with the state, not the party, as its core were aimed at creating a structure that would be not only easier to legitimate but, due to its non-ideological character, would be based on a broader coalition of social forces. Such a maneuver also makes it easier for the Soviet Union to avoid unwanted and costly military intervention: the redefinition of an institutional regime justifies the Soviet's lack of reaction even when the party's collapse is evident.

CHAPTER VI

Tragic Choices

THE FIRST YEARS AFTER THE SECOND WORLD WAR

The political fate of Poland was probably sealed long before the end of the Second World War. Two factors were decisive in that respect: the successful march of the Red Army toward Berlin through the East European countries and, connected with this, a change in United States' foreign policy from a philosophy of universalism to the concept of spheres of influence. Universalism was based on the assumption that all nations shared a common interest in all the affairs of the world. According to the second concept, each great power would be assured by the other great powers of an acknowledged predominance in its own area of special interest. The Four-Power Declaration, signed in Moscow in October 1942, was formulated in a universalist mood. However, the Foreign Ministry of the Soviet Union signed the declaration only after blotting out a clause that would justify the future intervention by the United States or Great Britain in Eastern Europe.

Eastern Europe had never been economically important to the United States. Before the Second World War, only 2 percent of American exports went to that region, and only 5.5 percent of United States capital was allocated to that area. What is more, in the United States at that time the concept of spheres of influence had very influential supporters: Secretary of State Henry L. Stimson, Vice-President Henry Wallace, and Soviet expert

George F. Kennan. Stimson, stressing the idea of "cooperation for peace," advised President Truman against any attempt to influence the development of the situation in Poland in late 1945.[1] Wallace advocated U.S. concessions to achieve Soviet-American conciliation, and he idealized motives of Soviet domestic and foreign policy.[2] Kennan argued for United States withdrawal from the Allied Control Commission: "Russia would probably not be able to maintain its holds successfully for any length of time over all the territory over which it has today staked out a claim. . . . The lines would have to be withdrawn somewhat."[3]

At the same time, in spite of the Yalta Agreement, Poland was under tough Soviet martial jurisdiction. A state of war was prolonged in Poland until October 1945; certainly that helped to stabilize the Soviet-backed Lublin government and gave the Red Army time to prepare the ground for future "free" elections (one of the conditions of the Yalta Agreement).

Earlier, on August 15, 1944, the National People's Council (KRN, supported by the Soviet Union), which granted itself the status of representative of the Polish people, passed a bill concerning the procedure for issuing decrees which had the force of law. On the basis of that bill, important acts were passed, such as the agreement between the PKWN (The Polish National Liberation Committee, the Council's executive organ) and the Supreme Commander in Moscow renouncing the sovereignty of civil law courts in liberated territories,[4] the agreements with

---

[1] Henry L. Stimson and McGeorge Bundy, On Active Service in Peace and War, New York, Harper, 1948, pp. 609–610.

[2] See Frederic M. and Edward L. Schapsmeier, Prophet in Politics: Henry A. Wallace and the War Years, 1940–1945, Ames, Iowa State University Press, 1970.

[3] George F. Kennan, "Sources of Soviet Conduct," Foreign Affairs (July 1947), pp. 566–582 (signed "X").

[4] The act was signed for Poland by Osóbka-Morawski and for the Soviet Union by Molotov, and published in Wolna Polska, no. 28 (Lublin, 1944).

Lithuania, Ukraine, and Byelorussia on the exchange of populations, and the decree on protecting the state (signed September 31, 1944, but valid retroactively from August 15, 1944). Together, these and similar legislative acts constituted, among other things, an instrument used by the new authority to destroy its potential enemies, and provided the legal basis for the trials of soldiers of the Home Army (AK). In that same year, 1945, some 5,000 people were sentenced by this procedure, and in the years 1946–1947 more than 12,000 people. These laws also provided legal grounds for the expulsion of the inhabitants of border regions (as part of the exchange of populations).

Such acts were, strictly speaking, illegal because the 1921 Polish Constitution, on which the KRN based its activities, gave no authority the right to issue decrees with the force of law on matters dealing with international relations. Under the circumstances, however, negating the legality of the activities of Polish courts and of the offices of public prosecution in the years 1944–1947 would have been tantamount to denying the legal status of the KRN itself. A peculiar situation ensued in which these actions were in accord with the laws; but the procedure by which these laws were passed was illegal. Thus, radical polarization followed, as one could either accept the situation of internal legality or else question the legality of the authority itself and of the whole system. The existence of such extreme choices (together with the presence of the Red Army) favored the stabilization of the Polish system, because attempts to oppose the legal status of the authorities were, in those days, acts of heroism. Silent consent to this internal legality, growing steadily and legitimating all the government's actions, was the first step toward the new identity of the system. Consent had been given (and probably there was no other alternative, especially since the Western powers showed complete indifference) to the still binding principle that the authority itself rectifies and defines its status vis-à-vis society, whereas the separation of powers of the judiciary, the executive, and the legislature is a fiction.

Separate armistices with Bulgaria and Hungary and full control of both countries by the Red Army made the Soviet Union's position in Eastern Europe still stronger, especially since the distinction between military and political periods of occupation was not clear. As Lundestad showed in his excellent analysis,[5] the British tried to speed up the conclusion of the peace treaties so that Soviet armistice organs could be abolished altogether, but that initiative was rejected by the United States State Department.

In spite of a clear contradiction between the political sense of the separate armistice on the one hand and the Yalta Agreement on the other hand, the American policy of non-intervention was fully consistent with its increasing recognition of "areas of political gravitation" (a euphemism for spheres of influence) and with contemporary United States priorities (to defeat Japan and Germany and to create the United Nations).

American policy toward Poland in the early and mid-1940s evolved from indirect support of the London émigré government to attempted neutrality (when the involvement of the Soviet Union in the Second World War became important from the United States' standpoint). On April 25, 1943, the Soviet Union broke off diplomatic relations with the Polish émigré government (over that government's well-documented accusation of Soviet involvement in the massacre of thousands of Polish officers at Katyń). The United States refused to make an issue of Katyń and declined Polish requests that the United States represent Polish interests in the Soviet Union after relations were broken off. Lundestad evaluated this situation as an

[5] Geir Lundestad, *The American Non-Policy Toward Eastern Europe, 1942–1947: Universalism in an Area Not of Essential Interest to the United States*, Tromsö: Universitetsforlaget; New York, Humanities Press, 1975, p. 86

"indirect invitation to form a Communist-oriented government of Poland."[6]

Franklin Delano Roosevelt's foreign policy toward Poland was inconsistent; he declared continuing support of the émigré Polish government claims for Lwów (a city located in the East of prewar Poland) in spite of his unpublished earlier agreement with Eden on the Curzon line.[7] Later, during the Warsaw Insurrection against the German occupation (August 1944) Roosevelt pushed émigré Prime Minister Stanisław Mikołajczyk to reach an agreement with the Polish Committee of National Liberation (backed by the Soviets), knowing all the while that the Russians not only refused to aid the Warsaw forces but refused permission for American planes to use bases in the Soviet Union. Between August 14–20, 1944, the Russians refused two American and one joint Roosevelt-Churchill request for support of the Warsaw resistance movement.[8] To the American government it was quite obvious[9] that Stalin's policy toward the Warsaw Insurrection, so strange at first glance, was based on the assumption (quite rational from his point of view) that the Polish (London) government forces in Poland (the so-called Home Army) must be destroyed. Perhaps Stalin was right from the Soviet imperial point of view; the failure of the Warsaw Insurrection cost Poland about 200,000 victims, most of them young members of the patriotic intelligentsia, and made it easier for the Soviet-backed government to control the country after the Second World War. But the American government, in spite of its quite realistic evaluation of the Soviet government's intentions, did not change its policy toward the Soviet Union.

[6] Ibid., p. 186.

[7] Ibid., p. 184.

[8] U.S. Department of State. *Foreign Relations of the United States* (FRUS), Washington, D.C., Government Printing Office, 1945, p. 454.

[9] U.S. Department of State, *The Conference of Berlin (The Potsdam Conference) 1945.* Washington, D.C., Government Printing Office, 1960, 2 vols.: vol. 1, p. 181.

Following these events, after Mikołajczyk's resignation as émigré prime minister, United States support for new Prime Minister Arciszewski's government was still weaker; official U.S. documents labeled that government "unrepresentative, uncompromising and therefore a short-lived exile group."[10] This opinion had a decisive impact on a key (from the Polish viewpoint) sentence in the Yalta Agreement: "The Provisional Government [backed by the Soviet Union (J.S.)] which is now functioning in Poland should be reorganized on a broader democratic basis with the inclusion of democratic leaders from Poland itself and from Poles abroad."[11] That statement was supplanted by a clause on free elections (but without an explicit formulation of institutional forms of control).

The bargaining that followed the Yalta Agreement dealt with the number of posts in the future government for non-Lublin Poles. Stalin proposed one-fifth (invoking the Yugoslav pattern) while President Truman insisted on a five-to-three proportion (in favor of the émigré government). The result reached in May 1945 was one-third for non-communist statesmen.

In spite of the lack of political success, the U.S. government hoped to use an economic lever in Poland (and in East Europe generally). But the new Polish government (with its pro-Moscow majority) quickly introduced strict state control of exports and imports and unfavorable rates of exchange for the United States dollar.[12] Also, the United States Congress refused to ratify the Charter of the International Trade Organization, to avoid tensions connected with dealing with a state-owned economy.

United States interest in the Polish situation seemed to decline. "After Potsdam Poland is hardly mentioned in the memoirs of Truman, Byrnes and Forrestal."[13] At the end of 1945

---

[10] FRUS, 1945, vol. IV, p. 478.
[11] Quoted by Lundestad, *American Non-Policy*.
[12] Baruch papers, Box 68, Clayton to Baruch, April 26, 1948.
[13] Lundestad, *American Non-Policy*, p. 111.

the U.S. State Department protested only verbally the Warsaw government's ban on all the minor parties.[14] However, in spite of this, a credit diplomacy was still in full swing. During January-February 1946 six conditions for U.S. credit assistance were formulated. They included, among others, Polish support for free trade, extension of most-favored treatment for the United States, access to information about Polish foreign relations, and one political condition — free elections.

On April 24, 1946, Polish government representatives agreed to five of the conditions, but not to free elections. U.S. credits were granted in the hope that financial aid would keep Poland more democratic. These credits were later stopped when Poland did not publish in the press information on the agreement and refused to keep anyone informed on its trade relations with the Soviet Union. At that time it became obvious that United States financial and technological aid to Poland was the only possible way to avoid the Soviet style of industralization.

In Poland in 1946 a peculiar philosophy of political realism appeared. In retrospect, it seems a pseudo-realism because it was based on false assumptions. But at that time it served as the basis for crucial political decisions and commitments. The clearest and most dramatic presentation of the political pseudo-realism of 1945 was the statement of Julian Hochfeld (one of the leaders of the Polish Socialist Party) at a meeting of the Young Socialists' Organization (ZNMS) in September 1946.[15] Hochfeld urged giving political support to the Communist party (Polish Workers Party — PRR) in the forthcoming elections "even if they are faked elections." The assumptions behind his statement were as follows:

1) The growing legitimacy of the Communist party (or window-dressing legitimacy to show to the Western powers) would improve Poland's chances of gaining financial help from the

[14] FRUS, 1945, vol. V, pp. 434–435.
[15] Samizdat journal *Krytyka* (Warsaw, 1979), no. 4.

West and of avoiding the Soviet method of industralization (the use of "inner colonization" and forced collectivization).

2) The only way to gain the Soviet Union's trust was by complete subordination of the Polish government's domestic and foreign policy to the Soviet Union's interests.

3) The Communist party would tolerate the Socialist party's autonomy, because it understood that the presence of two left-oriented parties with separate apparatuses would operate as a socialist version of the democratic checks-and-balance mechanism.

All of these assumptions turned out to be false. The Soviet Union's policy, aimed at the complete subordination of Eastern European countries, together with Cold War polarization pressures, eliminated all chance of obtaining Western funds and avoiding the Soviet model of socialism. The full allegiance of the United Polish Workers' Party to the Soviet Union's power (after sweeping purges of the "nationalistic" faction between September 1948 and December 1949) corrupted successive generations of the Polish ruling group. The Polish Socialist party ceased to exist after its forced unification with the communist party (December 1948), and thousands of Polish socialists paid a high price for their silent complicity in Stalinism in Poland and lost their moral right to judge communist policy.

The elections held on January 17–19, 1947, were "conducted more like a civil war," with repression designed to prevent the Polish Peasant party from organizing effectively. Its candidates "were stricken from the ballot in ten out of fifty-two election districts"; a new election law effectively disenfranchised at least a million people,[16] and some of the candidates were arrested. After the election, the regime began to tighten its control over society. The size of the security police force was increased, and thousands of political prisoners filled the prisons.

[16] Marian Kamil Dziewanowski, *Poland in the Twentieth Century*, New York, 1978, p. 153.

229

The last step in the consolidation of the communist regime in Poland was a compromise between the government and the Polish Catholic Church in April 1950. The political implications of that agreement are well illustrated by the following fragments of its text:

To ensure for the nation, People's Poland and its citizens, the best possible conditions for development and peaceful work, the Polish government, recognizing religious freedom, and the Polish Episcopate, having in mind the welfare of the church and the contemporary Polish raison d'etat, are to regulate their relations in the following way:

"The Episcopate will request the hierarchy to carry on its work in accordance with the principles of the church and to teach the faithful to obey the law and state authority. . . . The Episcopate will make clear to the clergy that it should not oppose the development of the co-operative movement in rural areas . . . the church, which in accordance with its principles condemns all anti-state activities, will especially oppose the abuse of religious sentiments for anti-state purposes . . . the church will punish under canon law clergymen guilty of participation in any form of underground activities and anti-state activities . . ."[17]

The tightening of the communist regime in Poland in the late 1940s was followed by a transformation of the economic system toward a Soviet-type, command economy. The period 1945–1948 had been years of slow economic recovery in Poland. Nearly two-thirds of nationalized industry and railways had been devastated. The Land Reform of September 6, 1944, created farms that were not only stripped of the means of production

[17] English translation of agreement by Hansjakob Stehle; the full text is in *The Independent Satellite; Society and Politics in Poland Since 1945*, New York, Praeger, 1945, pp. 306–307.

and transportation[18] but were too small for efficient agricultural cultivation. Economic rationality seems to have been sacrificed for political reasons. As a result, agricultural production was very low. If one takes the period 1934–1938 as a base (100), the level of agricultural production for 1945–1946 was 33, while for the years 1946–1947 it had risen only to 45. Shortages of both agricultural and consumer goods led to hyper-inflation, and the cost of living increased more than 50 percent between December 1945 and December 1946.[19]

The situation in heavy industry was much better, as territorial changes increased Poland's industrial resources. According to an UNRRA paper, "Industrial Rehabilitation,"[20] Poland gained 15 percent in coal production, 18 percent in the number of mines (an increase from 67 to 80), increased the number of steel mills (from 20-21), with a 7 percent growth in production potential. Small businesses, trade, and crafts also developed considerably in the mid-1940s.

But in the late 1940s (after the consolidation of the communist government) a rapid and major turn in economic policy was observed. That turn was preceded by a long economic dispute reminding Russians of a discussion between the so-called teleologists on the one hand and partisans of genetic planning on the other.[21] The approach represented by the apparatchiks (teleologists) won. They preferred a Soviet-type accelerated industrialization based on the inner colonization pattern. By the mid-1950s, leaders of this approach recognized their mistake, but it was too late. An institutional framework and deeply unbalanced

[18] In 1945 the horse population was only 35.6% of the prewar level, cattle were 31.5%, and hogs were 22.6%.

[19] United Nations Survey of Current Inflationary and Deflationary Tendencies, Department of Economic Affairs, Lake Success, 1947, p. 60.

[20] Edward H. Carr, *A History of Soviet Russia*, 4 vols., New York, Macmillan, 1951–71; vol. 1, pp. 486–498.

[21] Stanisław Kuziński, *Główne proporcje rozwoju gospodarczego Polski Ludowej*, Warsaw, 1960, pp. 48–50.

economic structure were already stabilized. What is more, it was evidently out of control and reproducing itself, in spite of the will of its own architect — the ruling group. Subsequently, this group tried many times without success to reform that structure and to restore the economic mechanisms destroyed by its own decisions in the late 1940s.

The victory of pro-Soviet teleologists was followed by a series of decisions that, from today's perspective, could only be called tragic choices. These decisions created the foundation of the present Polish economic system, characterized by a self-suffocating pattern of growth, structural bottlenecks, and repeated economic crises (see Chapter VII). Four decisions undertaken by the Polish ruling group in the late 1940s were particularly laden with negative consequences for future economic development. These were, in chronological order:

1) The Six-Year Economic Plan, presented to and approved by the First Congress of the PUWP in 1948, and revised upward in 1951–1952.

2) The replacement of relatively free and decentralized labor unions by a new central labor union, fully committed to the ruling group. This action was followed by a proclamation of a state monopoly on wage determination in December 1949.

3) Internal banking reform (1949) and withdrawal from the International Monetary Fund (March 1950).

The main purpose of the Six-Year Plan (1949–1955) was to transform the economic policy of 1946–1948, which had been aimed at a slow but balanced recovery and based on a decentralized market mechanism with a large number of small private businesses, to an accelerated-growth policy of the Soviet type, based on central reallocation of capital and on an "inner colonization" mode of accumulation. The techniques of the latter utilized, on the one hand, the repression of wages through political means (such as stripping workers of their right to strike and the captivation of labor unions), and, on the other hand, a forced, administrative decapitalization of agriculture in favor of heavy indsutry. The final version of the plan incorporated very high targets of accumulation and investment, which were revised upward in 1951–1952.

Eighty-five percent of investment funds went to heavy industry (as against the 75 percent originally planned). As a result, the metal industries' output almost tripled. But nearly 80 percent of that output went to make armaments, military equipment ("cold war"), means of transportation, and machine tools; only 20 percent was left to meet equipment needs of coal mining, power industries, and agriculture.[22] The result was a vicious and inflationary circle of production for production's and defense's sakes.

At the same time, farm output (which rose, on the average, 2 percent per year) lagged far behind the pace of industry. Investment in agriculture dropped to less than half of what it had been in 1949.[23] The result was an "investment retardation" of the private agriculture sector, introduced by administrative means (repressed prices, heavy taxes, and obligatory delivery of agricultural products below market prices). This forced decapitalization of agriculture led to a rapid decrease in productivity and marketability of that sector and to extensive use of the labor force (as labor was substituted for capital).

The deeply unbalanced economic structure created in 1949–1955 continued to reproduce itself. The repression of wages (real wages decreased in 1951–1952 and had barely recovered to the 1949 level by 1956)[24] reinforced the pattern of production for

[22] *Statistical Yearbooks*, 1951–1955, GUS [Central Statistical Office], Warsaw.

[23] Economic Bulletin for Europe, 1957, no. 3, p. 35.

[24] See debate on socialist economy calculation with F. A. von Hayek, ed. *Collectivist Economic Planning: Critical Studies on the Possibilities of Socialism*, London, Routledge & Sons, 1935, on one side, and Oscar R. Lange and Fred M. Taylor, *On the Economic Theory of Socialism*, Minneapolis, University of Minnesota Press, 1938, on the other.

production's sake (see Chapter 1). Low productivity in the agricultural and consumer goods industries, connected with their "investment retardation," created serious consumer market shortages. The broad substitution of labor for capital in those sectors, together with the reduction of resources formerly allotted to replacements, caused a serious technological backwardness that still had not been overcome in the late 1970s.

An Internal Banking Reform (1949) was a logical consequence of the shift toward a centralized, command-type economy. That "reform" conceded not only decentralized credits but also the control of local banks over efficiency of production and the investment process. The central allocation of investment funds ended the dependence of revenue on size of output. Economic, market competition was replaced by bureaucratic "competition" based on inter-organizational bargaining and information games. Central planning in the form created in the late 1940s (and existing until now) repressed both market mechanisms (when wages and prices were administratively settled) and entrepreneurial functions. Hence, there is no way that a centrally planned and controlled economy can collect and process all the information that is collected and processed naturally in an unrestrained market economy.[25] "The planners and managers of state-owned enterprises do not have available relevant indicators of the relative economic importance of the various factor services, in their various alternative uses."[26]

This situation has led to serious and repeated problems of allocation and to structural bottlenecks. Domestic "prices," which were decided and fixed by bureaucrats and not objectivized by market mechanisms, were exchange rates that served as units of account, rather than real prices. Rigid exchange targets and full separation of domestic prices from foreign market prices led to

[25] Israel M. Kinner, *The Perils of Regulation*, Law and Economics Center, University of Miami, 1978, p. 4.
[26] *Poland of Today*, March 1949.

a situation in which foreign importers (exporters) were not allowed to compete freely with local enterprises for products (markets) because such competition would disrupt the economic plan.

This situation created one of the main barriers to export-import development and increased the convertible currency shortages. We can call it a structural shortage, because it was rooted in the deep structure of the Polish economic system. The separation of domestic from foreign markets was deeply rooted in other activities of the late 1940s, not only bank reform. In March 1950 the Polish government took the Polish economy off the international banking system by withdrawing from the International Monetary Fund. In a statement justifying its decision, the Polish government labeled the World Bank "a submissive instrument of the government of the United States." The last brick that built a Soviet-type economic structure in Poland was monetary reform. The openly formulated objective of that reform was political; in the words of the reform architects, their aim was "the completion of the process of shifting part of the capital held by capitalists to the masses of workers and peasants."[27] But the main by-product of this reform was the mass bankruptcy of small private businesses, the reason being a formula of exchange wherein a new "zloty" was introduced to be exchanged for private persons and private enterprises, but at a ratio of 3 to 100 for cooperative and state enterprises and for savings deposits of workers. As a result of the decapitalization of the private sector, the share of private shops in trade fell from 78 percent in 1946 to 15 percent in 1950, and the portion of private business production of the total output was reduced from 21 percent in 1946 to 6 percent in 1950.[28] This method was

[27] Statement of Ministry of Finance, quoted by J. Taylor, *The Economic Development of Poland, 1919–1950*, Ithaca, N.Y., Cornell University Press, 1952, p. 185.
[28] *Statistical Yearbook*, 1946, 1951, Warsaw.

intended to get rid of the private sector by the use of an economic lever (in spite of the fact that the Nationalization Decree of January 1946 permitted the existence of private firms with less than fifty workers). The method seems to have been repeated in recent times. Government policy toward private farms, mandated in the late 1970s (e.g. administratively repressed prices, a shortage of basic means of production due to the profile of the machine industry, bureaucratic barriers to increasing the amount of privately owned land, despite a law promoting such increase) recalls "peaceful" drive of private industry to bankruptcy in the 1940s.

It is worth emphasizing, when describing the institutional framework of Poland in the late 1970s, that both the structure and the way in which the state administration functioned, were a far cry from Weber's model of bureaucracy, in which authority owes its validity to legal forms. A "socialist" administration is more reminiscent of the ritualized system of charismatic authority in a feudal society. In fact, none of the basic features of bureaucracy in Weber's model appears in the administration of a socialist state. Instead, we find there:

1) steering by uncertainty; keeping subordinated units in the dark as to their future legal status is aimed at neutralizing all attempts to gain autonomy by exploiting loopholes and inconsistencies in the regulations;

2) steering by exception and by individually addressed directives and solutions; the activities of the higher levels of the state hierarchy are carried out with a minimum of formalization;

3) the system of nomenklatura, which is the purest form of institutionalized charisma.

Finally, interference in the activities of the lower echelons, not only on the basis of specific regulations but more in line with the principle of "general supervision" (a privilege granted to the higher echelons of the hierarchy), is typical of the way Poland's administrative system is run. This is nothing more than the justification of rule by the possession of power — so typical of traditional legitimization of power.

TOTALITARIAN UTOPIA: MECHANISMS OF SELF-ENSLAVEMENT OF PARTY INTELLECTUALS

The social climate of the Stalin era (the early 1950s in Poland) has often been described. Most frequently, this has been a black-and-white picture of oppressor and victim told by the victim. The descriptions are usually confined to mass scenes and statistics of terror. Personal experiences in which the victim, under pressure, either had not managed to preserve his own dignity or had been horrified by the ordinariness of terror are carefully omitted. From the individual's perspective, terror often appeared to be just an endless series of petty, everyday efforts to survive, with their "good" and "bad" moments to which, after all, one could get accustomed. The majority of victims sought to keep their reactions to themselves. The most terrifying thing about their silence is that it reveals the far-reaching adaptability of human nature and its readiness to accept terror.

There have been all too few descriptions of this period from the perspective of the largest group in Polish society — the silent observers, the "extras," those who "voted unanimously," filled with a sense of guilt at their daily betrayals and looking the other way. It was these who tried to quiet their conscience with the slogan about "unavoidable victims of the period of change," and to justify their silence by the fact that they too, could at any moment become victims. Yet this fear cut them off still more from the actual victims, and made them carry out orders more zealously. Last, there were those who gave up their right to judge or even analyze the situation within the party "that knows best," and furthermore, found absolution and peace of mind in their voluntarily accepted incapacitation. It was these for whom, after the death of Stalin in 1953 and the "thaw" of the mid-1950s, the past was just a nightmare that could be forgotten when they awoke.

We also know nothing about the effect of the era of terror on the consciousness of so-called ordinary people. I am thinking here of the countless workers transferred to factories straight from their villages during the period of rapid industrialization and the mass migrations at the turn of the 1940s and 1950s. Bewildered by their advancement, even if they participated in the show of massive support, the workers remained indifferent, possibly because they had been made immune to all rituals by their peasant, ritualized religiosity. I also have in mind those peasants who remained on the land, and for whom the time of terror — which in Poland was directed primarily against intellectuals — seemed distant, affecting them only insofar as it reawoke their centuries-old fear of losing their land. The threat of collectivization reminded them, symbolically, of their fathers' dread of being dispossessed of their land by German settlers or of losing their farms because of unpaid taxes.

We also lack memories of those who were ardent preachers of "revolution from above," who were enchanted with the romantic vision of a Utopia and of "rebuilding" (even when the destruction was only preparing the ground for the "new"). These are the people we have described as totalitarian utopians. For them, the period of transformation was not the time to stand firm on matters of "secondary" importance (affecting only individuals and not the masses), or to be sentimental; after all, the "distortions" were only local errors or inconsistencies in implementing the guiding principle. Perhaps even if they had known the details of the mass terror and *gulags* in Russia, they would still have admired Stalin for taking upon himself the burden and responsibility of implementing the formula of Danton, who said, during the French Revolution, "let us be ruthless in order to ... save the people from cruelty." In their view, centrally directed and highly bureaucratized terror would protect the people from themselves, that is from anarchic acts of class vengeance and violence not sanctioned by the state.

The totalitarian utopians, who believed that revolutionary terror was the "lesser evil," indispensable in the struggle against an often imaginary "counterrevolution" and those who hindered "popular mobilization" (speculators, for instance), later themselves often became victims of party purges. Those who survived are either living quite comfortably as embittered party pensioners or have emigrated or withdrawn from public life (since, as "new revisionists," they criticized the regime with all the passion of "love turned to hate"). Those who were victims of the purges usually keep silent. Thus we know nothing about the horrifying mechanisms of mass self-accusation. Was self-accusation a result of the vulnerability of the stigmatized victims, unable to defend themselves because they did not know what they were charged with, while, at the same time, they knew full well the self-fulfilling power of labels from the time when it was they who tracked the victims? Was it perhaps the hope that they would be forgiven if they performed satisfactorily in the roles in which they had been cast? Or could they have stretched the logic of their own conduct prior to the accusation to absurd lengths? After all, they themselves so often claimed that the meaning of deeds, words, and even thoughts depended on the context, which could be retroactively construed and whose assessment by the party could change according to current needs. They may even have thought of themselves as "objective" enemies, since they did not know the context that the party assessed as "incorrect." Furthermore, unaccustomed to communicating their own thoughts after so many years of merely repeating official formulas, they may have had trouble articulating their views. Most of them to the very end identified themselves with the rulers rather than with the victims. This group probably presents the most bitter evidence of the mental degradation of the totalitarian era.

While pondering the fate of that group, it is worth tracing the still undisclosed process by which the rules governing relations between the party and the individual were fixed during the initial period of communist party activity. It is often forgotten that it was the party intellectuals who, in the early 1920s, themselves established the ethics defining their obligations toward the party. These ethics later became the source that somehow legitmated (even in their own eyes) the techniques that were used against them by the party machine during the purges of the late 1930s.

An interesting account of the evolution of communist party ethics governing its relations to the individual is contained in the documents of the so-called Polish Commission of the Communist International (headed by Stalin, his first public appearance in the Comintern). In 1925, the Commission, which consisted of Stalin, Molotov, Dzerzhinsky, Unszlicht, Milutin, and Skrypnik, carried out an investigation of the leaders of the Polish Communist party (Adolf Warski, Władysław Krajewski, and Vera Kostrzewa). Subsequently, they were accused of "revisionism" and "rightist deviation," and at the same time (although it would seem a logical contradiction), of supporting Trotsky, who in Russia was accused of leftist deviation. Other charges included so-called "Luxemburgism" (because Kostrzewa opposed "red terror") and a positive appraisal of a group in the German Communist party that the Comintern defined as "rightist." At this time, in the 1920s, the "political NEP" of a common front with social-democracy had just ended, and Trotsky still held the leadership of the Russian Communist party. Hence, the sanctions applied against Kostrzewa, Krajewski, and Warski by the Polish Commission, were limited to appointing new leaders for the Polish Communist party and recalling the defendants to Moscow.

Vera Kostrzewa's speech during the interrogations by the Polish Commission is very telling in this context.[a] Discussing the principles of conduct and party ethics that the intellectuals and party leaders had imposed on themselves, she reproved Stalin (albeit in a very veiled manner) for transgressing and violating the assumptions on which these principles were based. She insisted that the promises of obedience to the Russian Communist party that Polish communists had made of their own free will were being used by Stalin for his own ends in his power struggle against Trotsky. The following excerpt from Kostrzewa's speech is directly addressed to Stalin and is dramatic in its eloquence: "you know that it is impossible to fight you . . . if you brought matters at issue to a head; if you told Polish workers to choose — us or you, what do you think we would do in this situation? Well, the only course left to us would be to tell them to follow you. . . . And that is why — when there is a difference of opinion — there can be no question of struggle, of victory or of defeat. . . . For that is your special privilege and, consequently, the special responsibility . . . you bear. . . ."

What is striking in this statement is the assertion that any opposition to the will of the Comintern was simply unthinkable. It is all the more dramatic since, at that time, the group being criticized enjoyed the practically undivided support of the members of their party. They were even called the "majority." The "majority" group in the Polish Communist party did not fight, because they did not want to fight; certain rules of the game, including subordination of one's own interests to those of

[a] The author gives no reference for this information and the following quotation. The editor, however, had a conversation with Staniszkis at the time of her visit to the Hoover Institution in which she spoke of her readings of the Polish Commission transcripts in the Hoover Institution archives.

Russia as the first socialist state in the world, had been established and accepted by the accused themselves.

A similar process of entanglement in the self-invented rules of the game could be observed during the Moscow trials and the purges of the late 1930s in the U.S.S.R. The accused had been directly involved in the ideological operations of the 1920s and yet consented to the destruction of the communicative power of formulations from the standing repertoire of the Bolshevik and Marxist ideology. In the course of justifying pragmatic decisions dictated by the struggle for power and its perpetuation, the terms "leftist" and "rightist" lost their meaning, and attitudes toward controversial issues were determined not according to the substance of the issue but its context. This was one of the reasons for the defenselessness (semantic impotence) of the defendants before the Moscow tribunal. After all, they themselves had accepted the principle that the party, and only the party, had a monopoly on judging the context. As early as 1906, they had approved Lenin's formulation that the measure of the importance and the real meaning of a given position was the reaction to it of enemies of the party, and they had agreed with his stand on the prevailing party line. Also, without any protest in 1921, after Kronstadt, they accepted a principle banning factional strife within the Communist party, and at the Fourteenth Party Congress, December 15, 1925, they agreed with Stalin that disrupting the unity of the party was a crime against socialism. Zinoviev (later accused at the Moscow trials) was Comintern chairman when, at the meeting of the Comintern Commission in 1927, Stalin expounded his theory of social Darwinism. Stalin argued that the better adapted always wins (a peculiar revision of Hegel's thesis that what exists is rational) and that there could be only one correct party line. Hence, the slight improvement in Russia's economic situation at the time of the Moscow trials proved that the party was correct and not the defendants.

Furthermore, the perception of themselves as tools of the

party, so characteristic of communist intellectuals in the early postrevolutionary period, made it easier for the defendants in the Moscow trials to accept in good faith the prosecution's arguments. Some of the accused even went so far as to flare out at the incompetence of the prosecutors in carrying out their task and corrected them against their own interest. It is interesting that the accused frequently stressed that they had lost honor in their own eyes. "I am not fighting for my honor, which I have lost," said Kamenev in his testimony.[b] He was not thinking of the "crimes" that the prosecutor, Vyshinski, charged him with, but of the fact that in 1927 "he had taken the road of hypocrisy" in denouncing his own convictions in his self-criticism. With the "all or nothing" attitude typical of the "Russian soul," Kamenev decided that if he had lied then (for his self-criticism did not reflect his true state of mind), he could not be trusted now, either.

It is quite possible that Kamenev's and Zinoviev's accusers were aware of the guilt these men shared after they had denounced themselves in the late 1920s, and cold-bloodedly exploited this situation for their own purposes. I think I am justified in making such an assumption, on the basis of the "Letter by an Old Bolshevik," smuggled out of Russia in 1937 and published by Rand School Press, New York, that same year. This anonymous letter, apparently aimed at presenting a version of events in a form palatable to a Western reader (it also contained a rather mild criticism of Stalin), must have come from someone in a group very close to "official" circles. The author wrote: "We are all obliged to lie; it is impossible to manage otherwise. But ... there are limits which should not be exceeded even in lying. Unfortunately, the Oppositionists often went beyond these limits.... It had a very demoralizing effect inside the ranks of the Oppositionists ... it is impossible to believe them now" (page 49).

[b] No reference was supplied by the author.

The tendency to self-condemnation among party intellectuals (often expressed even before it was demanded of them) was widespread in the 1920s. The more intelligent ones even tried to think up various rationalizations to justify this self-denial. For a present-day Eastern European, for example, the confessions of Lukačs concerning the reasons for his self-criticism in the early 1920s are horrifying. What is horrifying is not only that the self-criticism was voluntarily given but that similar efforts to justify the denunciation of one's own opinion later occurred again and again and are quite common in Eastern Europe to this day. In his self-criticism Lukačs wrote: "When I heard from a reliable source that Bela Kun was planning to expel me from the Party as a liquidator, I gave up the struggle . . . and I published a self-criticism. I was, indeed, firmly convinced that I was in the right but I knew also—for instance from the fate that had befallen Karl Korsch—that to be expelled from the Party meant that it would no longer be possible to participate actively in the struggle against Fascism. I wrote my self-criticism as an entry ticket . . ." Further on, evidently to salve his intellectual conscience, he said: "How little this self-criticism was taken seriously can be gauged from the fact that the basic change in my outlook underlying the Blum Thesis from now on determined all my theoretical and practical activities . . ." (that is, the self-criticism was a symbolic, tactical move).[c]

IDEOLOGY IN A POST-TOTALITARIAN REGIME

Earlier I described two phases of the development of the post-totalitarian system. The first occurred in the 1970s and was characterized by ritualized crisis situations and an eroded ideology that had lost its utopian value and endured only as a magic

[c] The editor was unable to identify the source of this quotation, for which the author gave no reference.

system. The symbols that constituted this system were still used in the various games played between institutions, as levers with which to raise particular interests of the lower level, but their power no longer resided in passions and emotions but rather in the entanglement of the ruling group in traps of its own labels and legitimacy arguments. For instance: "workers' power" meant that every strike was fraught with political danger; "equal opportunity" was only an ideal, and therefore a reform based on the law of value and not feasible, as it would pose serious problems for non-competitive sectors of the economy. True, the symbols from this magical repertoire retained their ominous character as political labels and formulae of excommunication ("revisionist," "anti-socialist element") but resorting to them was less and less frequent because there were ways to rid the labels of their seemingly magic power as self-fulfilling prophecies. The new tactic of the political opposition in the 1970s was based on an open, lawful activity. The main strength of labels is their emptiness: when they are filled with concrete content, they loose their infecting power.

In this phase of system development, the galloping paranoia (to use a psychiatric analogy) of the era of terror has been replaced by mild schizophrenia, with which one can live and function almost normally. Characteristic of the 1970s was the unbridgeable gap between reality and misleading official definitions and images created by propaganda. This led to the constant clash between knowing and evaluating, in which personal experience, insufficient information, and often lack of interest in public life meant that the majority of people saw only isolated fragments of reality and argued in terms of rights being divisible. In fact, pressures exerted chiefly by the authorities but also by the opposition demanded that one constantly make choices and take sides according to the principle: he who is not with us is against us. The result was a general feeling that one's own choices, often accidental, were more extreme than one's

actual attitudes and could be more easily explained in psychoanalytical terms (as the projection of aggressiveness and complexes) than in the discourse of political behavior. One of the
results of this situation was the surreal result of a 1978 poll
when 30 percent of those questioned indicated that they had
opinions on social issues and, at the same time, not enough
information about them.

A second phenomenon in this same group, was a schizoid
uncertainty about the status of events. It was possible, for example, to know something both "officially"; and "unofficially" in
the latter case one did not have to react. This was a rather widespread method used by the government to avoid being trapped
in its own role as a strong authority, and is the administration's
defense against the traps of its own false definition of reality.

The last feature of the schizoid social reality of the 1970s was
a permanent discrepancy in everyday activities between an orientation to the situation and an orientation toward values. This
discrepancy touched even such a normative organization as the
political party, which would seem, by its very essence, to be
geared toward values and to indoctrinate its members accordingly. Yet, as was evident from the results of research conducted
in Poland in 1977 (by T. Kowalczyk and A. Rychard) precisely
the opposite is true. In the political organization of Polish youth,
which was the first step in reaching positions of influence in
the "adult" communist party, more emphasis was laid on creating readiness to conform to such imprecise concepts as "the
good of the organization" and "demands of the situation" than
on involvement in concrete values and norms. As the research
results clearly indicated, the organization's activists (full-time
employees) in particular were inclined to subordinate themselves to the "demands of the situation," 63.8 percent answered
affirmatively the question: "Do you think you should change
your opinion, even if you are sure it is correct, if the good of the
organization requires it?" Less than half stated that a person

should be guided by general values and that "unity of views" was important in a political organization. Putting discipline and readiness to submit ahead of ideological attitudes seems typical of the 1970s, when ideology had stopped being utopian and functioned only as a magic system. This ensured that organization members were at the disposition of the authorities amidst the tactical meandering of the ruling group.

The situation changed dramatically in the second phase of development of the post-totalitarian regime, after the August 1980 wave of strikes. Characteristic of this new phase was the end of labeling as the technique used by the ruling group; also communication rhetoric inside the ruling group changed seriously and became less free. The collapse of ideology resulted in it no longer being the only possible rhetoric in talking about social and political problems. A technocratization of rhetoric was also a result of the shift from the party-state toward the army-state.

CHAPTER VII

Three Decades of

Economic-Political Cycles

The seemingly accidental fluctuations in the rate of growth of the Polish economy between the early 1940s and the late 1970s and the hasty, apparently unrelated measures taken by the ruling group were, in fact, processes with a clear internal structure and logic. On the one hand, there were the economic-political cycles and, on the other hand, two mutually contradictory tendencies that appeared simultaneously and, what is more, originated from the same source — the ruling group: totalization and detotalization. Both of these interconnected processes shared an endogenous and dialectical character. Thus, the successive phases of the economic-political cycles were, to some extent, self-reproducing, and each contained the seeds of the subsequent phase. Parallel with the development of the constituitive tendency of a given phase of a cycle, the counteractive social forces and mechanisms also gained strength. This inevitably led to a turning point in the cycle, or a crisis, and to the emergence of a phase with opposite tendencies (which, like its predecessor, forecast another reversal). After all, the entire course of totalization and detotalization was similarly endogenous. The latter was simply an attempt by the power elite to avoid the traps it set for itself in the process of creating a totalitarian society.

The elite learned that its attempt to control and subordinate all aspects of social life, and the resulting elimination of independent mechanisms of self-regulation, had had exactly the opposite effects to those intended. The process of totalization not only did not increase the steerability of the system but, in fact, intensified its uncontrolability and led to a peculiar drifting. On the other hand, the limited detotalizing policy characteristic of the 1970s, the attempt of authority to restrict itself, caused tension and bore the seeds of a new wave of totalitarianism. For, as we saw in the previous chapters, the unofficial way of implementing that policy by the ruling group only aggravated statutory problems and the frustrations of the various levels of the executive branch. Under these circumstances, this pressure favored the recurrence of totalitarian tendencies.

Bearing in mind the endogenous character of the two processes, one must not lose sight of their interconnectedness. For example, the cyclical nature of economic growth was, to a large degree, an unintended effect of the mechanisms and institutional solutions created, among other things, in the name of a totalitarian utopia. The turning point of the cycle, or economic crisis, made the ruling group sharply aware of the traps of totalization and illuminated the weaknesses of the instruments it used for steering. In other words, a crisis might (though not necessarily) provide an impulse for detotalization measures.

In this chapter, I will discuss at some length the question of the periodicity of economic growth in the last three decades devoting particular attention to crises as turning points in the cycles, i.e., as specific moments at which the system was regulated.

REGULATION THROUGH CRISIS

Development cycles in Poland have had three characteristic moments. First, every cycle consists of two phases, distinguished by the opposite directions of the tendencies that constitute them. Thus, for instance, we first witness a high and then a low level of accumulation in the division of the national income, and, respectively, a lower and a higher level of consumption: a large share of investment outlays with priority given to sectors manufacturing the means of production, followed by phase containing a smaller share of such investments with a simultaneous increase of investments in consumer industries and in agriculture.

Second, the indicators characteristic of a given phase of the cycle have different turning points. For example, a downward revision of the share of accumulation and investments in the division of the national income is not automatically accompanied by an increased share of consumption (e.g. higher wages). The former takes place at a time of economic crisis, while the latter is necessitated by a political crisis. This lack of time correlation of the cycle's turning points (the gap averages about two years) serves, as we shall see later, to stabilize the previous balance of power, but it also eliminates any possibility of rationalizing the system while favoring the continuation of the socially expensive cyclical nature of economic growth. Rationalizing the system would require the simultaneous undertaking of a whole range of measures: a downward revision of planned accumulation, a change in the structure of investments in favor of consumer industries, securing credits, raising wages and consumption, as well as economic and political reform.

Third, a feature of the political crises that has reappeared in each consecutive cycle is a progressive ritualization. Two possible versions of the ritual exist, i.e., the "October" version (referring to October 1956) and the "December" version (December 1970). Furthermore, the behavior of the ruling group during successive crises reflects its effort to reduce internal tensions that have persisted since the preceding crisis. Therefore, the March 1968 crisis and, before that, the so-called cultural crisis of 1964, constituted the revenge of the faction that had played the role of "black sheep" during the "ritual drama" at the Eighth Plenary Session of the Polish United Workers Party's Central Committee in October 1956.

As I have already mentioned, the turning point of an economic-political cycle, i.e., the moment of transition to the subsequent stage, is a crisis situation. In a "planned" socialist economy, an economic crisis means that the official economic program (comprising the level and structure of investments, the share of accumulation in the distribution of the national income) can no longer be carried out because it would lead to a rapid fall of all indices of economic growth. This drop occurs despite the fact that investment efforts are maintained at an unchanged level (or even at a higher one) and irrespective of the manner in which the state appropriates surplus value (i.e., at a high rate of exploitation).

In other words, an economic crisis is precisely the moment at which the economy itself rejects a specific model of economic policy. The rejection is manifested in:

1) *A rapid decline in the effectiveness of investments.* For example, during the crisis of 1962–1963 the index of the effectiveness of investments (increase of GNP per zloty of gross investments), which amounted to 0.387 before the crisis (1960–1961), fell to 0.254.

2) *A drastic fall in the rate of growth of the GNP despite the higher level of accumulation and investment.* The most drastic situation of this type among the so-called "socialist" states occurred in Czechoslovakia in 1963, when the share of accumulation in the distribution of the national income was 25 percent while, at the same time, the index of growth of the GNP was negative and amounted to −2.5 percent. During the 1978 crisis in Poland, when the share of accumulation declined by 0.9 points as compared to the preceding period, the rate of

growth of created GNP fell by 3.9 points and of the divided national income, by all of 7.2 points.[1] This proved, among other things, the erroneousness of the decisions taken during the preceding period. It is worth noting that the falling rate of growth of the national income took place at a time when the share of investment in the national income was very high indeed (31.5 percent in 1975), thus involving considerable costs borne by the society (such as the standard of exploitation, deferred consumption). It is almost as dramatic a picture as that of Czechoslovakia in 1963.

3) *Mounting difficulties in the sphere of raw material supplies and in cooperation between enterprises.* An indication of these difficulties is the drastic increase in the number of cases brought before arbitration commissions for failure to adhere to the provisions of agreements, as well as the rising percentage of cases in which the targets set in the quarterly plans were not met (stoppages caused by shortages of raw materials). An example is the index of stoppages in Polish industry, which, in 1974–1978, oscillated from 10 to 30 percent of work time depending on the branch of industry.[2]

4) *A declining index of the productivity of fixed assets in industry* (this is the relation of the value of fixed assets, the gross, in current prices to the value of net output in fixed prices). A constant fall of the productivity index, totaling 4 percent was observed in 1974–1977.[3] This is evidence not only of stoppages caused by faulty cooperation but also of the advancing petrification of capital as a result of a faulty investment policy.

[1] *Statistical Yearbook*, 1978, GUS, Warsaw, p. 59.

[2] Studies conducted by Andrzej Żuk from the Maria Curie-Skłodowska University of Lublin, paper for the conference, "Qualitative Factors of Growth" of SGPiS [Main School of Planning and Statistics], Warsaw, March 1979.

[3] Calculated by Andrzej Żuk on the basis of the *Statistical Yearbook of Industry*, 1976, pp. 96, 98, 310, and the *Statistical Yearbook*, 1978, pp. 116, 140.

5) *Mounting tensions in the consumer market linked with market imbalance and inflationary processes.* Such tensions were linked with the chronic under-investment in agriculture and consumer industries during the first phase of the cycle and with the tendency typical of that phase to invest excessively while underestimating the duration and the cost of investments, thus also underestimating the amount earned by persons employed at investment projects. These indications of an economic crisis were a signal for the rejection of such economic policy by the economy itself but not by the people. During periods of economic crises, society, although frustrated, was silent (due to increased rigid police surveillance during such periods).

The rejection of an economic policy by the economy itself signified on each occasion that the tendency to reproduce an unbalanced, self-suffocating economic structure, unverified by objective economic mechanisms such as the market, had stumbled upon insurmountable barriers (structural bottlenecks).

At times of recurring crises, the ruling group took extraordinary decisions, contrary to the tendency typical between crises to reproduce self-suffocating structures. Such exceptional decisions usually included a downward revision of investment plans and a redistribution of means and resources between different sectors, thus temporarily removing the bottlenecks in the economic system.

Four such economic crises have occurred in Poland in 1953–1954, 1962–1963, 1968, and 1973–1974, creeping until 1978, and later developing with an accelerated speed. Each crisis brought exceptional regulations, when decisions from above revised downward both production and investment plans. Each revision was accompanied by personnel changes and shifts in the economic administration. The crises determined the turning points of economic cycles and marked the moment of transition from

253

the first to the second phase of the cycle, from a program of accelerated accumulation and investments to one that reduced their share in the division of the national income.

The regularities of pulsating economic development, with crises as the turning points, are well illustrated by Table 1 showing the mean annual rate of growth in Poland from 1950 to 1977. It is interesting to note a phenomenon that cannot be

TABLE 1. Mean Annual Rate of Growth*(%)

Periods	National Income	Divided National Income	Accumu- lation	Invest- ments
1950–53	9.8	9.0	19.1	14.8
1954–57	9.2 −**	9.8 +	5.4 −	6.6
1958–63	5.4 −	5.1 −	7.2 +	8.7 +
1964–68	7.1 +	6.8 +	8.0 +	9.4 +
1969–70	4.0 −	4.7 −	5.9 −	6.0 −
1971–75	9.8 +	12.0 +	19.0 +	20.7 +
1976–77	5.9 −	4.8 −	0.9 −	2.5 −

	Consumption	Foreign Trade Turnover	Employment
1950–53	5.0	6.7	7.7
1954–57	12.3 +	5.5 −	4.0 −
1958–63	4.3 −	14.2 +	2.2 −
1964–68	5.8 +	9.8 −	1.9 −
1969–70	4.6 −	9.4 −	1.5 −
1971–75	8.7 +	13.3 +	3.4 +
1976–77	7.8 −	6.0 −	1.2 −

Calculated by G. W. Kołodko "Ogólne cykle rozwojowe" in *Gospodarka Planowa*, March 1979.

* Prices are controlled for inflation.
** "+" accelerated growth, "−" slowed down growth

detected by studying the figures in the table, which represent long-term averages. At the moment when a cycle reached its turning point, the decisions to revise the accumulation and investment plans downward, to raise consumption (e.g. wages), as well as efforts to reform the economy, were not taken all at once. The first steps were taken by the ruling group during the actual economic crisis. Decisions concerning wage increases and reforms were taken after a period of "suspension" that lasted one to two years, and only under social pressure which came into the open during a political crisis. This separation of crises and the entry of frustrated social forces upon the scene was, as I have said before, a precondition for the stabilization of the power ratio. So far, it has prevented the linking together (and cooperation) of all the frustrated social groups. Consequently, it has become one of the elements contributing to the stabilization of political relations in their present form via the disintegration and segmentation of society. The methods by which social protests are absorbed and the symbolic gestures used by the ruling elite at times of political crisis have only aggravated the "status uncertainty" within the middle levels of the economic and political administration. In turn, the methods the ruling elite has used to reduce tensions among the executive levels during economic crisis, such as the transfer of means and resources and creeping inflation, have been taken at the expense of society.

This separation of economic and political crises led to a lack of correlation of decisions that, if they were really to rationalize the economy, should have been adopted simultaneously. For as a rule, by the time political pressure had forced a rise in wages there was not enough money available for this purpose because the funds obtained from cutting down the share of accumulation and investments in the national income had already "evaporated." The delay was so long that people regarded the increase in wages and salaries as a normal, even if inadequate, compensation for past sacrifices. Furthermore, efforts to reform the system of management that are not made until after a political crisis, are doomed to failure. Economic reforms require a different logic in the allocation of financial resources from those made under vengeful political pressure by society.

Thus, decentralization and workers' self-management established in 1956 became chiefly a means of pressing for higher wages. In 1971–1972, a dual logic of the allocation of means appeared. On the one hand, the ruling group yielded to popular pressure for higher wages and also to industry's demands for greater investment outlays, which were reasonable after a prolonged period of stagnation. On the other hand, its attempts to rationalize the economy were based on the principle of granting "wage increases only when the enterprise achieved additional production." This duality made it impossible to carry out geniune economic reform. What is more, the party's new First Secretary, Edward Gierek, remembering the tactical mistake made by Gomułka at the time of so-called selective growth in 1968–1970, was afraid of displeasing powerful sectors of the economy, and failed to come out against the institutional forces responsible for an unbalanced economic structure.

It should be emphasized, at this point, that during the 35 years of the People's Republic of Poland, sizable wage increases were granted only at times of political crises (20 percent in 1956–1957 and 22 percent in 1971–1972). In the latter period, however, the high rate of inflation (about 8 percent annually) greatly reduced the effect of the wage increase. In other periods, plans that provided for wage increases were not implemented while, at the same time, plans for expanding the sectors that manufactured means of production were systematically exceeded (see Table 2). This illustrates how inadequately the interests of society were supported in the course of making decisions on the distribution of means and resources, and how interests of institutions were over-supported.

What causes economic cycles in socialism? The causes are to

TABLE 2. Planned Increases of Real Wages and Reality

1950-55		1956-60		1061-65		1966-70		1971-76	
Plan	Actual	Plan	Actual	Plan	Actual	Plan	Actual	Plan	Actual
40%	4%	30%	20%*	22.5%	8%	10%	8%	20%	30%**

Source: GUS *Statistical Yearbooks*, Warsaw
*The entire increase occured during the 1956–1957 crisis.
**22% of the increase occured during the 1971–1972 crisis.

be found in the sphere of politics and are mainly connected with the way the economy and the state are run. Another set of causes is linked, in my opinion, with the vulgar interpretation of Marxist economic and social doctrine. However, it is striking to what a degree the system that is a projection of the doctrine has objectified itself, and the participants have virtually forgotten the ideological roots from which particular solutions spring. The ideology, conjured up in a system of institutions and decision-making procedures, has lasted through all the changes and revisions in the verbal sphere. To wit, the social sciences in socialist countries have long questioned the theory that all conflicts automatically disappear when the means of production are nationalized. Yet the foundation of all planning still remains the so-called general interest of society, and the planning procedure is still based on the premise of the uniformity of needs. In this situation, the diversity of interests, not properly taken into consideration in the planning process, spontaneously makes itself felt as the plan breaks up when individual enterprises divide general indices into the assortments of products most convenient for them. Usually, this is done at the expense of economic balance. In another example, the procedures and techniques for calculating industrial costs and fixing prices are based on the Marxist theory of value, conceived as proportional to the outlay of socially necessary labor. Such an approach, perhaps analytically fruitful in itself, in economic practice leads to a steady expansion of outlays when it becomes the foundation of the price-fixing procedure. To put it in a somewhat exaggerated way, in enterprises accountable for the value of their production (when the latter is proportional to the amount of outlays), maximization of outlays becomes the goal of activity. This, in turn, causes distressing waste and inefficiency in the Polish economy. The roots of these phenomena are sought in the sphere of motivations, while a blind eye is turned to the fact that they lie much deeper in the economic philosophy operating in the magic circle of institutions and procedures.

The Marxist interpretation of the law of value rejects systematic consideration of the role of the sphere of realization, the market, which it treats merely as a source of upward or downward deviation of the price, from the actual cost. Marx's theory was formulated to describe a capitalist economy that had a market. Under the conditions of a socialist economy, however, the theory has become less an instrument of analysis than a theoretical justification for the elimination of the market mechanism. The truth is that it is labor and not exchange that is the source of value. But given a situation of free competition, the rules of exchange express the objectification of different labor outlays and determine the relations of value. So far, there is no way to objectify labor outlays that could be generally applied in economic practice. Hence, the elimination of the market mechanism has not only made it impossible to objectify the effectiveness of outlays but has led to arbitrariness in establishing the basic categories of economic semantics (the cost of labor and of the product), and, consequently, to the purely artificial character of such categories as profit or economic effectiveness. For these categories compare values determined not by an objective economic mechanism but by bargaining between the state planning commission and the enterprises. If we add that this takes place under conditions of advanced monopolization of the economy, it is obvious that the degree of arbitrariness in establishing these categories (as well as the artificiality of the entire economic terminology) must be considerable. The high level of monopolization of the socialist economy is, after all, chiefly a political phenomenon. The ruling group assumed it would be easier to direct centrally an economy made up of various branches if the branches (in fact, monopolies) affiliated all enterprises that have identical production profiles into one big complex.

Among the primary roots of centralization trends should be included not only the extensive philosophy of power but also a specific utopia which I have called a totalitarian utopia. Its characteristic feature is a vision of a swift transformation of the economic and social structure. It was precisely this purpose that was to be served by concentrating all resources in a single, decision-making center. In order to be organizationally feasible, such a high degree of centralization required that the previous economic system must first be destroyed by atomization and the disruption of horizontal links. It was also a question of eliminating economic self-regulators, which, being autonomous mechanisms, resisted political control. It is virtually impossible to eliminate objective economic laws, yet decisions were made as if these laws did not hold in a socialist economy. Actually, they continued to function, but were, in a way, moved out of the institutional sphere in which decisions are made; also, as we have seen, they did not influence the establishment of the basic categories of economic semantics. Under these circumstances, the only way these laws asserted themselves was in cyclical recurring crises, when the economy itself brought into the open the inherent contradictions between the arbitrarily adopted economic policy and the law of balanced growth. Thus, as I have noted before, the artificiality of the entire economic rhetoric makes it impossible to evaluate objectively the effectiveness of expenditures incurred by the economy. At best, we may give only very intuitive assessment of this effectiveness.

It is also impossible to assess the effectiveness of particular economic sectors and undertakings. Until recently, the only available method of verification (negative) was the rejection of the prevailing economic policy by the economy itself during economic crises. The rejection manifested itself in the five indices presented above. Lately, however (because Poland's economic development in the 1970s was based on foreign credits), the criteria for verifying economic effectiveness were the difficulties encountered in meeting the conditions for repaying the debts.

The impossibility of evaluating outlays objectively creates a trap for the ruling group itself. It finds it very embarrassing, indeed, to refuse demands for additional resources by the lower levels. As I have already pointed out, a partial assessment is impossible, which makes it easier for the enterprises to implement their strategy of extensive investments. It should be stressed, at this point, that this strategy does not arise out of economic motivation; centralization has destroyed all such motivations and mechanisms for capital accumululation at the enterprise level. Rather it emerges from organizational interests. To be in the process of investing is, from the point of view of enterprise management, a very convenient organizational position. It makes it possible to put off the moment of evaluation by higher authorities by using such arguments as "We have not yet reached full productive capacity." It is a source of additional allocations for current activities and provides trump cards in bargaining with local authorities and in dealings within the enterprise. The relative weakness of the ruling group's opposition to the widespread tendency to invest extensively, aside from their difficulty in saying "no," is the result of other factors connected with the specific social atmosphere in which this ruling group and its philosophy of governing function. Above all, the following should be mentioned:

1) The premise that very tight economic planning plays an integrating and mobilizing role.

2) The psychological need for economic success. Success is supposed to be a compensation for the absence of legal legitimacy for the assumption of power by the communists in the 1940s, on the one hand, and a point scored in the competition with the capitalist world, on the other hand.

3) The internal struggles for power within the ruling elite. Each faction "buys" the support of the various interest groups with material (and investment) goods, which are distributed by its members, who occupy various posts in the central apparatus of the political and economic administration.

All three factors favor excessive investment, which cannot help upsetting the balance of the economy.

The alleged general interest of the community, which theoretically is the primary goal of economic management, is only a fiction, a veil to conceal the "true" nature of the planning. The real objective of the planning (albeit never fulfilled) is to strike a balance between the activities and counteractivities of the parties concerned (i.e., between the decisions and directives of the ruling group on the one side and the defensive mechanisms and pressures exerted by the enterprises on the other). In the sphere of investments with which we are concerned, such balance between the pressures by enterprises and counteractions by the ruling group simultaneously produces unequilibrated economic growth. Thus and not otherwise did the relationship between the steering center and the enterprises evolve empirically, and this is the effect of the center's inability to say "no," its devious intentions with regard to the policy of investments, and the strong pressure exerted by the enterprises. Over-investment, so characteristic of the first phase of each cycle, inevitably causes serious economic imbalances in the market, raw materials, and foreign trade, and, in effect, leads to such an aggravation of tensions (crisis) that the ruling group feels compelled to take extraordinary measures.

Another factor, aside from excessive investments, that disturbs economic equilibrium is the planning itself, in its present procedural and institutionalized form. In a socialist economy, planning functions as a fetish. It has been forgotten that it is not planning as such, but planning within a rational system of institutions, that produces economic effectiveness. Yet this rationality is virtually impossible when the planning procedure is based on two mystifying assumptions: that "the general interest of society" can be defined and that there are no conflicts between enterprises.

True, both assumptions have now been dropped in the verbal sphere; but the institutions remained unchanged and the decision-making procedure has not been altered. This leads to the surfacing of divergent interests in the form of informal bargaining, not only during the drafting of the plan but right up to the very last day of its implementation. The price paid is an increase in randomness and economic imbalance.

Economic planning in Poland, in its current institutional and procedural form, leads to economic anarchy for other reasons as well. First there are the unexpected consequences of a situation in which the fulfillment of the plan is the main criterion in evaluating enterprises. Enterprises manipulate the range and quantities of production so that, in the end, the plan, though centrally balanced with regard to large groups of commodities, ceases to be a balanced plan when it is put into practice.

Economic equilibrium is also seriously endangered by the fact that the indices that hold the plan together and are decisive for its over-all balance are fixed in an arbitrary, administrative manner. These indices, which concern such matters as the presumed increase in labor productivity and saving of materials, are usually calculated much too optimistically by the ruling group. For example, in the draft plan for the last five-year period (1976–1980), the rate of annual reduction of the cost of production was fixed at 3–4%. In practice, however, as Minister of Finance Henryk Kisiel admitted in a press interview, the actual reduction amounted to barely 0.3–0.4%. The difference was a result of, among other things, spending thousands of millions of zlotys on raw materials, which had to be purchased in order to maintain the necessary material balance. The increase in labor productivity and the more effective and more efficient exploitation of machinery and equipment were planned with the same unwarranted optimism. The ruling group, as usual, overestimated the effects of its own symbolic measures and of the wage increases granted after the political crisis of 1970, which led also to the planned tasks being raised by about 80 percent as compared with the original version of the Five-Year Plan, from 1.2 billion to 2.2 billion zlotys in the value of production and investments. The failure to implement such overly optimistic goals (even in the absence of the other, above-listed factors) could not but bring the disruption of economic balance, aggravated tensions, and in the final account, the crisis and the extraordinary decisions taken in 1974 and then in 1978.

The bargaining character of the entire planning process imperils the economic balance not just because of its unpredictable effects and its anarchic influence on the economy. Equally ominous is the fact that industrial enterprises and branches that manufacture the means of production hold a clearly stronger position in the bargaining. This, in turn, is to a large degree the consequence of the still valid ideological dogma of the first half of the 1950s, the so-called "objective law of socialism," which stressed the need for the faster expansion of this particular sector of the national economy. True, the dogma was officially revised in the early 1960s but, again, only verbally and not in practice.

The accelerated growth of the branches manufacturing the means of production has, in my opinion, deep roots in the system itself, and is a kind of a vicious circle resulting from political methods of financing economic growth.[4]

---

[4] Compare K. Ryć, "Problemy wzrostu dochodu narodowego i spożycie w warunkach napięcia inwestycyjnego" in *Ekonomista* (1967), no. 2.

Postwar reconstruction and the subsequent expansion of Poland's industrial potential during the 1940s and 1950s at the rate planned by the central authorities would have been impossible had they been based solely on the capital surplus the industry could produce itself. Hence, the economy had to extract the necessary capital resources (the repressive state acting as intermediary) from the sphere of consumption; collectivization of land, compulsory deliveries of farm produce at below-market prices, and keeping wages at a very low level, all served this end. This policy was made possible by the monopolistic status of the state as the only employer, by the elimination of independent trade unions, and by depriving the working class of the right to strike. The political methods used to finance growth (at the expense of consumption) gave seemingly excellent results. It had taken the United States 55 years to increase its per capita output of steel from 50 kg (1887) to 574 kg (1942). As late as 1946, Poland's per capita output was equal to that of the United States in 1887; but it took her only 33 years to attain the same level of production for which the American economy needed 55 years (574 kg in 1979).[5] This example illustrates not only the intensity of the investment effort but also the extent of the society's sacrifices.

At the same time, however, the political methods of financing growth very soon resulted in the rise of barriers to further economic and social development. The underinvested agricultural sector reacted with a decline in productivity, while the "syphoning off" of resources from consumption prevented the emergence of effective consumer demand that would stimulate continued and structurally balanced economic expansion. The delay in satisfying consumer needs (e.g. the unsolved housing

[5] Per capita output of energy and raw materials in Poland as compared with average output in four highly developed states of Western Europe. Source: A. Karpiński, "Socjalistyczne uprzemysłowienie Polski," in *Nowe Drogi*, 1979, no. 3.

problem) and the generally low level of income (a high proportion of the family budget is spent on food) has concentrated demands on a few items, such as meat and housing, which in any case have always been bottlenecks in the economy. What is more, in the absence of effective and broad consumer demand, the economy, in order to continue expanding (steadily incrementing the national income) must be self-propelled and create needs in the sphere of production, such that their satisfaction will stimulate the further expansion of productive potential.

Production per head of population	1950	1977	1977 production as % of 1950
Electric power			
4 West European states	890	4394	494%
Poland	379	3152	832%
Poland, as % of the 4 capitalist states	43%	72%	—
Energy raw materials			
4 West European states	2229	2051	92%
Poland	3222	6018	187%
Poland, as % of the 4 capitalist states	145%	293%	—
Steel			
4 West European states	223	446	210%
Poland	101	514	506%
Poland, as % of the 4 capitalist states	45%	110%	—

The table shows Poland's huge investment outlays in the raw materials sector of the economy. (In the consumer commodiites sector, the level of production — according to the same source — is only 30 percent of per capita output in the highly developed states).

A large part of the increment of raw materials production is swallowed up by the raw materials industry itself. (For example, 50 kg of pure steel are needed to extract 1 ton of coal.) Furthermore, the consumption of raw materials, such as steel and cement, is some 20–30% higher than in the highly advanced states because of obsolete equipment or chosen technologies (e.g. large-panel construction). Source: Report of experts from the Polish Academy of Sciences, quoted by T. Podwysocki, Życie Warszawy (March 22, 1979).

This is precisely the origin of the mechanism of production for the sake of production, when a powerful industrial potential (the per capita output of cement in Poland amounts to 122 percent of that in the four most highly developed states of Western Europe; of steel, 110 percent; of energy raw materials, 203 percent) devours its own products. Besides, when production is occurring for production's sake, conserving raw materials and energy does not really make sense. On the contrary, a high rate of material and energy consumption by industry provides a strong incentive for further expanding the raw material base and, consequently, the sector that manufactures the means of production. In this way, "production for the sake of production" coupled with faulty economic management do stimulate growth, but a growth that does not bring about social development. The enormous economic potential makes only an insignificant contribution to better meeting social needs.

The mechanism of a self-propelled economy has now become autonomous and uncontrollable. The overheated economy imposes heavier demands for raw materials and energy than it can itself satisfy. On the other hand, incomes have risen, and the condition of market imbalance is further increasing.

Thus, the policy that was to accelerate growth has become one of the main reasons why the economy constantly strangles itself. There are tensions and crises and, in effect, slower growth than should be attainable with the same expenditures. The allocation of 85 percent of all capital investment outlays during the Six-Year Plan (1949–1955) for the expansion of heavy industries stemmed from the logic of this mechanism of stimulating the economy by "production for production's sake." At that time, the need to rebuild Poland after the devastations of war may have justified the shortages of consumer commodities. At present, however, when the very same mechanism has led to a fall in real wages by 2.8 percent (1978) and to acute market disturbances, the authorities find it increasingly difficult to justify convincingly the existing shortages and to induce people to accept more sacrifices.

So far, despite efforts in this direction (inconsistent as usual), the ruling group has not succeeded in halting the stimulation of the economy by production for production's sake. This mechanism is too deeply rooted in formal and informal decision-making processes and is also backed by powerful interest groups.

The emergence of this mechanism was facilitated in the past by both the government's totalitarian aspirations and the cold-war climate of the early 1950s. For in fact, means of production, being the end result of the manufacturing process, raise the value of the national income, which the ruling group controls. Furthermore, the ability to decide how those means are distributed is one of the fundamental instruments of power and allows the ruling group to buy the support of chosen branches by granting them special privileges.

The means of production as the final product can also easily be used for the needs of the arms industry, simply by shifting them to the appropriate branch of the economy. Thus, production for the sake of production, however impossible it would seem, means a simultaneous increase of the national income and of the country's defense capabilities.

All these elements combine to make up the endogenous mechanism that has led to excessive investment and unbalanced growth during the first phase of the cycle and, consequently, to the recurring economic crises. The crises, in turn, act as peculiar regulators, since they make it possible to stop the action for a while.

When extraordinary measures have been taken, in response to a crisis, the temporarily suspended mechanisms begin to function again, though starting at a lower level of tensions within the system of economic institutions. The tensions gradually mount until the time of the next crisis and of new extraordinary decisions. The tendency to unbalanced economic growth

267

is additionally reinforced by a factor introduced after the second turning point, a political crisis. Credits from the West are repaid in part symbolically when the government in question installs a slightly more liberal leadership. But such credits can also be repaid mostly in raw materials (70 percent of Polish exports consist of raw materials, mostly coal and copper). This is a strong motivation for investing in heavy machinery for mining and generally in heavy industry. Thus, as we have seen, all these elements which constitute the endogenous mechanism of cyclical economic development are political in nature. The influence of this mechanism is also enhanced by external factors.

In this connection we should, first of all, mention the international situation and the state of agriculture. All economic crises in Poland were preceded by a breakdown in agricultural production. Such breakdowns, incidentally, were also caused, at least in part, by politics, specifically by abrupt changes in the policy toward private farming. In 1973, 69 percent of the land acquired by the State Land Fund from farmers who were retiring was sold to individual farmers; in 1976, the figure dropped to barely 4 percent (with a stronger incentive for collectivization).[6] This coincided with the difficulties in procuring sufficient fodder and a shortage of the means of production for agriculture, a consequence of the previous method of distributing investment capital. Food problems and a rapid decline in livestock brought about a change in agricultural policy. Thus, in 1978, the share of land sold to farmers rose to 50 percent, and 70 percent was planned for 1979. The latter level was not attained due to informal, but systematic obstacles created by local authorities. Nevertheless, chiefly for doctrinal reasons, cattle restocking has not taken place on private farms but on state farms, which utilize fodder much less effectively. As a result, with virtually the

[6] See Edward Gorzelak, "Zasady realizacji polityki agrarnej" in *Wieś Współczesna* (January 1977), also Bolesław Strużek "O konsekwentnej realizacji polityki rolnej" in *Wieś Współczesna* (March 1977).

same number of cattle, twice as much fodder was purchased abroad, constituting a major hard-currency drain in the form of imports (one billion dollars every year).

The most characteristic feature of the economic cycle in the 1970s was the creeping type of economic crisis. During the present, prolonged crisis, all the instruments used in the past to balance the economy have been exhausted. In addition, the economic crisis merged with the political one generating, among other demands, a demand for higher wages. In the past the time-lag between economic and political crisis was at least one and a half years. The current lack of balance in the industrial sector leading to a rapid decrease of productivity (in 1981 the GNP will be 20 percent less than in 1980) is combined with a 125-billion-zloty increase in wages (in line with the Gdańsk Agreements), plus an additional 100 billion zlotys for social policy (an increase in old-age pensions, etc.). The gap between consumer demand and the supply of goods increased rapidly from 50 billion zlotys in 1980 (before August) to 450 billion at the end of 1981. The full disorganization of the market accelerated political tensions. One reason for the slow-down of productivity is a serious cut-back in imports, which paralyzes an economy as import-dependent as Poland's. The balance of trade is maintained mostly by such cuts: in 1979 the participation of Poland in the world trade decreased to 1.03 percent, its level before the Second World War, from 1.28 percent in 1976. In 1981 this relation worsened.

The signs of the self-suffocation of the economy were already evident in 1974. These were an increase in foreign debts and in import dependence combined with increasing deficits in foreign trade, an increase of compulsory savings (due to a lack of balance on a consumer goods market), and a strong inflationary pressure. In spite of these signals, the first decisions to decrease the percentage of GNP devoted to investment funds came very late, at the end of 1977. Earlier, in 1976, the only reaction had been to freeze the level of investment at the very high numbers of 1975.

The cuts that came later were not very high (averaging 10 percent per year). Chapter II described the reasons for such behavior of the ruling group.

Regulation through crisis is very costly. The most important cost is that involved in the downward revision of the investment plan and in the extraordinary decisions taken at times of economic crises. We have to take into account both the material losses that result from the freezing of already launched investment projects and the drop in morale caused by frustration and unfulfilled hopes. Another serious consequence is the confusion in management. For example, a major problem in the Polish economy is low productivity and the inefficient use of machinery and equipment. In such cases, enterprises are supposed to pay a fine amounting to 30 percent of the value of unused, imported machines, but in practice such penalties are waived because, when investment cuts have been ordered by higher authorities, it is hard to determine the extent of the enterprise's responsibility for failing to use the already-installed machines.

The third price paid for the cyclical character of growth, is the emergence of a peculiar philosophy of leadership that regards crises as the normal (or even the only possible) occasions for regulating the system. This approach calculates the listed costs, and it also concentrates on ways to maneuver in crisis situations, rather than on ways to rationalize the system and eliminate the causes of cyclical growth. In other words, it is an example of the authorities learning about crisis as a way of regulating without learning anything in the course of repeated crises that is new and could rationalize the system once and for all.

Why the Polish System Was So Stable in the 1960s and 1970s.

What were the stabilizing mechanisms working in the last three decades? After all, the system existed and worked in a relatively unchanged structural form. If nothing else, the example of the state's organization shows that despite the evolution in its functioning from Stalinist terror to the gentle ritualization of the 1970s, it remained structurally unchanged or even reinforced its legal identity.

The fundamental factor in stabilizing the system was the consolidation of its structural identity and the development of informal mechanisms and structures that served as shock-absorbers (see Chapter IV). At the same time, a number of techniques were developed to enhance stabilization. Most of these techniques had become useless at the end of the 1970s, producing more tensions than they absorbed. But in the 1960s and 1970s, their scope was wide, ranging from the lowering of tensions through symbolic actions during the periodically recurring crises to measures aimed at neutralizing and subjugating society, down to the level of language.

Generally speaking, the relatively stable situation in the 1960s and 1970s was not the outcome of a consensus of values or the absence of tensions, but rather the effect of specific techniques of control and manipulation used by the ruling group. Due to such techniques, the conflicts between social groups (except for short, violent periods of crisis, often used by the ruling elite to effect changes within the power elite), were played out as a highly sophisticated system of undercover games between institutions. These techniques effectively prevented the emergence of conflict outside the framework of institutions. They operated on several planes. First, steps were taken that led to stabilizing the status quo by promulgating a peculiar definition of reality that saw no alternatives to the current institutional form of social life. Other measures, not without influence, were intended to keep conflicting interests below the threshold of articulation. This was possible not only because society was atomized but also (indicative of much more advanced control) because various notions traditionally linked with the so-called liberal ethos were kept from being openly advanced. When such notions were monopolized by the superficial official language and grew devoid of meaning, they were no longer regarded by the population as an instrument of communication. Hence, such notions as democracy or self-government dropped out of ordinary usage. Control of the vocabulary in which needs were formulated (and, in the long run, perceived) also created a polarized structure of alternatives for self-identification. This was another way—aside from creating an equally polarized structure of possible actions (he who is not with us is against us)—to consolidate the political status quo.

An aversion to radical commitment, in which everyone stands to lose something, in this situation caused the majority to adopt an escapist attitude in the broad sense of the term. Public activity was limited to necessary rituals, activist postures were avoided, and hopes and ambitions focused mainly on basic levels such as the family.[7]

The second group of techniques used by the rulers to stabilize the system was intended to shift and reallocate tensions by administrative means. The setting up of shock-absorbers, a sys-

[7] Research conducted by Professor Stefan Nowak, Warsaw University, 1978. Jürgen Habermas noted the emergence of such attitudes and postures in capitalist society (*Legitimacy Crises*, Boston, Beacon Press, 1976). In his analysis of contemporary capitalism, he writes about two characteristic and mutually reinforcing trends, an orientation toward the family and the pursuit of "privatism." In privatism, the main motivating factor is an orientation toward a career, understood as status rivalries, usually within a class and disrupting the feeling of a unity of interests. Similar observations were made by Robert Lane in his description of the phenomenon of "escape from equality" ("The Fear of Equality," *American Political Science Review* [March 1959], pp. 35–51). Lane points out that rivalry in the sphere of consumption is becoming a substitute for class conflict (channeled through intraclass competition); instead of a revolution, we have indefatigable consumers and borrowers, working wives, and overtime. The stabilizing effect of the consumer attitude seems to be beyond dispute.

In this connection it should be stressed that the emergence of consumer attitudes in a socialist society had a simultaneously stabilizing and destabilizing effect. The former was the outcome of status rivalries; the latter of growing aspirations.

tem of exceptions and local "buffer" solutions, arrived at in the course of bargaining between institutions and corporatist development was often reached at the expense of the efficient functioning of the system; at the same time it promoted the system's stabilization. The same stabilizing effect was attained through separating complex conflict situations into a number of less complicated ones, which were differently resolved at different points of the system, or through algorithms that changed over time. Such techniques helped get rid of conflicts, or rather prevented their intensification. All these measures stabilized the system at least in the short run, so long as the dispersed tension did not start rebuilding. This submerged functioning of social conflicts, shielded by the system of institutions and usually hidden, produced a number of psychological effects. It strengthened the general feeling of self-regulation by creating a peculiar ethics of the system, without a subject (and without responsibility), and also strengthened the impression of game-playing with the system, i.e., a contest with an unidentifiable opponent.

The third feature of the periods between crises in the 1960s and 1970s was the absence of direct confrontation between social groups with conflicting interests. All conflicts took place through institutional intervention, usually disguised as various kinds of games, manipulation, bargaining, and countermoves. Thus, workers' wage demands were sent "up higher" by the enterprise, as part of its game with its superior authorities, in which an easier production plan and more favorable assessment were at stake. It is true that such pressures indirectly modified the principles of distribution of income, but they also helped avoid a direct confrontation between conflicting forces. Furthermore, the model of conflict between the different levels in the system of institutions had a very specific form. The strategy pursued by individual levels and institutions, subordinated to diverging interests (and decision prospects) and connected with their place and role in the process of production and distribution, was aimed chiefly at minimizing their own tensions and uncertainties, and was resorted to in response to actions undertaken by the other side. We can thus speak of a never-fulfilled striving to bring about a balance between the defensive mechanisms of the parties concerned. In other words, this model of conflicts served to balance the mutually obstructing forces.

A seemingly paradoxical phenomenon, which favored the emergence of stabilizing compensatory actions and made the existence of a basically absurd system feasible, was that the possibility that decisions would be disobeyed was quite consciously taken into consideration. Polish economic practices reveal that, in making decisions that could seriously aggravate tensions, the ruling group often set aside an area for possible bargaining. This was done either by indirectly indicating fields of activity that could be the subject of bargaining (by less rigid formulation or by using ambiguous and weak wording that allowed for reinterpretation of the decisions, not necessarily in accord with their spirit) or by leaving time for "politicizing" and bargaining during the time the decisions were actually implemented. All these moves were meant to act as shock-absorbers and to perpetuate the spontaneous games and bargaining, to some extent they changed the substance of the decisions, but, at the same time, they alleviated tensions and stabilized the system. Sometimes the area left open for possible bargaining was only a front, meant to shift the emotions of the parties concerned to a group of problems that were less important to the decision-making center, which, at the same time, rigorously exacted the rest of the solution. Occasionally, the decision maker included the opportunity to countermand his own decision in order to preserve the outward appearance of power. This happened when the decision-making center was aware that it did not possess all the necessary information but either was unwilling to pass on its prerogatives to lower levels or wished to make a given decision for purely symbolic reasons.

One can look at shock-absorbers and their role in a socio-economic system from another angle as well. Observing the course of social policy pursued throughout the 35 years of the People's Republic of Poland, one notices a more or less conscious selection of different social groups to fulfill the function of shock-absorber. The cost of rapid industrialization, for example, has been borne by such selected groups. In Poland, until the mid-1950s, the peasants chiefly provided the means of primary socialist accumulation of capital. One could even risk defining internal colonization as the period when the peasants, forcibly collectivized and deprived of land, provided foodstuffs with which industrial workers were paid. The peasants themselves were starving, but, like the colonies for Western European countries, they made it possible for the country to embark upon the process of industrialization, first in war-devastated Russia and later, according to the same pattern, in other East European countries.

The ideological premises underlying the selection of specific social groups for the role of shock-absorbers deserve deeper analysis. At this point, however, I want only to note that in Poland the choice of shock-absorbers is made with the aid of administrative mechanisms. Therein lies its fundamental difference from a society based on market mechanisms, in which the distribution of the cost of industrialization is a spontaneous, uncontrolled process and an outcome of the play of market forces.

Another way to stabilize the system and to reduce tensions without naming the contradictions producing them was to resolve conflicts indirectly by trying to alleviate tensions that apparently concerned quite another sphere. Students of the Polish industrial system have pointed out that one of the basic, though not directly formulated, questions for the enterprise in selecting a variant of the production plan was whether it guaranteed the payment of bonus money to the personnel. For in the very rigid Polish wage system, the bonus was a major instrument for reducing tension. When it was impossible for enterprise management to reduce tensions over wages, a bonus fund provided a safety valve. The indirect solution of conflicts also lay at the root of one of the mechanisms that determined the logic according to which organizational structures developed. As was evident from surveys conducted in Poland from 1973 to 1975, the unjustifiable multiplication of managerial posts and the resulting excessive fragmentation of functions could be explained, at least in part, as an indirect attempt to reduce tensions resulting from the rigid wage scales by providing the possibility of additional payment for those holding managerial positions. Ten percent of those employed in the Polish economy (19 percent in the administration) hold management posts.

Another stabilizing factor for the system was the fact that, since the activities of the interest groups were local and specialized, negotiations dealt mainly with partial issues and only a few elements of a solution, but not with comprehensive solutions. This resulted in concentrating emotions and efforts on tactical and operational decisions, and turning attention away from strategic issues. The latter was an essential factor in stabilizing the system, as it hindered the proper perception and exposure of social contradictions in all their complexity. It should also be borne in mind, that the fragmented way in which the rationality in each sphere took concrete form was linked with the institutional shape of the system. There were no vertical ties (and no forms of political democracy) that made it possible to coordinate views and interests and transmit them to the higher echelons of the hierarchy. Actions by specific interest groups therefore did not require clear identification of the opponent nor even the open naming of the subject of controversy. Actions were intended simply to thrust away tensions and uncertainties. Under these circumstances, tensions were redistributed spontaneously in the course of the planning process at the expense of the system's maneuverability, on the one hand, and of greater tensions and uncertainties among those participants in the system who were in a weaker bargaining position, on the other hand. The latter, in such a case, turned to the steering center for intervention and help. The steering center strengthened its influence in order to reallocate tensions successively. Its aim was to set up a protective screen around the weaker partners in economic activities and to compel the stronger ones to implement the tasks arising from the division of labor, even if they found it undesirable in the light of the rationality belonging to their own sphere. This led to the adoption of a new defensive strategy and compensatory actions by the lower levels, and in turn to the automatic repetition of the whole process.

These activities stabilized the system because they disguised conflicts and kept them below the threshold of articulation; they separated the mechanisms of controversies into a number of conflicts of purely local significance. This made it possible to shift tensions and solve problems partially, according to the prevailing alignment of forces, as well as to set individual participants in the system against each other.

CHAPTER VIII

October 1956 as a Ritual Drama:

Case Study of Artificial Negativity

The process of de-Stalinization in Poland in 1956 — particularly its most spectacular moments, the seventh and eighth plenary meetings of the party's Central Committee — was until quite recently the most mythologized period in the current history of Poland.[1] A notable feature of the process was the invocation of public opinion by the ruling group in order to introduce the changes necessary for the smooth functioning of the regime and the personal safety of the ruling elite. This feature, which I have called "artificial negativity," had not been discussed enough.

In this chapter I will describe one of the most characteristic techniques of the tactic of artificial negativity, namely the ritual drama. In speaking of a ritualization of conflict situations or politics as such, I do not mean the binding, compulsive and rigid behavior that is a neurotic reaction to uncertainty. Such neurotic behavior serves chiefly as an escape from ambivalence. I am thinking of the opposite situation, when the ritual not only does not repress ambivalence but helps to identify it for the ben-

[1] Compare Tadeusz Kowalik's article in *NTO* (February 10, 1981) — a Solidarity weekly in the Mazowsze region — on the role of the party apparatus in the origin of the idea of a workers' council in 1956; also a description of the Poznań 1956 events that underlines the elements of political provocation: Łucja Łukasiewicz, *Poznań: Czerwiec 1956*, Poznań, 1981, published on the 25th anniversary of Poznań riots.

efit of a social group, or at least for some of the members of that group.

I am interested here in those historical moments when, from the point of view of the ruling group, a ritual becomes a safe vehicle for introducing changes, restructuring symbols, and articulating new attitudes and emotions.

The use of the ritual as a vehicle for changing the system is a convenient way for the ruling group to forestall or even control the future actions of the participants in the ritual. The maintenance of a stable configuration of social roles and a consistent method of appointing actors to those roles (for example, by labeling), is sufficient to control the whole process. To know and control the exact content of the roles is not nearly as important as, for example, maintaining their polarity. This polarized structure produces its own dynamics called "amplification processes," in which the extremes become still more extreme and labels become self-fulfilling prophecies. Such dynamics also generate lively emotions in the observers, particularly when the extreme positions have strong good and bad emotional connotations. An active public opinion is a necessary element of the process; labeling does not work without witnesses.

The second advantage the ruling group obtains from introducing change through ritual drama is that a by-product of the method is social amnesia, in which a society is separated from the memory of its past. In moments of ritual drama, new value judgments are assigned to the previous experiences of a particular group, or a society as a whole, but the experiences are not re-evaluated. The ruling group can continue to use most of the instruments and institutional structures from the past, because the instruments are not linked in social consciousness with those social facts, which can now be given a negative stigma by the ritual drama. What is more, this public negative re-evaluation (usually in terms of black and white) maintains the illusion that a return to the former "wrong" practices is impossible. The

279

inability to learn from one's experience is not new in the history of societies. But ritualization of political crises makes the inability still more extreme and also more obvious. The tendency to substitute a symbolic representation of social mechanisms for their real nature, combined with strong emotions (a combination typical of ritual drama), is the best recipe for forgetting these mechanisms. It works especially well when a system has left no one without guilt, except perhaps its victims.

Ritual drama is not only the safest mechanism for introducing changes from above, it also serves a number of other functions. Ritual can rearrange the order in which values are held and thus also of the symbols that represent them. It prepares new social roles for individuals and groups. Very often ritual drama marks the end of a process of reform. However, for most of the social groups who were invoked to participate in it, the very same moment is perceived as the beginning of so-called "renewal." Such illustrations and wishful thinking help to smooth the re-establishment of a "harder line." By the time people recognize it, the power apparatus (demobilized during ritual drama) is already consolidated. This lack of a correlation between real processes and their perception by society was evident in Poland in October 1956, when the Eighth Plenum of the party's Central Committee was ending a series of reforms that had begun in 1954. Public opinion (mobilized only in the last stage of the whole process) perceived the very same plenum as the beginning of a political liberalization. As we see, the ritual drama in politics not only reanimates the group for whose benefit it is staged but, at the same time, works as an instrument of political control. The ritual makes possible a manifestation of conflict and a way of introducing reforms that does not endanger the stability of the political system.

Ritual thus conceived therefore becomes integrated with social practice, through trial and error, by molding modes of behavior and expression so that they are in accord with the symbolic imagination of the society.

Within ritual drama, the response to problems and stresses shifts away from actions aimed at genuine solutions toward pseudo-reactions and pseudo-solutions. This sometimes works as follows: the ruling elite (or some faction in that elite) deliberately plans and provokes a crisis, which it therefore can control. By means of this crisis, the ruling group hopes, first, to provoke strong reactions from dissatisfied or dissident elements against whom it will then be free to invoke strong sanctions. A good example of such a situation was the March 1968 crisis. Second, these controlled crises enable the ruling group to channel existing social frustrations against targets that it selects.

In order to invoke such artificial crises, the ruling group must correctly understand the emotional impact of various semantic labels and accurately predict the sensitivity of particular social groups to concrete gestures. For instance in 1968 the managers of the crisis knew that intellectuals and students, rather than workers, would react to an anti-zionist and anti-revisionist campaign. The provocation was the cancellation of a performance of the play "Dziady" (Ancestors) by the greatest Polish romantic poet Adam Mickiewicz at the National Theater in Warsaw. The play described the situation in Warsaw when a third of partitioned Poland was ruled by Czarist Russia. On another occasion, just before Christmas 1970, when a faction in the ruling group specifically wanted to provoke workers, it raised the price of the cheapest sausage, the basic mid-morning snack of the workers.

The invocation of artificially created negative reactions to artificially introduced crises results in artificial solutions, such as canceling a sanction introduced during the crisis. Once the crisis has reached the desirable duration and/or intensity, the ruling group must give society signs that they, the ruling group, are about to solve or alleviate the problem. They want to emphasize the turning point, so that they can use this moment to establish new roles and symbols or at least to execute the palace revolution. The ritual drama is the most convenient way of signaling such turning points.

DE-STALINIZATION, 1953–1956

Such a chain of trial and error in the course of learning the ritual of change through crises was contained in the Polish ruling group's three-step de-Stalinization maneuver in 1953–1956. From the beginning, the Polish pattern of de-Stalinization differed from the same process in the other East European countries. First there occurred in Poland, after Stalin's death, a strong countermobilization of the ideologically oriented totalitarian utopians directed against the "bureaucratic class-oriented terror of the early fifties," as well as the activization of internal security forces.[2] The latter were anxious to prevent changes similar to those observed at the time in Hungary, where the Minister of Internal Security had been charged and received a life-sentence, or in East Germany, where Minister of Internal Security Zeisser was dismissed. In Poland, the uncoordinated but clearly parallel pressures by the two forces led to a hardening of politics toward the Catholic Church. A few hundred priests were arrested: Bishop Kaczmarek was given a show-trial on September 14, 1953, and Cardinal Wyszyński was imprisoned. At the same time, internal security forces began searches of the members of

[2] The departments of security police, threatened by the possibility of liberalization and the questions being raised about personal responsibility, launched a counteroffensive almost immediately after Stalin's death. At the PUWP's Central Committee Plenum on March 28, 1953, Stanisław Radkiewicz of the Public Security Ministry called for "greater vigilance" and informed the meeting about the discovery by his department of more "saboteurs" and "illegal organizations," *Nowe Drogi* (1953), no. 3.

the narrow power elite. A trial was prepared, for example, against the personal secretary of Jakub Berman, who was himself responsible for internal security police in the Politbureau. The only way the ruling group could defend itself was to try to disarm the internal security forces by disclosing the practices of this force. The escape of one of the higher officers of internal security, Józef Światło, was arranged (December 1953).[a] His first press conference in Washington took place on September 18, 1954.

Światło's revelations reinforced pressure within the party to "reorganize" internal security. A meeting of the party's activists in Warsaw in November 1954 seems to have been the first serious step in the policy of de-Stalinization. During this meeting two incidents are worth noting because they involved future scapegoats of the October 1956 ritual drama. Wiktor Kłosiewicz demanded that the imprisoned Gomułka [jailed on charges of "nationalist deviation"] be set free. Bolesław Rumiński made a speech urging that Security Minister Radkiewicz be brought to trial. Gomułka actually was released from prison a few days later on December 13, 1954 (though remaining under house arrest), but the party apparatus was not informed of it until June 6, 1956.

The Third Plenum of the Central Committee, which met on January 21–24, 1955, followed the policy formulated during the meeting of November 1954. What was more, a few leaders of the totalitarian utopian group in the apparatus (especially the Young Communist Association, ZMP) were coopted to the ruling group, including Stanisław Matwin and Jerzy Morawski.

At the same time the ruling group, headed by Bolesław

---

[a] Światło was deputy chief of the Tenth Department of the Ministry of Public Security, in charge of investigating the party cadres. On a visit to East Berlin with his superior Colonel Fejgin, Światło escaped to the West. He was privy to intimate details of secret police activities throughout the Stalinist period. He began broadcasting these revelations to Poland through Radio Free Europe in 1954. His broadcasts had a tremendous impact on Polish public opinion.

Bierut, attempted to redirect its economic policy, discarding the principles of economic management it had advocated since 1949. The first step had been taken at the Ninth Plenum of the PUWP's Central Committee on October 20–30, 1953. The issue dealt with at this plenum was the elimination of the "inequality" (a euphemism for deep disequilibrium) of the economic branches and sectors manufacturing consumer and investment goods. Other topics were "raising the people's standard of living more quickly" and making up the "backlogs in agriculture."[3] This change in economic policy was the Polish version of a strategy just being launched in the Soviet Union by Malenkov. The strategy was aimed at satisfying consumer needs by reducing the share of accumulation and of arms expenditures in dividing up the national income. A peculiar feature of this maneuver in both countries was the introduction of changes while maintaining the appearance of continuity and refraining from any criticism of past economic policies. It is true that "structural difficulties linked with conditions of the transitional period" were mentioned, but the myths that previously served to justify economic policy were fully upheld at the same time.[4] The pragmatic conclusions drawn by the plenum from the situation were that: outlays for production goods from the national income must be reduced still further (they were already lower than in preceding years); agriculture (cooperative and state-owned farms) must be provided with additional means of production and credits; and an attempt must be made to revitalize rural self-government (the farmers' self-help cooperatives).

[3] *Nowe Drogi* (1953), no. 11. According to data presented at the plenum, industrial production grew by 115% between 1949 and 1953, while agricultural output during that time increased by only 9%. What was more, the manufacture of the means of production was 21% above the planned target, which meant that the plan for consumer goods production had fallen short of the target.

[4] Ibid. Thus it was claimed that, during the period under review, real wages went up by 27%. Not until 1956 was this figure corrected and blamed on a "mistake" made by the Central Statistical Office.

In Russia, Malenkov's consumer-oriented policy soon encountered opposition from industrial groups connected with the sector that manufactured the means of production as well as from the armed forces, who believed their interests were threatened. His new policy was defined in the Soviet Union as a rightist, "Bukharinist" deviation, and Malenkov resigned from his post as first secretary following an attack by Dimitr Shepilov, printed in *Pravda* on January 24, 1955. These events in Russia could not have failed to influence the implementation of the resolutions adopted at the Second Plenum of PUWP. By the time the Second Plenum took place in 1954, criticism of Malenkov had already begun. Therefore, the Polish ruling group become even more cautious in its attempt to continue the more pragmatic policy formulated at the Ninth Plenum in 1953. The label applied to the entire range of changes was reduced to the innocent-sounding phrase: "to stop letting any land lie fallow, and more effectively use pasture land,"[5] even though much more was actually being done. The establishment of new collective farms was practically halted, arms spending was curtailed, and the importing of consumer goods, books, films from the West began.

This first "approach" to de-Stalinization allowed the Polish ruling group to see the extent of the opposition, both within its own ranks and in various interest groups in the state administration and in the economy. It also learned how far it could go in introducing changes without invoking apprehension and anxiety in its neighbor to the East. It was also the first attempt to face a dilemma that was to recur in all subsequent attempts to introduce reforms. The problem was that the ruling group believed it could not openly acknowledge some of its moves and activities either because of its entanglement in formerly used formulae and rationalizations or because it feared that the acknowledgment itself would turn into an autonomous social fact that could provoke outside intervention.

[5] *Nowe Drogi* (1954), no. 2.

Nevertheless, the ruling group also realized that unless its activities could be named openly, no new political line could enter social awareness and thus play its part in mobilizing social support and reducing tensions. Furthermore, the unofficial way in which the new internal policy was introduced greatly facilitated the situation for groups opposed to it. They could not be overtly attacked, and direct appeals could not be made to society urging support for attempts at de-Stalinization and the rationalization of the economy.

The first visible signals of the "thaw" occurred in the cultural sphere; this seemed the safest way to inform society that the policy was now somewhat different. In 1955 Adam Ważyk, formerly one of the court poets of the regime, published the poem "For Adults . . ." which contained strong anti-bureaucratic accents, an effort to demystify everyday life in the early 1950s, and the characteristic claim: "Let's demand changes *through* the party." To maintain balance and to avoid "swinging" society too far, Paweł Hoffman, editor of *Nowa Kultura*, the weekly that published the poem, was immediately dismissed.

To understand the specific atmosphere of the thaw, we must be aware of its peculiar a-ideological character. The critique of Stalinist practices was conducted in philosophical rather than ideological or political institutional terms. Two articles published at that time were especially characteristic. First was Leszek Kołakowski's criticism of the "Platonic elements" in dialectical thought, its arbitrary character due to the magic of "one correct line," and perception of "evil" as a necessary part of dialectical processes.[6] The next was Jan Kott's speech during the Nineteenth Session of the Culture Council on March 25, 1956, when he asked that Marxist tools be used to analyze socialism, not only capitalism, and underlined that during Stalinism art was used to justify the existing regime, not socialism as such.

---

[6] "Platonizm, empiryzm i opinia publiczna," *Po Prostu* (Spring 1956).

The next attempt to carry out de-Stalinization, which still envisioned no changes in the ruling group but (unlike the 1954 Plenum) already contained some verbalization of the ritual of change, was the Seventh Plenum on July 18, 1956, with its efforts to assess the preceding period and the self-criticism offered by a few members of the Politbureau. Three major events had separated the two plenary meetings of the Central Committee. The first was Khrushchev's speech at the Twentieth Congress of the Soviet Communist party, February 14–25, 1956, which revealed the excesses of Stalinism.[7] It is claimed that Khrushchev sought thus to undermine the position of the Molotov group, which was unfavorably disposed to him, and that the speech also reflected the attempt of the power elite to protect itself from any future purges within its own ranks (Khrushchev was speaking mostly about victims among communists). Putting the full blame for criminal policies on the period of the "cult of the individual" and the exposure (and thus demystification) of the techniques applied during the purges, served the same purpose.

The second important event was Bierut's death on March 13, 1956, and the ensuing struggle for succession between Roman Zambrowski and Zenon Nowak. This struggle accelerated the process of political change. It should be noted that both competitors had been responsible for implementation of Stalinism in Poland, but they now chose different tactics in order to survive. Nowak proposed radical personnel changes but opposed vigorously the participation and mobilization of society (his tactics were similar to Khrushchev's in the U.S.S.R.). Zambrowski decided on a riskier strategy of ritual drama (partly in order to disarm his opponents through a war of labels). At this stage of

[7] Khrushchev blamed Stalin with repressions against the party cadres in the 1930s (when 70% of the 139 members of 1934 Central Committee was shot), an extermination of whole nationalities, and liquidation of the high officers of Red Army just before the Second World War.

conflict, however, a compromise candidate won, Edward Ochab, who later joined the Zambrowski group. The tactical differences found public expression in a polemic between Stefan Żółkiewski, who defended the position that the Communist party should keep a "leading role" in the "renewal" process, and Arthur Sandauer, who demanded "the right to be critical also for people who were not members of political Establishment."

The third element that appeared between the two plenary meetings was a political amnesty declared on April 27, 1956. During the following month 40,000 political prisoners (out of 70,000) were set free.

But the most important factor accelerating the process of change and reinforcing the need for the ritual drama to lower social tensions was a massive demonstration of workers in Poznań that turned into a street battle with an assault on the local Security Police Office, the participation of army units, and many casualties on both sides.[8]

[8] The Poznań riots took place at the end of June 1956. The immediate cause was a broken agreement between a workers' delegation from Cegielski (at that time "Stalin's Factory") and Minister of Machine Industry Fidelski, who had been negotiating compensation for unjust decreases in piecework payments. (Over three years, workers lost nearly 11 million zlotys.) There is some evidence of political provocation, probably directed by those members of the ruling group who sought to accelerate changes in the country. Events took place in two separate phases. The first phase was a peaceful demonstration, during which the 18-member workers' delegation led by St. Matyja met in Warsaw with Fidelski. A very primitive coordination had been arranged with other factories: mass marches to the center of the city started at the sound of the morning siren, set to ring a few minutes later than the usual 6 a.m. During this phase, the police were calm and occasionally fraternized with the workers.

The situation changed rapidly when an unknown person began to speak through a loudspeaker in a police car that had been taken over by workers. The unknown speaker announced, falsely, that the Cegielski delegation had been arrested and urged the demonstrators to march on the Security Police building on Kochanowski Street. The crowd of 100,000 divided. Some went to the building housing the city court and prison, set free 257 prisoners and secured 76 pieces of armament, 48 grenades, and 23,325 pieces of ammunition. The other group went directly to the office of the Security Police. At 10:40,

VIII. OCTOBER 1956 AS A RITUAL DRAMA

The Poznań riots compelled the authorities to state publicly their position with regard to the causes of the events and also to assess properly the mood of the country. Their assessment differed basically from the optimistic assertions made at 1954 Plenum. Ochab spoke of the "delays in eliminating the mistakes and shortcomings in the system by which the national economy is run" and of "bureaucratic abuses in the administration." He stressed the "unsatisfactory living conditions of the working class" which, in his opinion, resulted not only from the "objective need for rapid industrialization" but also from "inadequate efforts by the authorities." The earlier enthusiastic appraisals of the implementation of the Six-Year Plan were revised at this time, and the wage growth index, earlier put at 27 percent by GUS, was corrected. The real increase amounted to barely 13 percent, over a period of six years, and the increase was unevenly divided, so that some social groups felt no improvement whatever in their situation. It was also revealed that real wages actually fell in the period 1951–1953. Among the mistakes of the economic policy of the Stalin era, Ochab listed: "adoption of arbitrary indicators of increase in agricultural production," a mistaken policy toward peasants coupled with "elements of adventurism in the attitude to kulaks," lack of analyses of the effectiveness of investment projects undertaken, and too much centralized planning. It should be noted that all these mistakes persist in the Polish economy to this very day.

At the same time, Ochab clearly set limits to the changes

---

shots from the police building took the first victims. At the train station, the crowd murdered a policeman, Izdebski. At 12, three tanks from Poznań's officer school arrived; unwilling to fight, the officers turned the tanks over to the workers. At 2, tanks from the IV Corps from the Silesian region arrived, and regular battle began, with barricades, bottles of gasoline, and a few aeroplanes. By the end of the day, nearly 200 people had been killed (according to official data, 38). Hundreds of workers were arrested. A trial of the first group—the Poznań 9"—began on September 27, 1956, with sentences varying from 1.5 to 6 years.

admissible by the ruling group. He stated that the "movement toward democracy cannot be conducted in a careless way," and that "freedom to criticize does not mean freedom to criticize everything." As for the causes of the Poznań tragedy, he named the "dilatoriness of the authorities in redressing the wrongs" and also "lack of moderation on the part of the press, which failed to grasp the objective reasons for the difficulties." Ochab openly blamed the press for "arousing society's mistrust in the party" and for bringing about "internal demobilization of the party." The measures proposed by the Seventh Plenum in order to improve the situation included the following:[9]

1) Greater emphasis was placed on wage increases (30-percent increase by the end of 1960).

2) Rural self-management was extended, and a new policy was formulated toward peasants who were not members of collective farms; the policy was defined as "giving the kulaks the chance to become middle peasants."[10] This was progress, insofar as they were not collectivized or treated as enemies of the state.

3) The number of commands was limited, and the role of material incentives in industrial management enhanced.

4) "Compulsory Sunday work" in the mining industry was ended.

5) The constitutional rights of Sejm were respected as the institution established to control the activities of the government.

6) The system of Workers' Councils as "organs for democracy of the workers" was reactivated.

The importance of sternly opposing "irresponsible actions by unstable individuals, who strike at the whole of our achievements" was stressed, and the concept of political pluralism was rejected on the grounds that "democracy must reflect the aspirations and activities of the masses led by the party."

[9] *Nowe Drogi* (1956), no. 10, Resolution of the Seventh Plenum.
[10] "Middle peasants" were those with 3–7 acres of land.

The resolution adopted by the plenum contained two significant elements which, in my opinion, indicate a continuation of the Stalinist philosophy of leadership. First, irrespective of all the clearly evident internal differences and factional divisions, the resolution sought at all costs to preserve the myth of the unity of the ruling group. Second, an injunction was strongly formulated not to involve non-party people in conflicts within the bosom of the party. The injunction, I think, was an effort to keep crises separate from each other, a feature especially characteristic of the Stalinist era. During the debates in the Seventh Plenum, some Politbureau members who were the chief culprits in the eyes of the people offered ritual "self-criticism." "Ritual", because, as certain members of the Central Committee insisted in the discussion at the Eighth Plenum, this was rather a justification than an admission of guilt.[11] Additional evidence for the ritual character of this self-criticism was that, in this first version of the drama, no changes in the composition of the ruling group occurred. Thus, the seventh plenary meeting of the PUWP's Central Committee in July 1956 constituted the first version of the ritual of change, a version that, as we will see, has been continuously perfected ever since.

This was also the first attempt to use public opinion as an instrument of factional games. Zambrowski's faction circulated an unofficial "letter to the party units" that was full of accusations against "neo-Stalinists" and "anti-semites" in the ruling elite. However, in order to use public opinion, it was necessary to reconstruct it. Beginning in Spring 1956, some less compromised members of the party apparatus began to organize discussion clubs among non-party members. Within a short time 130 such clubs originated, some of which formed spontaneously. Król, a professional apparatchik from the Central Committee was elected chairman of the Federation of the Clubs, whose

---

[11] *Nowe Drogi* (1956), no. 10, p. 81.

main task was to send a telegram supporting Gomułka, in October 1956. After fulfilling this task, the Federation and many clubs were dissolved.

It must be reemphasized that the earlier attempts at de-Stalinization (in 1953 and 1954) did not have such a ritual character, for the naming of the new tendencies was consciously avoided. At that time, the party attempted to launch a new policy under the guise of continuing the old one, whereas the concept of the ritual of change is just the opposite, continuity under the guise of change. The situation changed at the Seventh Plenum: the verbalization of the whole process, long after action had been undertaken, made possible the regrouping of symbols peculiar to ritual drama and the emergence of new configurations to social roles. It also facilitated moral self-cleansing. An element of catharsis predominated at the Seventh Plenum, though still to a rather limited degree. No new institutions had been established, so there could be no question of a new configuration of roles. Some elements of such a new configuration became apparent only during the Eighth Plenum in October 1956. This was the second version of the ritual of change which in its initial version had failed to fulfill its expected function of lowering social tensions. At the Eighth Plenum, the ruling group took a decisive step forward in the process of establishing the ritual of change. First of all, there was a more effective appeal to society's symbolic consciousness, with the result that, even though it was near the final stage in the process of change, the Eighth Plenum has remained in public consciousness to this day as the turning point from which these changes began. Also, unlike the Seventh Plenum, it was a complete "ritual drama" as defined at the beginning of this chapter. It was preceded by a new distribution (in some instances even imposition) of roles, a regrouping of symbols, and, to a limited degree, by a new configuration of social positions and institutions.

The process is worth closer examination, as it illustrates the phenomenon of the ritualization of crisis and also reveals the characteristic features of how so-called, liberal opinion, that is to say that of the "general public" sometimes called upon to act as catalyst in the ritual of change, functions in a post-totalitarian society. The ritual was apparently directed by that part of the ruling elite that was aware of the urgent need for some symbolic gestures, if only to relieve social frustrations that had been further aggravated when, after the death of Stalin, hope for liberalization dawned. The directors of the ritual drama wanted to inform society that a turning point in its history had passed, and, at the same time, they sought to retain their positions of power.

The starting point for that particular group had been the Seventh Plenum. True, it failed to pass the test as a ritual drama because the measures proposed by the ruling group were not sufficiently radical or "perceptible" in the range of the society's symbolic imagination to lower the level of tensions and emotions. Yet, the plenum did become a convenient platform from which to prepare for the ritual drama at the Eighth Plenum. For even though the resolution adopted by Central Committee members at the Seventh Plenum ostentatiously stressed unity of opinion on all questions under discussion, by resorting to gossip and insinuation spread through "public" channels, reanimated since 1955, steps were taken to polarize in the public consciousness the different positions taken at the plenum. This maneuver was facilitated by the fact that the debates were held in closed sessions and that full texts of the speeches were not published, but only an allusive and ambiguous "Letter of the Central Committee to party organizations." It is worth noting that the polarization was not applied to issues vitally affecting the country's future or as a result of past differences in attitudes and behavior. On the contrary, by extensively exploiting rumor and gossip to pin such labels as "anti-intellectuals," "anti-Semites," "yokels," and "enemies of democracy" upon certain Central Committee members, new divisions were created, often along imaginary lines, thus turning the people's attention away from fundamental problems. The labels were based on word-of-mouth versions of speeches at the Seventh Plenum, very often at variance with the real statements. This artificial polarization was indispensable for creating the inner dynamics of the ritual drama; it also neutralized, after a fashion, demands by those "yokels" who insisted that personal responsibility for actions taken during the "cult of the individual" era should be more scrupulously accounted for. After its authors had been labeled "anti-intellectuals," this demand was interpreted as a longing for iron-fisted rule and a "return (sic!) to Stalinist methods." It should be emphasized at this point that some of the "popular" leaders were personally involved in the "errors" and "distortions." Among these was Staszewski, secretary of the Warsaw Committee of the Polish United Workers Party who arranged the popular "spontaneous" support for Gomułka. Staszewski, for example, was actively involved in carrying out collectivization in the country.

Furthermore, the maneuver to some extent whitewashed and certainly diverted public attention from such members of the ruling group as Cyrankiewicz (who after the Poznań events of June 1956 called for "cutting off hands" raised against Soviet power), Zambrowski, Zawadzki, Szyr, Ochab, Starewicz, and some others who had not been given any of the above labels. "Yokels" like Kłosiewicz, Łopot, Jóźwiak-Witold, Krupiński, Rumiński, and Nowak, were labeled "neo-Stalinists" and "anti-intellectuals," and were thrown as prey to the public.

Kłosiewicz and his colleagues were only the "second string" of the ruling elite. They may have thought their demands that full responsibility be taken for the excesses of Stalinism would be a lever for their own upward mobility to leading positions in the party apparatus. But the labeling maneuver neutralized the effect of their outspoken demands. Thus, for example, the objections raised by Bolesław Rumiński and Stanisław Łopot, that the "self-criticism" of Jakub Berman, who was responsible for internal security, and Hilary Minc, responsible for the economy, were largely of a ritual character and self-justifying rather than self-criticizing, were countered by claims that they themselves were "anti-intellectuals" and "anti-Semites." The latter accusation had its roots in a peculiar interpretation of a statement by Zenon Nowak, who pointed to the potential source of anti-Semitism inherent in the cadre policy of the Stalin period. The core of that policy was the appointment of communists of Jewish origin to leading posts in "unpopular" sectors like security, because they were the most trusted "comrades," who spent the war in the Soviet Union, the only place they could have survived. A similar argument was repeated in 1968 by Andrzej Werblan in *Miesicznik Literacki*, and ten years later by Andrzej Szczypiorski in a samizdat publication, and yet no one accused them of anti-Semitism.

Attempts to defend the labeled individuals were hindered by the fact that they themselves voted at the Seventh Plenum for a motion prohibiting the involvement of non-party opinion in any conflicts within the party. Attacked, they sought to defend themselves during the debates of the Eighth Plenum. Rumiński spoke of "actions and games prompted by personal ambitions." Wiktor Kłosiewicz referred to a "compromising letter that presented the course of the plenum in an ambiguous and insidious way and has been exploited to launch a slander campaign, distorting the statements made by some members of the Central Committee."[12] He requested the publication of the complete texts of all statements made during the discussion at the Seventh Plenum. If that were not possible, he asked for permission to publish his own speech, because, he said, "it is very hard to bear the burden of unfounded, slanderous accusations." He further

[12] Ibid., p. 97.

said that he took "full responsibility for every word he uttered, and rejected the allegations of anti-democratic and anti-intellectual sentiments which some comrades from the Warsaw Committee sought to ascribe to him."

Zenon Nowak, accused of anti-Semitism, said: "in local party organizations a lot of effort went into misrepresenting my attitude to democratization." He offered his views once more, stating: "The comrades know all about it, but I think that our cadre policy has often enhanced anti-Semitism. Comrades may disagree with me; that's too bad. But my opinion is that in our policy we should avoid anything that might arouse anti-Semitism. . . ." "I know," he continued, "of a number of comrades who disagree with me, but they protested when charges of anti-Semitism were leveled against me in local party organizations. The point is, however, that a lot of noise has been made on that issue and that it helped to divert the attention of a large proportion of our party organizations away from fundamental issues."[13]

Other Central Committee members who were labeled "anti-democrats" tried to defend themselves by questioning the sincerity of the charges made by "half-baked liberals." Łopot said "It is rather difficult to understand those who, until quite recently, were such zealots and nothing but 'yes-men,' and who now so suddenly and just as passionately are anti."[14] It has been also pointed out that the atmosphere prevailing at the Eighth Plenum, where everything was attributed to "factionalism," tended to stifle discussion. All critical voices that had not been written into the scenario of the ritual of change were interpreted as signifying affiliation with a group or a faction, "which is something the comrades fear like the devil."[15] The division of roles in the ritual drama into "good" and "bad" characters was most expressively analyzed in a speech by Central Committee

[13] Ibid., p. 75.
[14] Ibid., p. 65.
[15] Ibid., p. 208.

member Stefan Matuszewski, who was not himself directly connected with any faction. He stressed that "as became evident
from the way in which the party was informed about the course
of the Eighth Plenum, its primary objective was to indicate to
the rank-and-file party members an artificial line of division in
order to divert party attention from criticism of our policy up to
now."[16] Matuszewski showed how the mystification and over-
generalization of the problem of "anti-intellectual" attitudes
within the Central Committee shifted the focus of public opinion, which wanted scapegoats, onto individuals who were certainly not among those most guilty of the "errors and distortions" of the Stalin era. In fact, these were the very people who,
as the text of the debates reveals and despite the gossip, themselves strongly urged that everyone should accept the responsibility for their activities during the Stalin period and who
demanded, for instance, that not only Berman but also Zambrowski be removed. Yet, as a result of "operation labeling" and
to their own great surprise, these people turned from being the
attackers into objects of transferred social aggression. The aston-
ishment of the victims of this manipulation, especially Kłosiewicz, Rumiński, Nowak, and Łopot, might be compared to that of
the victims of the purges in the governing apparatus and at the
executive levels in 1968, who asked in amazement "how could
they resort to such methods against us?" The 1968 provocation
was apparently among other things, a form of revenge for the
maneuver at the Eighth Plenum in 1956, taken by those who
were made scapegoats at the earlier plenum.

The labeling procedure (Stefan Matuszewski called it a "cun-
ningly devised political campaign," p. 208), confirms my thesis
about the Eighth Plenum being a ritual drama. Matuszewski
pointed out that "repeating the fairy tales about a revival of Stalinist trends" by creating new divisions, is intended to divert

[16] Ibid., p. 101.

attention away from responsibility for the past. By providing an easy, artifically construed object of attack, it also helps "the former advocates of servility to gain a reputation as heralds of independence" (p. 210). Matuszewski concluded his statement with a dramatic warning, "let no one dare to criticize and, in particular, to discuss the matter in the light of individual responsibilities, for whoever does so will be surrounded by an atmosphere of terror and such a label will be pinned on him that he will not be able to show himself among certain groups of people who have access to the press and propaganda media. These typically Beriaist methods were brought unchanged into the process of democratization. At that time, people had to face the courts on the basis of fabricated accusations; now they faced public opinion. And like that earlier time, it was very hard for the comrades to defend themselves. For how can you influence public opinion when the entire propaganda and information machine is still in the hands of the old guard, who were tested in the battles against all kinds of deviation" (p. 210).

Yet, even this open naming of the maneuver in the most conspicuous way possible, and the attempt to describe its mechanism, did not result in the demystification of the labels, nor did it prevent artificial polarization. Was this because the skillfully chosen labels were so emotionally loaded? Or perhaps the need to go through a ritual drama (with its "bad" characters — no matter who they were) was as strongly felt by the society as it was among those who directed it and had a vested interest in it? Finally, could one expect full political maturity and culture from an inadequately informed public?

I would like to emphasize very strongly that my intention in treating the above events is not to defend any member of the group that ruled Poland during the Stalin era. I believe that each of them, without exception, had a share of the responsibility. But ritual dramas have a tendency to repeat themselves simultaneously with the techniques described above: appeals to, and

exploitation of, public opinion together with artificial polarization. Therefore, I think it is worth taking a closer look at these
techniques. In describing the method by which the stage managers of the spectacle at the 1956 Eighth Plenum managed to set
the characters in artificial opposition, I have tried to show how
the ritual of change developed and what the origin of its mythicized social perception is. This spectacle distracted public attention from essential issues and helped whitewash some members
of the Stalin era ruling elite.

This maneuver, even though it was carried out under the slogan of democratization, contained two elements characteristic of
totalitarian power: first, the contempuous exploitation not only
of society as a whole but also of yesterday's allies; second, the
power elite's use of labeling, against which there was no
defense. The maneuver was feasible not only because of the
devious way it molded public opinion but also because it skillfully blocked articulation inside the party through the myth of
party unity.

Hence, it is absolutely necessary that the role which the public is supposed to play be changed, however painful and demys-
tifying the operation may be, if the ritual of change is ever to
be replaced by real changes.

The Eighth Plenum not only alleviated social tensions by
staging the ritual drama (and that, as I have pointed out, was the
least painful way for the ruling group) but also accomplished a
regrouping of symbols. It signaled the end of the "liminal"
phase of the process of change (see concluding remarks of this
chapter), and marked the return to "normal work." It was no
accident that these were exactly the words of Władysław
Gomułka, immediately after he was elected first secretary of the
Central Committee during the Eighth Plenum. All those who
were disappointed with such a rapid shift were punished in a
spectacular, "didactic" way. The ritual of change was over.

Later a new wave of discontent took place, probably provoked by the losing faction at the Eighth Plenum. This included the attack on the Soviet Union consulate in Szczecin on December 10, 1956, and the clash with police on November 18, 1956. Both incidents forced Gomułka's team to take hard measures against the dissent and eroded his legitimacy. The epilogue of the Polish "thaw" was the summer strikes of public transportation workers in Łódź on August 12–14, 1957; Gomułka's attack on "revisionism," and on his former allies, and the liquidation of *Po Prostu*, a weekly that was a symbol of "renewal," in August 1957.

The Eighth Plenum not only allevatiated social tensions by staging the ritual drama but left a new institutional body — workers' self-management group on the factory level. The resolution adopted by the Eighth Plenum contained a section dealing with the establishment of workers' councils. The new bodies were to "take decisions on basic economic problems such as the elaboration of the enterprise's production plans and an assessment of its implementation, expansion of the plant, technological progress, organization of work and of production, work norms and wages, bonuses, etc., within the framework of the enterprise's directors."[17]

Discussions during the Eighth Plenum, stressed the "risk of effecting changes at a time when tensions are very high"[18] and, in connection with the creation of workers' self-management groups, the danger of "the enterprises largely ignoring the central plan and the necessary minimum indicators, excessive layoffs of workers which could result in unemployment in certain regions, fixing economically and productively unjustified profits, and the distribution of profits which the workers did not actually produce."[19]

Other speakers noted the danger of an emergence — following the creation of self-management bodies — of far-reaching wage

[17] Ibid., Resolution of the Eighth Plenum, p. 6.
[18] ibid., p. 55.
[19] Ibid., p. 118.

demands that could further aggravate economic imbalance. But as Ochab said, warnings given by an authority that does not enjoy society's confidence are not heeded, for the people perceive it as yet another attempt to defer long overdue change.[20]

The failure to work out the legal status of workers' councils in 1956 resulted in the virtual suspension of the activities of these bodies acute economic imbalance and constantly raised wage demands. Thus, Gomułka's speech at the Twelfth Plenum in 1958 contained remarks about "crystallization of the idea of self-management in contact with life" and about "the need for help for the self-management bodies by the enterprise's administration." Gomułka stated that the party "has not yet mastered the machinery of self-management" and concluded emphatically that "self-management is the most important organ which the party should practice handling" (in order to mobilize the workers for more intensive work).[21]

My analysis of the events of October 1956 in terms of ritual drama has a simplicity that makes it both profound and suspect. Have I said at once too much and too little, overrationalizing the activity of the ruling elite and at the same time underestimating the social forces bubbling beneath the surface of events at the October Plenum? Trying to dig beneath the appearance of facts to their real significance, but concentrating on the manipulations of the power holders, did I dig only in one direction?

With these doubts I asked two important and active participants in the events of October 1956 to comment on my line of reasoning.

The first of them, Mr. XY, was a leading journalist of the party's daily *Trybuna Ludu* in the 1950s, and, if my scheme is

[20] Ibid.
[21] *Materiały XII Plenum*, Książka i Wiedza, Warsaw, 1958, pp. 18–22.

correct, he had taken part in at least few turning points of the ritual drama I described.

The first turning point was a phase of separation, very important in every *rite de passage*, when behavior and symbolism are momentarily liberated from the norms and values that govern public life.[22] The mass media's role in this phase was mainly to "rock the boat" by introducing subtle changes in both the language of their reporting and in the way the facts were evaluated, with the help of critical articles or voices from "our readers." Such critical texts, printed perhaps with permission of the ruling group or some part of it, when censors were instructed to be more liberal,[23] on the one hand informed society that the ritual of change had begun and on the other hand marked out the areas of allowed criticism. During the spring and summer of 1956 both the *Trybuna Ludu* and the student weekly *Po Prostu* were full of such previously forbidden topics as "the bureaucratic tendencies in the party and administration," "voluntaristic decisions in agriculture," etc. Texts underlining the need for self-government and intraparty democracy "as instruments for the restoration of links between a vanguard and the masses" were widely publicized. Also articles about new tendencies in Western culture (abstract painting, jazz, rock, modern theater) were now printed, together with some signals of reconciliation with the "old intelligentsia" prosecuted in the early 1950s,[24] as

[22] Victor Turner, *The Ritual Process*, Ithaca, New York, Cornell University Press, 1966, p. 166.

[23] Professor W. Adamski, Institute of Sociology, Polish Academy of Sciences, who worked in the censorship office in 1956 states that the well known, critical letter by "Polish Journalists" that was unexpectedly published in *Życie Warszawy* in Summer 1956 was printed with the special permission of somebody from the Politbureau. However, in order to keep a balance, the censor who signed that agreement was immediately fired and quietly reallocated to a better position.

[24] J. Ambroziewicz, W. Namiotkiewicz, Jan Olszewski "Towards the People of Home Army (AK)" *Po Prostu* (March 25, 1956).

well as with the national tradition, previously passed over in silence as deprived of a "progressive class content."

In the next, liminal phase (an ephemeral, transistory stage) of the ritual after the Seventh Plenum (which participants described later as a moment "in and out of time"), a characteristic ambiguity of formal structures was evident, and, in contrast, a communal, national comradeship was strongly emphasized. In that phase of the ritual drama, its stage managers used the mass media to disarm their opponents in the Central Committee with the help of such labels as "hard liners," printed of course without names but with the magic word "group." The mass media also helped in that phase to alleviate the popular and widespread frustration connected not only with the Stalinist past but also with the process of transition. The psychological aspects of the process of change initiated from above in totaltarian regimes are very complex and difficult to reconstruct. Subtle psychological insights are almost impossible a quarter of century later, but the problem is even more complicated. Even for scrupulously honest, modest, and sensitive people, it is difficult to confess that the October 1956 euphoria and hope for political relief and communal regeneration were interlaced with deep tensions and with an ambivalence that they could not explain then and cannot now.

I believe it is this very psychological ambivalence of people exposed to the process of transition that gives the moments of change (or rituals of change) in totalitarian systems their sharpness and drama. The hope for change and the joy of intense social encounters during the liminal phase of the *rite de passage* was mixed during October 1956 with strange, at first glance, elements of popular and widespread auto-aggression. People were torn by feelings of guilt and shame. Now, the same mass media that for years had convinced them that an order based on "objective laws of history" was unavoidable suddenly described that very same order as the product of "mistakes and distortions." What is more, the prime minister for many years now called himself the "leader of a renewal" (Cyrankiewicz's speech in the Sejm on April 23, 1956).

At the same time, a different shade of shame appeared as, in spite of the invitation to "public discussion," most people remained silent because of an instinctive and deeply imprinted fear of using words and epithets so long forbidden. This shame combined with the self-hatred of a people who, having been raised in a totalitarian regime, were trained to think in terms of power (as the small animals in a jungle). Now, with their heightened perceptivity of weakness, they could not help but jump from yesterday's servility to a cruelty toward their former bosses. Almost everyone found himself in such a situation. In the past, subordinated members of the society were often encouraged by their supervisors to terrorize weaker fellows. Now nearly everyone, even those of relatively low status, was at the same time a victim and a flayer. Such feelings were followed by self-contempt of those who remembered their own servility and the fact that, just yesterday, they had been afraid of the same people who today were afraid of them. To realize that everyone is weak is a shock for somebody brought up in an authoritarian culture.

These emotions, together with the lack of tolerance for ambiguity, characteristic of people who have lived for a long time in an authoritarian situation, led to the labyrinthine psychological reactions to the political changes of 1956, reactions that were often a far cry from the joy of resurrection.

In addition, living for a long time in a totalitarian world leads to certain limitations of cognitive capacity. Most of the people were unable to analyze their own psyches for fear of what they would find; such an inability to label their own feelings created an amnesia concerning that time. Because of this amnesia, my thesis can serve only as a hypothetical explanation of the tension of transition, confessed by nearly everybody.

I would like to stop here to avoid an oversimplified psychological profile, but I want to underline a characteristic similarity of those tensions to the feelings reported by anthropologists at the moments of *rites de passage* in primitive societies. To illustrate, I will use a long quotation from Victor Turner's analysis: "Life crises provide rituals in and by means of which relations between structural positions and between the incumbents of such positions are restructured, often drastically. Seniors take the responsibility for actually making the changes prescribed by custom; they, at least, have the satisfaction of taking an initiative. But juniors, with less understanding of the social rationale of such changes, find that their expectations with regard to the behavior of seniors toward them are falsified by reality during times of change. From their structural perspective, therefore, the changed behavior of their parents and other elders seems threatening and even mendacious, perhaps even reviving unconscious fears of [...] punishment for behavior not in accordance with parental will."[25]

Wizards in primitive societies were conscious of the presence of tensions associated with change. To lower them, they decorated people of low status with masks that made it easier for them to participate in the *rite de passage*. They also organized rituals of status reversal that "mask the weak in strength and demand of the strong that they be passive and patiently endure the symbolic and even real aggression shown against them by structural inferiors."[26] Nearly the same techniques were used in Poland in October 1956, and the role of mass media was influential here. To eliminate feelings of self-hatred, numerous arti-

[25] Turner, *The Ritual Process*, p. 175.
[26] Ibid., p. 179.

cles underlining the role of the masses in the transformation of the system were printed. Widely publicized self-criticism of high officials, together with stories about unpopular managers "being carried away from factories on wheelbarrows" introduced some elements of status reversal, or rather status leveling, in which "the high must submit to being humbled and the humble are exalted through the privilege of plain speaking."[27]

Mr. XY told me, that the mass media received detailed instructions at turning points in the process of change: "print such and such materials," "let them speak about a, b, c but not d," etc.

In the last phase of the ritual of change, the formal structure was reborn by emphasizing (again with the help of the mass media) that society, to survive, must be organized in an hierarchical and functionally segmented order, and that the time of "lampooning liberty"[28b] was over. The danger of *anarchy* and the need for control was exposed. To make that transition from a liminal to a rigidly structured phase less painful, some elements of the *communitas* for a while masqueraded as structure (for instance, by creating the institution of self-government in factories). In that last stage of *rite de passage*, some extremists from the previous liminal phase were punished. Interestingly, these sanctions were divided between two sides of the ritual: the second-rankers in the party hierarchy who took too seriously the moment when the formal structure was suspended and tried to capture places at the top were as severely punished as those

[27] Ibid., p. 176.

[28] Bosman's phrase quoted by Turner, ibid., p. 178.

[b] Bosman was a Dutch historian of the coast of Guinea. As quoted in Turner (p. 178), he says: "There is a Feast of eight days accompanied with all manner of Singing, Skipping, Dancing, Mirth, and Jollity; in which time a perfect lampooning liberty is allowed, and Scandal so highly exalted, that they may freely say of all Faults, Villainies, and Frauds of their Superiors, as well as Inferiours without Punishment or so much as the least interruption (Letter X)."

who too vigorously criticized that formal structure. My collo-cutor found himself in the second group and was dismissed from *Trybuna Ludu*. *Po Prostu* ceased to come out in 1957, and its editor-in-chief, Eligiusz Lasota, lost his seat in Sejm during the next election (1961).

Jerzy Morawski, the new secretary of the Central Committee who was introduced to the ruling elite with the help of the October wave of anti-bureaucratic restoration of the PUWP, was dismissed in 1961, together with other relatively young mem-bers of the Politbureau who had obtained their positions after the 1956 events (Stanisław Matwin, Jerzy Albrecht). Karol Mo-dzelewski and Jacek Kuroń, who organized the Young Revolu-tionaries Association at the Warsaw University in 1956, were imprisoned in 1964 for circulating an anti-bureaucratic mani-festo. The *rite de passage* was definitely over. Nearly all mem-bers of the previous ruling elite survived: some of them came back; for instance, Zenon Nowak and Julian Tokarski received new seats in Sejm during the same elections in which Lasota lost his.

Mr. XY generally supported my scheme of ritual drama with the creation and later dismissal of public opinion. He under-lined, however, that it was more an instinctive and spontaneous act of manipulation than a fully conscious and systematically planned plot. What was more, the performers, both totalitarian utopians and liberals, who animated the public, were them-selves motivated by the hope of change; they decided to act even when elements of manipulation were obvious.

Another reviewer of that chapter was Władysław Bień-kowski, a long-time collaborator of Gomułka. He was one of the founders of the Polish Workers' Party during the Second World War. Later, in the late 1940s he, together with Gomułka, was pushed from power and accused of "nationalistic deviation." He returned to the Central Committee of the PUWP after October

1956 and for a few years held the post of Minster of Education. In the early 1960s, he resigned his position after a conflict with Gomułka.

After reading an early draft of this book, Bieńkowski wrote a long and mostly positive review that circulated in Poland in samizdat form in the summer of 1980. He formulated, however, two serious accusations concerning my description of the October 1956 events that I feel obliged to answer.

He contended that I gave insufficient attention to the role of the Soviet Union. Specifically, he suggested that a tactic chosen by the defeated faction (Nowak, Kłosiewicz, Rumiński and the others) was a repetition of Khrushchev's strategy of system transformation from above, with passive society. Zambrowski's and Gomułka's pattern was opposite, an active society but mostly a ritual of change on the central level.[29]

Another, and more basic, accusation made by Bieńkowski was that I overestimated the abilities of the ruling group to manipulate. Bieńkowski wrote: "The author embraced in her vision of society the same approach as a ruling elite. According to that approach, a history of society disappears in the socialist system and all that happens is and could be only and exclusively a result of the rulers' actions. . . . An underestimating of the history of society is particularly obvious in her analysis of Polish October."[30] Later Bieńkowski agreed with me that, when talking about the 1950s, it was nearly impossible to write social history understood as a "sequence of crystallization of ideas and aspirations" because one of the first consequences of the totalitarian-type power was the elimination of all possibilities for such crystallization by the atomization of society and a mystification of reality. What is more, only the ruling elite left a trace of its activity; society remained mostly silent, "only rarely emitting

---

[29] Wł. Bieńkowski's samizdat review of my book, p. 13.
[30] Ibid., p. 15.

fierce grumbles or impetuous impulses."[31] But, Bieńkowski argues, "It should be underlined that, together with a thickening of the atmosphere, a revisionist tendency appeared in the party that tried to articulate the needs of society."[32] He added, however, that, from today's perspective, this tendency seems to be so "incoherent, that it is easy to evaluate it as a mere manipulation of the ruling elite, trying to survive with the help of simulating a revision of the past."

Bieńkowski concluded the above fragment of his review with the general reflection that the young generation of critics of the totalitarian system, who were brought up and educated in such a system, not only feel obliged but find a peculiar pleasure in exposing what they call a "myth of subjectivity of society." It is a peculiarly ironic remark because Bieńkowski was himself Minister of Education during my high-school years.

I agree with Bieńkowski that at least three levels of social activity must be distinguished — elite, public, mass — and that my analysis of October 1956 has been preoccupied with the elite. My fascination with the manipulations of the ruling elite and with the ritual drama of October 1956 is, I believe, a function of the real nature of the events, but it could be also the by-product of having lived all my life in an authoritarian system. On the topic of public opinion, however, I cannot agree with Bieńkowski that the revisionist tendency in the PUWP was fully spontaneous and detached from factional games and, on the other hand, that it was the only active element of a so-called *public*. A peculiar feature of 1955 and 1956 in Poland was that particular segments of the public crystallized, articulated, and organized themselves *against each other*.

For instance the revisionist tendency in the PUWP and in the Association of Polish Youth (ZMP) with its "pure" Marxism

---

[31] Ibid., p. 17.
[32] Ibid.

and anti-bureaucratic program was very similar to the totalitarian utopians of 1970s. They were antiliberal and opposed not to terror as such but only to bureaucratic, "random, idle" terror that did not build a new society and a new culture. They believed in the possibility of a renewal of the communist party from within by a return to the ideological orientation and purity of the first years after the revolution. Their aim was to democratize the party and clear it of members who were not ideologically oriented. They were against mass mobilizing organizations; they arranged for the liquidation of the mass Youth Association and in its stead created a cadre Revolutionary Youth association. The latter was depoliticized in 1957 and later liquidated. Revisionists were violently anticlerical; their influence on party politics caused increasing pressure on the Catholic Church between 1953 and 1956. The decree of February 9, 1953, obliged all priests to swear their allegiance to the state. According to a letter of the Episcopate on May 8, 1955, these steps broke the 1950 agreement between state and church. An activization and further differentiation of the Catholic community was a reaction to these pressures. A new Catholic group was organized around the weekly WTK (Wrocław): the intelligentsia around the Catholic weekly *Tygodnik Powszechny* in Cracow was rapidly politicized. A split deepened in the Catholic association PAX, which collaborated with the government; the difference concerned with the choice of a tactic against government pressure.

All these activities had an impact on the activation of the public, but the latter remained segmented, agitated, without any influence on the dynamics of the situation on a national level. At the same time some members of the party machine (not ideologists connected with the revisionist stream, but professional apparatchiks linked with the faction that directed the ritual drama) began to activate public opinion outside the party. A few discussion clubs were organized: the founder of the Poznań club

"Zielony Semafor" (Green Semaphore) was Orchoń, manager of the propaganda division in the district party committee. An analogous club in Warsaw, "Krzywe Koło" was taken under the wing of Stefan Staszewski, first secretary of the Warsaw party committee. Members of the Federation of Clubs (most of them not party members), pragmatic and motivated by a dream of a real citizenship in their country, sent a telegram to the Eighth Plenum supporting Gomułka. Shortly afterwards the ritual drama was over, and most of the provincial clubs were liquidated and their members returned to political apathy.

The workers' councils were demobilized by 1958. The initiative to elaborate the idea of workers' councils had also come from the party apparatus. From late Spring 1956 (long before the Eighth Plenum) a group of party members, a few journalists (Hajnicz, Brodzki from *Trybuna Ludu*); writers (Jacek Bocheński, Jerzy Broszkiewicz, and Jerzy Putrament), as well as the Warsaw party committee secretary St. Kuziński and Lechosław Goździk, a worker and secretary of the party unit at the Żerań Automobile factory, met a few times to work on this idea. Before the plenum a special government commission was created "to help in a further development of the self-management initiative. Its members were Jaroszewicz, Jaszczuk (Minister of the Machine Industry), Goździk and Professors Brus, Lipiński (at that time chairman of the Polish Economic Association), and Kalecki. Responsible for the work of this commission was the chairman of the Department of Industry in the party's Central Committee.[33]

The most lasting, but less politicized, event was a movement of restoration in culture.

All these events of public life were more or less elitist: this was characteristic of the pattern of artificial negativity that at best invoked a part of the public. A history of the society still remains an open question.

[33] Compare Kowalik, *NTO* (February 10, 1981).

Bieńkowski is correct in saying that a preoccupation with power and manipulation is characteristic of my book. Bieńkowski's criticism raises troubling questions not only about my analysis but about my generation as well. Perhaps this is so because a core experience of this generation was the experience of being objects of manipulation (March 1968) on the one hand, and, on the other hand, of maturing to public life in a decade of repressive tolerance. The generation who was active in the 1950s had the illusion that terror could be the force of creation. The generation younger than we, those active in the 1970s now have their period of political activity, when most of our generation serves as "experts." Our main experience was a detachment and the faint satisfaction of a lack of illusions. This is also the reason for the peculiar sensitivity of my generation to the technical side of power.

CHAPTER IX

Concluding Reflections

[Completed on November 30, 1981]

It is too early to answer the questions: has the Polish revolution already been aborted or is it yet incomplete?

At least two phases of a classical revolutionary pattern have already been accomplished.

First, the old party-state has collapsed. The collapse began in the late 1970s as a result of the confused reactions of the power apparatus to the policy of totalization spearheaded by Gierek's team. As we remember, the basis of this policy was a peculiar mixture of strengthening the regime's legal identity (through the formalization of the "leading role of the party," a one-list election procedure, and intraparty mechanisms blocking free articulation) and the development of informal corporatist arrangements and lame pluralism.

This collapse of the party-state deepened after August 1980, when its structures, based on the myth of the unity of the state's and society's interests, made it impossible to meet the new problems of a highly mobilized and politicized society. The mechanisms that blocked the articulation of interests different from the official formulas no longer worked.

The power vacuum that followed this collapse was the rebellious masses' opportunity. But as Jeremy Brecher wrote: "In fact, revolutionary movements rarely begin with a revolutionary intention: this only develops in the course of struggle itself."[1]

---

[1] Jeremy Brecher, *Strike*, San Francisco, Straight Arrow Books, 1972, p. 240.

This was the case in August 1980. At the beginning, the main aim of the workers' movement was to detach itself from the hated regime with the help of its own, independent organization, Solidarity. Solidarity would function as an organized society, with its own information and protection systems, its own educational arrangements as well as internal mechanisms of upward mobility and of restoring dignity. At this stage the workers were not interested in taking over the political functions of the state. To the contrary, the escapist-type, utopian perspective, characteristic of traditional status-oriented societies, blended with the rejection of politics (due to its compromise-building character) and rooted in a fundamentalistic-moralistic mentality prevailed in Solidarity. Not until a year later did the movement's activists begin to be interested in political power. By that time, however, the regime had consolidated itself, and the rank-and-file members of Solidarity had become demobilized, passive, and not very enthusiastic about organizing self-management groups or "active strikes" as a way of taking over economic power. They were even less interested in fighting for the new institutional arrangements like the "Social Council on Economic Problems." That initial lack of interest in politics (except the symbolic politics typical of the first stage of Solidarity's development) was reinforced by the tactic of "self-limiting revolution" chosen for the first months of the movement's functioning.

Another opportunity to fill the power vacuum, through the stablization of a more liberal form of regime that would be based on broader cooptation of the marginal political elites (from the Catholic groups as well as democratic and peasant parties) did not work either. This possibility depended on the success of a maneuver of redefining the institutional regime. But this maneuver did not succeed. As I showed in the introductory chapter, this attempt to redefine the regime was linked to a shift from the party-state toward the army-state.

The advantages to the narrow power elite of this move were evident. First of all such a state would be easier to legitimate. Its reductionist, not instrumental, formula based on the National Unity Front (where all participants have to agree on basic decisions), plus its a-ideological character make it a much more capacious form, able to absorb a wider range of interests. This redefinition also seems to be very convenient from the Soviet Union's point of view: if it is completed, the Soviet Union does not need to invade, even after the complete collapse of the PUWP. This transformation of the political regime increased the tensions within party apparatus. At the time I wrote the introduction to this book I asked how the countermobilization of this apparatus could be avoided. Today such countermobilization has become a fact. Above all, the apparatus received its own "operational" groups[2] parallel to the military groups, created by Jaruzelski a few weeks ago in order to control local authorities. Second, the strong polarizing pressures introduced by the "hard liners" to the resolution of the Fourth Plenum[3] led to a characteristic counterreaction of Solidarity: a demand that the party withdraw from industrial enterprises.[4] The latter pushed Premier Jaruzel-

---

[2] Students of the party school, WSNS, were sent to small towns and a return to institutions of "commissars" in industry as well as on district level, was discussed during the Sixth Plenum on November 27–28, 1981.

[3] This resolution forced party members who were also members of Solidarity "to choose their identification." As a result, many rank-and-file members of the party gave up their party cards. In some factories the party apparatus reacted by withdrawing its support for ex-party members in managerial positions. This led to a rapid acceleration of conflict.

[4] Two parallel techniques were used here: first a decision undertaken by a factory commission of Solidarity or a meeting of delegates asked that the party be moved from factory to territorial level on the basis that industry should be "apolitical." This method was used at Warski's shipyard in Szczecin in mid-October, after several months of conflict over the way the party should execute a "leading role." Another, more radical method, undertaken on November 24, 1981, in Ponar factory in Żywiec was a referendum of all workers on the question of retaining a committee on the factory level. The answer of 92% of the workers was "no." A visit of the district prosecutor following this event did

ski to defend openly the status of the PUWP. This move complicated, if not blocked, his own strategy of redefining and broadening the base of the regime.

The apparatus began its own offensive with militant speeches during the Sixth Plenary meeting of the Central Committee.[5] One of the most aggressive speakers, Julian Kraus from the Bielsko Biała automobile factory, demanded "a transparent dictatorship, based on keeping order, but in an open, public way."[6] He then found himself in a very complicated situation. His own party cell, which a few months ago elected him to the Ninth extraordinary Congress, has recently dissolved. Cutting itself off from the party's base seems to be a peculiar strength of the apparatus; it is not interested in feedback from the rank-and-file members and is no longer controlled by this feedback. The only barrier to the evolution of a party synonymous with the appa-

not change the situation; workers asked the party to move out of their factory. In fact, it is extremely difficult to argue that the party's presence in factories is legal. The general formula of the "leading role" is not followed by an operational concrete legal instructions. On the contrary, during the Sixth Plenum the Secretary of the Central Committee, Mokrzyszczak, said that this "leading role," formulated in Constitution, "cannot be limited by legal regulations on the lower level" (this sounds like a classical type of legitimacy). The party side — the local party committee — decided to take such step. It will be very difficult to win the case against Żywiec Solidarity in the court. The only possibility of winning is to use pressure on the court; during the Sixth Plenum the first voices about a necessity to change cadres in legislative system and courts were formulated.

[5] See *Trybuna Ludu*, November 29, 1981, with transcripts of speeches by Kraus, Drabik, and Mokrzyszczak. The latter reported for instance more than 350 searches recently undertaken against Solidarity activists, nearly 200 of them for circulating uncensored information.

[6] Kraus — in connection with a recent incident (in which a few prisoners escaped from arrest, climbed the chimney of an old factory and negotiated revision of their trials with negotiators from the General Prosecutor office) — asked for a public, "televised overturning of the chimney." He and others also supported an initiative of the Central Committee Secretaries repealing a demand sent in late October to the PUWP's Parlimentary Club to use its right of legislative initiative in order to bring before the Sejm a vote to empower the Government to issue special anti-strike legislation.

ratus are the democratically elected secretaries from big factories and universities. But, to solve this problem, an initiative was formulated during the Sixth Plenum to send members of the central (most conservative) apparatus to party organizations that seem to be weak. When this group of relatively liberal, young secretaries gives up, a gate to decision-making positions would be open for those who had no chance to be elected in a democratic way.

This rapid revival of a caricature of the Leninist idea of a party as a vanguard also invoked some elements of the old rhetoric. One of the speakers at the Sixth Plenum used, for example, the phrase "a dictatorship of proletariat," meaning a hard line directed against Solidarity (in other words — against the majority of Polish workers).[7]

This shift from pragmatic semantics toward ideological phraseology completed the second phase of the Polish revolution, characterized by an increasing politicization of claims and a deepening polarization. The stabilization of the regime on the basis of the illusion of a social contract seems to be less and less possible. This was also the phase typical of the general revolutionary process, in the same extent, as the first, power-vacuum phase.

The ideologization of conflicts between the ruling elite and the party on the one side and Solidarity on the other, is reinforced by a new development within Solidarity. We could observe recently the accelerated ideologization and politicization of many members of Solidarity when the original, fundamentalist or pragmatic mentalities that initially played the role of ideologies crowded into a network of 35 illegal political parties and organizations.[8] Mechanisms of identification are very

[7] Compare the speech of Ignacy Drabik from Skarżysko Predom factory during the Sixth Plenum; *Życie Warszawy* (November 28–29, 1981), no. 278.

[8] Central Committee Secretary Włodzimierz Mokrzyszczak's speech on television during the Sixth Plenum, November 27, 1981.

often random and occur by chance, but later on an organizational logic reinforces differences between political groups and orientations. This process can be interpreted as an escape from the formula of Solidarity, when it became obvious that the formula contained elements of false articulation. This recent radicalization (at least on a verbal level) is also caused by a prevalent atmosphere of unreality. The centrally conducted negotiations did not change the course of real events. The few victories, which were mostly in the sphere of social policy, were instantly appropriated by the party. When nothing seems to be possible, anything is possible. When one has no knowledge of political process (which would make clear both barriers and possibilities), the imagination is radicalized. This is the process we can observe in Poland.

Wendell Phillips commented that "Revolutions are not made, they come."[9] It is important to remember that the rebellious masses quite often act on their own, without being directly organized or ideologically inspired. As I show, radicalism can as well be a problem of imagination, and accelerated politicization can be the result of blocked articulation inside Solidarity.

The logic of the present complicated twist of multiple conflicts is not controlled by any class, group, or organization, and it is nearly impossible to forecast. But for me it seems obvious that we are now in the middle of revolutionary process, not at its end.

[9] Wendell Phillips quoted by Theda Skocpol, *States and Social Revolutions*, New York and Cambridge, Eng., Cambridge University Press, 1979.

Epilogue

[*Completed on November 30, 1981*]

During the night of December 12, 1981, the confrontation became real. The Military Council of National Salvation, chaired by General Jaruzelski, was constituted. The Council of State (Rada Państwa) proclaimed a "state of war."[1] The justifications were "the needs for inner peace, security, and defense of the state."[2] Confrontation politics had clearly transferred the decision-making center of the political system outside the previous institutional regime in order to stabilize the system by introducing rules of the game more favorable to the ruling group. Solidarity and other labor unions as well as 48 nationwide associations were suspended. Nearly all the members of the National Commission of Solidarity were arrested,[3] as well as KPN, KOR, ROPCIO, and "Young Poland" activists and their

[1] The most important features are: a military-type summary jurisdiction, the militarization of a large sector of the economy, suspension of most organizations and labor unions, severe limitations on movement and communication, closed borders, and internment of thousands of people.

[2] The state of war was voted by the Council of State nearly unanimously; only Reiff, from PAX, opposed it. The vote took place between 1:00 and 2:00 a.m., December 13, when the whole operation was already in full swing. In spite of obvious legal problems—the Council of State cannot vote any decree when the Sejm is in session—at its plenary meeting on January 25, 1982, the Sejm decided, with 5 abstentions, that the entire operation was legal.

[3] Except Bujak, Kosmowski, Frasyniuk, and Janas, who escaped entirely, and few who left Gdańsk but were arrested within a few days—Słowik in Łódź, who received a 4½-year sentence for trying to organize a street demonstration against the state of war, and Waszkiewicz and Krupiński, who organized the National Strike Committee in Gdańsk shipyard.

followers among the workers. The key to the arrests became obvious after a few days: these were the people who would be able to function in a conspiracy. The leaders of the August 1980 strikes; printers of samizdat papers before and after August 1980; regional activists with high prestige and good contacts among workers; and people who were the objects of resentment by the party and internal security apparatuses in the late 1970s (such as the founders and lecturers of the Flying University, people with "clean hands," who functioned as a social consciousness or perceived themselves a "collective conscience" of the nation). Official sources claim that 5,067 people are in 49 internment centers;[4] Catholic Church information indicates that the number is at least twice that.

It is obvious that the reasons for this military coup were much more complex than the official explanation. Prior to the event it is likely that two scenarios had been prepared simultaneously, due to the fact that the camp of the ruling group is and was riven with deep inner contradictions and dramatic challenges.

The first of these, already described in this book, was the scenario formulated by the Jaruzelski regime to redefine the institutional regime and to move from a party-state toward an authoritarian-bureaucratic, non-ideological army-state based on the cooptation of marginal elites and the demobilization of the masses. The military operational groups sent by Jaruzelski in mid-October [to inquire into regional problems] were supposed to fill the power vacuum and to build from below a new control structure at the expense of the party. As we see now, this scenario was open-ended: the very same network could be used in a "liberal" as well as repressive, "state-of-war" manner. Probably shortly after the PUWP's Fourth Plenum at the end of October

[4] Statement by the Minister of Internal Security before the Sejm commission, January 6.

1981, when polarization pressures became obvious and the social contract notion less feasible, Jaruzelski's group began to reorganize its scenario into a more hard-line type.[5]

Another scenario, probably prepared by the ideologically oriented section of the party apparatus was directed against Solidarity as well as against Jaruzelski. This group consisted of several factions. Some had been labeled hard-liners in the past — Tadeusz Grabski, Stanisław Kociołek, Michta (rector of the party school), Stefan Olszowski. Also involved were real hard-liners — Andrzej Żabiński, Mirosław Milewski, Albin Siwak — hostile toward the "refining" maneuver, supplemented by part of the security forces, which had been kept on a leash and frustrated in the late 1970s by Gierek's policy of repressive toleration, and the political branch of the army linked with the daily *Żołnierz Wolności*. The Russians probably supported both scenarios as alternative solutions to the Polish problem that would not require Soviet intervention. The second scenario repeated the 1968 Czechoslovak pattern in the sense of both strong ideological pressure with the destruction of the previous cultural and scientific social fabric as having been infected by "renewal," and the repression of the liberal wing of the party which comprised Kubiak, Barcikowski, Krasucki, horizontal structures activists, and many others. This scenario also proposed much more severe repressions toward Solidarity leaders and experts than were actually used.[6] This scenario was going to be activated around December 17, 1981, when Jaruzelski would be in Moscow for Brezhnev's birthday celebrations. The pretext for this

[5] The joint operational council was organized in Lwów (SU) in late August or early September 1981. A list of interned individuals that contains names of a few people who left Poland in early October and the mention as a destination the prison in Kamienski that was burned in late October serves as a good indicator of the timing.

[6] One of the bulletins of the Warsaw Party Committee, December 1981, contains the sentence: "we decided not to use public executions."

scenario would be the rally and street demonstration planned by the Mazowsze Region of Solidarity on the eleventh anniversary of the events of December 1970.

The tactics of the promulgators of this version of confrontation were evident from the Fourth Plenum: the polarizing pressures and undercutting of the possibilities of social contract by the provocation and extension of local conflicts.[7] They counted on the militant reaction of the radical wing of Solidarity to justify their own countermobilization. And they got it: the November 27th militant resolution of Gdańsk shipyard's Solidarity, which demanded a referendum on the government's credibility, and, above all, the December 3 resolution formulated by the regional leaders of Solidarity during a meeting in Radom.[8] The rapid but to this time apparently mostly verbal radicalization of the pragmatic leaders of Solidarity had several causes. Before the Radom meeting they received the information (in leaflets probably prepared by the authors of the second scenario) about the Sixth Plenum's claim of special powers for the government that had been put to Sejm and was going to be discussed during the December 15 meeting.[9] What was more, Solidarity leaders felt that their status had been offended and not taken seriously.[10] The violent resolution of the strike in the Fire

[7] For instance the conflict connected with the nomination of Professor Hebda in Radom, when even the Commission of Rectors had asked for his dismissal.

[8] The concluding document demanded "free elections," rejected so-called "provisorium" in economy, and asked for a permission to create the Social Economic Council and free access to mass media, especially television.

[9] Among these competences were some legal regulations used later on in the "state of war" scenario.

[10] The recent negotiations with the government were more and more perceived as a smoke-screen for the ruling group. The last negotiations on the "provisorium," on November 28, ended with an agreement to meet once more; in spite of that, the government undertook the final decision alone, on November 20. This action was perceived as a sign of disregard, a serious threat from the point of view of the status-politics so important in the activity of Solidarity's leaders.

Officers school two days previously also added to their rapid radicalization.[a] It must be added that the mass media of both sides played a key role in this period of escalating confrontation. The media became the principal exponents of the most extreme views. During the last weeks before the "state of war" it was impossible to separate the real issues from the symbolic battle of the media, in which all events were distorted and politicized.

From Jaruzelski's point of view, the pressure of time was more and more evident. The scenario of the rival apparatus group focused on December 17, the moment when the final regulation of the February 1982 elections to People's Councils would be decided (Solidarity demanded free elections). The international meeting of student organizations scheduled for December 15 in Wrocław was perceived as a threat to the Moscow-controlled International Student Federation. What was more, December was the last month of service of soldiers from the previous induction; the new group would be "infected" by Solidarity. Ironically, probably the final element that accelerated the military coup was the letter sent on December 6 by Primate Glemp to the Sejm, in which he asked that they not vote for the extraordinary powers for Jaruzelski's government.

Jaruzelski's first step was to neutralize the party as far as possible: it was probably his people (Woźniak and Mokrzyszczak) who, as the Central Committee secretaries, prepared and determined the temporary limitation on December 10 of some parts

[a] Students in the Warsaw Fire Academy went on strike on November 25, 1981. They demanded that their school be included among institutions of higher learning covered by the new legislation concerning higher education, which was being presented to Sejm. Their Academy, though under the authority of the Ministry of the Interior rather than the Ministry of Higher Education, was until this time subject to civilian law. According to the new project it was to become part of the system of military schools, and subject to military jurisdiction. On December 2, the peaceful sit-in strike was broken up by a helicopter assault by the military police. It was a massive show of force and a rehearsal of strategy that would soon be used to break strikes in numerous factories after December 13.

of the PUWP's statute: the right to demand the party congress; the right to control apparatus from below, and the right to recall district secretaries by elected bodies. Power inside the party was centralized in the bodies loyal to Jaruzelski ready to neutralize "trouble-makers" of all kinds. The next step was to forge an alliance with the authors of the second scenario, probably advised by Marshal Kulikov, who spent a week in Warsaw at the beginning of December. The alliance between the two groups was based on a peculiar trade-off: Jaruzelski contributed his name (which guaranteed the appearance of continuity and prevented division within the army) and his operational groups with their knowledge of and access to factories and local authorities. The managers of the second scenario gave up their dreams of repression. It is interesting that at the beginning of the operation some repression touched the very same men who had been perceived only a few weeks before as candidates for Jaruzelski's National Salvation Council, Professors Szaniawski and Bartoszewski. These repressions signaled the deep frustration of the authors of the second scenario and were, in a sense, a message sent to their supporters in the lower echelons of the party indicating that the faction still had political power. The WRON military council contains members of both groups and serves above all as a broker and a guarantee of Soviet Union's interests in Poland.

Several features of the political life in Poland during the last months are especially pertinent to an understanding of the reasons for the military coup and the relatively weak reaction of the rank-and-file members of Solidarity.

Of particular importance was the existence of two parallel streams of political life. The first of these was politics at the center, characterized by polarization over major institutional issues and a centrifugal tendency, reinforced by symbolic battles in mass media; the second stream comprised local, particularistic politics that repeated the corporatist network of the previous years, not fully eroded by values of national solidarity. The gap between the sphere of expression with its symbolic polarization and everyday practice was responsible for the inner incoherence of the rank and file's attitudes and their relatively smooth (after the initial shock) entrance into the new social order without Solidarity. The heterogenous base of Solidarity's support still reinforced the important role of particularistic politics that was a shameful but necessary addendum to the union's tactics of solidarism. These transactions were more common in the last months, when the economic crisis rapidly deepened.

A second feature of the political life of the period was the important role of status politics. This, together with a narrowing of communication channels (due to symbolic constraints on both sides and the polarization game played by the mass media), led to a situation when the behavior of both was unpredictable. Neither side reacted to material gains, and both overreacted to status issues. Nor did either side have a clear picture of what the final result of the game would be. What was more, Jaruzelski and Wałęsa were under continuous pressure from some of their more radical and militant supporters. Thus, neither side was sure that the other would be able to keep an agreement. In the last weeks the situation seemed to be fully out of the hands of both leaders. This situation accompanied the erosion of the position of the Sejm, a quasi-neutral institution serving as an accommodation mechanism. This erosion was accentuated by the purposeful politics of the mass media, linked with the faction interested in further polarization. The media (especially television and *Trybuna Ludu*) magnified every difference and conflict between Sejm commissions and Solidarity negotiators, and systematically undermined the images of the prominent figures of the opposite faction (Rakowski, Barcikowski). These were the last officials willing to talk with Solidarity; ironically, they became the most unpopular and most attacked by Solidarity government figures.

Before I describe the reactions of Polish society to the "state of war," I would like to discuss some errors made by Solidarity leaders that made the coup so smooth. The most important were two mistaken assumptions:

1) Solidarity leaders believed that the power vacuum (the ruling group's inability to control the real processes in society and the economy) was synonymous with the ruling group's inability to use repression. Interestingly, this assumption closely paralleled the position of the ruling group itself. Ironically, the latter has also mistaken the ability to repress for an ability to govern.

2) Leaders of Solidarity also assumed that, even if confrontation were to come, the ruling group would begin with mild and legal methods and that its options would be limited by the present form of the institutional regime, with its characteristic situation of stalemate. At worst a "state of emergency" would exist with the delegation of extraordinary powers to the government by Sejm, not a "state of war," preceded by a military coup. The latter seemed improbable because, from the perspective of Solidarity leaders, no immediate threat to the government itself existed: the proposed referendum would not take place until February 15, 1982. They did not take into account the tensions and contradictions within the ruling group and between its institutionalized sectors. The assumption that parliamentary procedure would precede eventual confrontation not only created the feeling that they possessed a time-reserve, but led Solidarity to overestimate the ability of the National Commission to control the situation and its ability to choose the most convenient terrain for confrontation.

Another mistake of Solidarity leaders was rooted in their underestimation of the problems within Solidarity itself. Recent surveys made by the sociological research center of Mazowsze Region[11] show among members of Solidarity not only a low will-

---

[11] One reason this evidence was not taken seriously enough was that A. Maciarewicz, a head of the research office, was in conflict with Kuroń and probably Z. Bujak, the leader of Mazowsze region Solidarity.

ingness to strike (even if the right to strike were in danger),[12] but also deep differences within the union,[13] the ambiguous relationship between the rank-and-file members and their national leaders,[14] and, above all, the increasing passivity of Solidarity members.[15] The ruling group appears to have read this evidence much more carefully; especially the data showing the relatively high prestige of the army among Solidarity members[16] as well as their ambivalence toward at least some proposals popular among Solidarity activists.[17] On the basis of this evidence

[12] The data collected at October 30, 1981, show that 12% of the representatives polled, thought that the recent strikes were "necessary"; 41% thought they were "important," but some of them could be avoided; 27% thought that most of them could be avoided; and 7% thought that all strikes could be avoided. This was the very same day when the Sejm was discussing the eventual limitation of the workers' right to strike. When asked what to do if strikes were forbidden, 14% answered "accept it"; 23% felt it should not be accepted but negotiated, 22% thought a warning strike should be organized and negotiated; and only 22% thought a general strike should be called immediately. When asked about their own reaction, 12% declared that they would go on strike, 43% would participate only in a warning strike, and the rest (less than half) would join a sit-in strike. This survey took place before severe sanctions for participation in strikes were announced.

[13] A good indication of the inner differences in Solidarity is revealed in the October 1981 survey research, when 18% of the delegates to the Solidarity Congress perceived their organization as a "labor union" and 69% saw it as a "social movement." Among the rank-and-file members, however, 47% perceived Solidarity as a "labor union" and only 19% as a "social movement."

[14] During research conducted in November 1981, the ambiguous relation of the rank and file toward the National Commission was evident; 30% declared that the prestige of the latter had increased; 26% that it had decreased; 74% did not know who from their region was elected to the National Commission, except the region's chairman.

[15] Fifty-eight percent did not know who was in the new Presidium of the National Commission; why should they risk their lives when the former were interned? Concerning the First Congress of Solidarity, 45% declared weak interest, and 9.2% no interest.

[16] Sixty-nine percent declared trust or "some trust" in the Army, with 95% trusting in Solidarity, and 94% the Catholic Church.

[17] For instance, the idea of referendum: according to the October poll, a small percentage of Solidarity members were against it, but among those who were for it, nearly half did not know what to ask in an eventual referendum.

one could predict the variety of radicalism in Solidarity. I wrote about it in the Introduction when describing the non-institutional character of the fundamentalist orientation typical of the rank-and-file leaders of Solidarity. The rapid radicalization of Solidarity members in Radom led mostly in the direction of institutional solutions (a social-economic council, new regulations of elections on the city council level) or was based on issues not understood by most of Solidarity members.[18] Both worked to the advantage of official propaganda after the coup.

The third mistake of the national leaders of Solidarity was in accelerating a "paper war" (an exchange of statements and resolutions) without any real preparation for the eventual consequences of such an escalation of claims. A feeling of strength based on its membership of nearly 10 million was one of the basic reasons for the "safe game" attitude of most of Solidarity's leaders. They did not take into account how easily the union could be paralyzed by cutting off communications and arresting activists.

These mistakes, together with the oppressive sanctions introduced by the "state of war" decree[19] (and workers were aware of the sanctions they faced if they decided to go on strike) was the reason for the relatively weak wave of protests. In many cases, referendums at factory levels revealed an unwillingness to go on strike. Three interfactory strike committees were organized: in Gdańsk shipyard (49 enterprises) on December 14–15; at Szczecin shipyard (with some links to the Lenin steel mill in Cracow and a few mines in Silesia); and in Gorzów. The National Strike Committee was organized on December 16–17 in Gdańsk by a few members of the National Commission.[20]

According to official data, strikes were organized in 199 enterprises and institutions;[21] other evidence cites nearly 300 strikes.

---

[18] For instance the "provisorium."

[19] The punishment for organizing a strike was up to 5 years.

[20] Waszkiewicz, Krupiński, Konarski, Maciarewicz were arrested.

[21] *Trybuna Ludu* (January 6, 1982).

Strikes took different forms: from 12-hour, sit-in strikes that made no demands and had no leaders but demonstrated sadness at the aborted revolution, through one to two-day occupational strikes that usually ended with police intervention,[22] toward more dramatic strikes that lasted several days in Nowa Huta or the Katowice steel mills, with barricades and warnings that workers would blow themselves up if police intervened (Nowa Huta), and use of gas and blank cartridges (Katowice steel mill), to the tragic events in the Wujek mine where nine were killed in battles between police and miners.

The latest accord reached so far ended a strike that lasted nearly three weeks in two mines: Ziemowit and Piast. The latter strike ended on December 28, when workers had been underground for three weeks and had rejected Church advice to quit. There was among the striking miners a fanatic atmosphere of moral obligation, sanctions on those who decided to go up.[23] deep faith that the whole of Poland was on strike, and intense shock when they discovered that they were the last ones. After the end of the strikes, a new drama emerged. Workers were pressured to write new applications to get back their jobs; those who blamed the leaders of the strike also got back pay for the time of the strike. Those who rejected the offer to sign loyalty oaths were fired: this included 5,000 at the Katowice steel mill, 1,400 at the Gdańsk shipyard, 3,000 at the Szczecin shipyard, and many, many others. The problem of maintaining personal dignity became most crucial; immense help came from local priests who stated during Sunday mass that "what was done under pressure is not valid." Of those who went on strike, 33,609 were punished additionally with financial penalties

[22] In the Warsaw automobile factory (FSC) on December 16, 1981, small groups of workers were forced to walk along a few-hundred-meters-long line of armed policemen. After making it to the end, some of the workers were unable to stay on their legs. Despite the fact that they were not beaten, this was an effect of the mental stress.

[23] They were warned by their colleagues that they would go up naked.

(administrative tribunals sentence those brought before them to pay 5000 zlotys each), 1,713 people were sent to prison. Hundreds of strike organizers were arrested and put under "war decree" trials, with sentences as high as $7\frac{1}{2}$ years (for strikes at the Katowice steel mill) and an average of three years. From my personal acquaintance with more than ten sentenced strike leaders, I can confirm that they are not radicals, but people with highly developed feelings of dignity and obligation toward the roles they took on themselves.

In three towns, violence exploded in the streets: in Gdańsk, where many were injured and at least few killed, and in Łódź and Warsaw, all on December 16 and 17. Small scenes of these moments: three tanks standing under the monument of the December 1970 victims bearing large Solidarity signs and red flowers in their barrels (December 16): the fate of these soldiers is unknown. Candles in windows (December 17). Black armbands. But, above all, the sadness of compulsory muteness in the face of the lies of official propaganda. The slow adjustment to continuous fear; punishments can be used against those wearing Solidarity badges; the Ministry of Education instructs school teachers "not to go beyond school textbooks in their interpretation of literature and history, and, what is more, to report on their co-workers not observing the rule." Doorkeepers are obliged to report when "strangers" visit their houses. Policemen are instructed to destroy (during house searches) "all materials and publications of Solidarity and all they are unable to understand." A mechanical voice that repeats, when you try to call friends after three weeks of silent telephones, "your conversation is overheard."

The present circumstances make it impossible to work on this text very long so I will leave this description of everyday life under the "state of war," the peculiar aesthetics of the latter revealed in the mass media, the initial shock and slow adjustment, and, above all, the inner dynamics of the state of war, with tensions between the party apparatus and the junta, between police and army, and the slow but unavoidable compartmentalization of the terror machine. Such important topics as the impact of the state of war on the economy as well as the junta's relations with the Catholic Church will be described in another book.

In conclusion, I would like to suggest briefly two possible developments of the present situation in Poland as they look at the beginning and to show their further modifications.

One possible development is connected with the position represented by the sector of the PUWP apparatus and other groups linked with the second scenario that I described earlier. Its main characteristics were "Czechization," with severe repressions directed against the more liberal party functionaries as well as the intelligentsia. Some steps of this scenario have already been executed, but were recently slowed down by Jaruzelski's group.[24]

There will be a tendency to punish Solidarity activists (especially those of middle-class origin, who constitute more than 70 percent of elected union functionaries) but to protect workers,[25] or even to build emotional links between "the party and its class." The latter is especially characteristic of the ideologically

[24] The III program in radio was dissolved; more than half of the journalists of *Kurier Polski* were fired. On *Życie Warszawy*, only 7 of nearly 100 were fired, but here the "verification" came a few weeks later.

[25] The most spectacular case was the defense of FSO workers by their director, a member of Warsaw Party Committee, during the trial of the strike organizers. They were found "not guilty" although this should have been impossible given the minimum 2-year sentence under the state of war regulation. This was the first open test of force between the two groups, the founders of "Czechization" scenario and the Jaruzelski group (January 6, 1982). The second evidence was Brych's speech in the Sejm commission opposing an increase in food prices: he is an eminent party apparatus member. Also the so-called "social commissions" organized by the PUWP committees on the factory level tried in a demonstrative way to break through some limitations imposed by the state of war.

oriented segment of this group, which includes some totalitarian utopians who now call themselves the "Workers Platform" — an analogy with the Workers' Opposition of the early 1920s in Russia. In its December leaflet, this group attacked not only WRON (for its "mechanical — not class — terror") but also "liberal" and "technocratic" factions in the party itself — the latter for using economic repressions in order to exploit workers.[26] This group seems interested in reconstructing unified labor unions; its ideological branch also stresses the need for self-management and a return to the traditions of Network (as the pure workers' branch of Solidarity). The utopian and orthodox character of these plans is notable; they do not take into account the real processes that have taken place during the last two years in Poland.

This group has also demanded severe sanctions against KOR, KPN, and NZS (the Independent Student Union) activists: KOR is perceived as the most dangerous opponent due to its social-democratic orientation (the old communist assumption that the nearest enemy is the worst enemy).

Another element of this conception is a proposal to dissolve the present party and to organize a new, highly politicized and ideologically oriented party reminiscent of the party that was characteristic of the totalitarian phase of the system's development. A very important part of this tendency is a re-Stalinization of the economy with compulsory requisitions of food or even collectivization of agriculture, serious limitations on private craftsmen and trades, as well as a cutting off of relations with Western economies.

The last element in this plan is a serious worsening of the relations between state and the church.

The above vision, similar to the first, ideological phase of Sta-

---

[26] In some districts where the apparatus members sympathetic to the "Czechization" scenario are in decision-making positions, the use of economic repressions is limited, for instance in Łódź.

linism in Poland in 1948–1951, would be very different from the plan of the Jaruzelski group, which recalls rather bureaucratic Stalinism, non-ideological and based on the state not the party. The tensions between the two groups are rooted not only in differences in the patterns of repression that they would use but in the everyday problems connected with a presence of military commissars even in district party committees.

Another possible course of events is the scenario favored by the Jaruzelski group: Among its basic features are the reinforcement of the "holding" function of the military regime and such paternalistic practices as an increase of lower monthly wages from 2600 to 3300 zlotys, a continuation of old-age pension reform, special protection for young people, and an increase of state-delivered credits to 100,000 zlotys.[27]

The legitimacy of this plan would build on an attack on corruption, instituting proceedings of a state tribunal against the members of Gierek's team, interned at the same time as Solidarity activists, and claims that order has been established with a slogan that the rigorous laws are aimed at the defense of peace for citizens.

Another feature of repressions can be labeled as a "mild hungarization" (that is with broad, not class-oriented sanctions and economic reforms). This pattern conflicts with the proposal of "Czechization" described before. Characteristic of the Jaruzelski group's pattern of terror is extensive use of economic repressions as a method of worker pacification: massive dismissals from jobs, reallocation to worse jobs, an increase of work norms, financial penalties such as the loss of year-end bonuses as a result of participation in strikes after December 13. Increases in prices often as much as 200–300 percent to begin February 1 plays a very important role in this scenario; it not only reinforces the eco-

---

[27] The special commission was created to look into problems of the young people.

nomic repressions (when you lose your job you have to live on 3,300–4,300 zlotys, without "compensation" refunding a part of price increases). Price increases (together with changes in the tax system) serve also as a remedy to the fiscal crisis of the state and make it possible for the junta to play its "holding" role. Third, price increases will probably limit consumption of food, making possible an additional export. All these measures require the continuation of the terror, especially severe anti-strike legislation, helping to demobilize the angry masses. In a sense this pattern has imprinted in itself a spiral of repressions, in spite of Jaruzelski's declarations.

In blocking "Czechization,"[28] the Jaruzelski group does not seem to be as interested in a spectacular discontinuity in prop-aganda as is the apparatus faction nor in dismissing mass media stars of the previous period. On the contrary, it would like to incorporate them into its own service through intimidation as well as buying them off. For instance authors' fees were increased after the state of war was introduced; this technique also recalls the bureaucractic phase of Stalinism.

The Jaruzelski group is apparently trying to maintain rela-tively good relations with the Catholic Church. This underlines the non-ideological character of the regime.[29]

An important part of the described scenario is to protect indi-vidual farmers and craftsmen and to use economic instruments as long as possible.

[28] On the advice of Jaruzelski's supporter, Kubiak, the Rector of Warsaw University Samsonowicz (expelled recently from the PUWP by the Warsaw party apparatus) wrote an appeal to the higher-level commission; that gave him some time and held up for a while the nomination of a new rector with his "Czechization" program.

[29] During a meeting with professors of Warsaw University informing them about the state-of-war regulations, a very characteristic remark was made: "we will look over all subjects taught to see which can serve as ideological lec-tures," mutual winks suggesting that both sides are interested in a minimal level of the ideological pressure in spite of the position of the apparatus faction (January 15, 1982).

At first glance this group seemed to be interested in the recon-struction of Solidarity as the channel for negotiations and as a necessary buffer in the crisis situation;[30] it also sent out signals of its interest in a "political solution" to the situation (for instance through formation of the Christian-Democratic party).[31]

A very important part of the Jaruzelski scenario is a contin-uation of the policy to demobilize the PUWP and to reduce its apparatus.

The tensions between the authors of the two scenarios is increasingly evident. A few days before Christmas, Jaruzelski rejected the anti-apparatus warnings delivered by the small group of party "liberals"—Tejchma, Werblan, Wiatr, Do-bieszewski, Zawadzki, Markiewicz, Sufin. Now, only a few weeks later, he has tried without success to dismiss one of the most important directors of the apparatus scenario, Stanisław Kociołek, first party secretary of Warsaw. Recently we could observe a strengthening of a characteristic of a system that has no institutional mechanism to solve internal conflicts—com-munication through signs. Both groups need to inform the lower echelons of party and state apparatuses about their pref-erences in the mode of repressions; but they cannot talk openly about differences. For instance the daily *Rzeczpospolita* (linked with Jaruzelski) recently printed letters from a few people attacked by the apparatus faction—Krasucki, Gniech, and oth-ers. On the other hand, we can observe a slow but continuous modification of the Jaruzelski scenario, driving it closer toward that of the apparatus.

[30] During the first few weeks of the state of war, some efforts were made by members of Jaruzelski group such as Ciosek and Rakowski, to contact moderate Solidarity activists to discuss the possibility of new elections and a reconstruc-tion of Solidarity. Now all contacts have stopped.

[31] Meeting of Rakowski with some Solidarity advisers from circles close to the Catholic Church, before Christmas 1981.

The very weak reaction of farmers to economic incentives (due to a lack of goods they would like to buy) makes it more and more probable that Jaruzelski's administration will use a method of compulsory requisition, already legalized by the state of war decree.

The success of its pacification methods makes the Jaruzelski group less interested in restoring of Solidarity as a channel for negotiations. The position taken by Jaruzelski in his Sejm speech on January 25, 1982, was that craft unions, the most segmented working-class form of the unions, can be slowly organized on the plant level. Nothing was said about Solidarity, with its territorial structure. Also the possibility of the creation of a Christian-Democratic party seems to be weaker. One of the authors of this idea, Reiff, chairman of PAX, was recently dismissed from his position. What is more, much evidence suggests that the Jaruzelski group is interested in building a typical authoritarian-bureaucratic state, based not on political parties or other forms of representation but on the mechanisms of cooptation and an articulation of social needs inside the state machinery (for instance through quasi-simulation with the help of experts; which recalls the "lame pluralism" of Gierek in the mid-1970s). The recent rapid shift in a proposed pattern of refunding price increases that is more favorable for workers is a good example of such a technique of ruling when a paternalistic state is itself defending citizens against state machinery. This was also a clever move, forestalling a possible countermobilization of the opposite faction on the basis of social protest against an increase of prices.

The last modification of Jaruzelski's scenario, making it very similar to the apparatus scenario, is caused by two factors: U.S. economic sanctions and the Soviet Union's strong demand that production in Poland meet the COMECON countries' military and consumer needs. This modification seems to go in two directions: first, to restructure the economy in order to maximize exports by repressing the domestic market and manipulating food rationing, work norms, and work hours. All these moves make terror a necessary part of economic policy. A second approach is to create an economic system that is more independent of the West. The only possible way to meet both the Soviet Union's demand and the United States' sanctions is to use a pattern of a dual-sector colony, with one sector exclusively based on Soviet energy and raw material and working mostly to meet the needs of the Soviet Union and other East European countries, the other sector, working in much worse conditions, full of bottlenecks and with a decreased supply of Soviet energy and raw materials producing for domestic use. The relative high prosperity of the first sector would have no impact on the well being of the society; on the contrary, it would produce additional inflationary pressure due to higher wages combined with a lack of production on domestic markets.

This economic policy is followed by the invention of some possible ways to circumvent Western economic sanctions — for instance with the help of a quiet transfer of money through Brazilian and Greek banks by financial circles not interested in the bankruptcy of Poland, and the end of the export of cheap Polish steel, copper, and coal. The latter, together with short-term credits, possible due to an increase of exports from the repressed domestic market, would make it possible for the economy to vegetate. Of course severe repressions to pacify society are a necessary part of the above pattern.

The possible Polish alternatives for the near future, thus, seem to be either ideological, utopian, and very repressive Stalinism or bureaucratic Stalinism, also oppressive, but in a different manner, with some aspiration to enlightened authoritarianism.

The violent character of the last change of the regime (taken in order to save the system) shows how much was at stake in the conflicts that preceded the implementation of the "state of war." The dialectical process of attrition of forms of domination (as well as forms of protest) and the development of the sytem's contradictory logic are full of the unexpected and ambiguous. "The ambiguities of politics give ground for hope" wrote Fernando H. Cardoso, describing the authoritarian-bureaucratic regime his society must live through. We in Poland also can hope for the emergence of social forces within the established order that will eventually undermine authoritarian rules, in spite of their relative elasticity due to minimal ideological constraints.

Warsaw, January 26, 1982

Index

Library of Congress Cataloging in Publication Data

Staniszkis, Jadwiga.
Poland's self-limiting revolution.
Includes index.
1. Poland — Politics and government — 1980–
2. NSZZ "Solidarność" (Labor organization)
3. Poland — Politics and government — 1945–1980.
4. Poland — Social conditions — 1945–
I. Gross, Jan Tomasz.   II. Title.
DK4442.S72   1984   943.8'055   82-61387
ISBN 0-691-09403-9